Poseidon Press
Simon & Schuster Building
Rockefeller Center
1230 Avenue of the Americas
New York, New York 10020

POSEIDON PRESS is a registered trademark
of Simon & Schuster Inc.

POSEIDON PRESS colophon is a trademark
of Simon & Schuster Inc.

Designed by Liney Li
Manufactured in the United States of America

10   9   8   7   6   5   4   3   2   1

Library of Congress Cataloging in Publication Data
Sachar, Emily.
    Shut up and let the lady teach: a teacher's year in a public school/by
Emily Sachar
        p.   cm.
    1. Poor children—Education—New York (N.Y.)—Case studies.   2. Afro/
American children—Education—New York (N.Y.)—Case studies.
3. Public schools—New York (N.Y.)—Case studies.   4. Elementary school
teaching—New York (N.Y.)—Case studies.   5. Brooklyn (New York, N.Y.)
—Social conditions—Case studies.   I. Title.
LC4C33.N5S33   1991
371.96'7'097471—dc20   91-7872
                                                                                               CIP

ISBN 0-671-69034-5

PHOTO CREDITS: #3—© 1989, Fine/New York Newsday; #4, 5, 17, 18, 19—
© 1989, Dietrich/New York Newsday; all others are from the author's
collection.

*In the interest of privacy, the names of students and members of their families
have been changed.*

SHUT UP
AND LET THE
LADY TEACH

A Teacher's Year in a Public School

Emily Sachar

 POSEIDON PRESS

New York - London - Toronto - Sydney - Tokyo - Singapore

*For the kids I taught
and the teachers I admired*

Contents

It's a very ancient saying
  but a true and honest thought,
That if you become a teacher,
  by your pupils you'll be taught.

—Richard Rodgers and Oscar Hammerstein II,
"Getting to Know You" *(The King and I)*

1

Of Basketballs
and Crowded Halls

Shut the fuck up and let the lady teach.

—Tameeka, one of my students at Walt Whitman
Intermediate School, Flatbush, Brooklyn.

The basketball sailed over my head—from Andre to Clement, back
to Andre, over to Rodney, then to Clement, and so on.

"Okay, that's enough. Will you please take your seats?" I shouted,
my voice cracking. "The period started ten minutes ago."

My math class in Room 327 had turned into a gym. It was just
past 9 A.M., only an hour into the school day, but I felt like I'd been
working for hours.

"Dribble," mumbled Andre. "Dribble, dribble, dribble. Up and
score!" The ball banged against the back wall, landed on a desk, and
bounced to the floor.

Andre reached high into the air and pretended to shoot again.
Rodney yanked the basketball off the floor. "Dribble, man, dribble,
dribble," he shouted. The ball smacked on the old wooden floorboards. "Score, baby, score." Again, the ball ricocheted off the back
wall, then dropped to the floor.

"In your seats, boys," I tried again. Other students were milling
around the room, laughing and glancing at me, obviously anxious for
my reaction. I had to get the boys in the back to settle down. *Sit
down. Now,"* I yelled to the basketball trio. They ignored me.

As I marched angrily to the front of the room, my attendance book slipped out of my hand. Rodney, a chunky kid with a mean streak, raced up and grabbed it, dangled it in my face, then threw it Frisbee-style against the blackboard. The boys with the ball broke into hysterical laughter.

Andre, a tall lanky fifteen-year-old, sat on top of a desk, whistling and twirling his basketball like a Harlem Globetrotter.

"Okay, enough!" I stood at the front of the room behind my desk. "Now sit down and get to work."

No one paid attention. Instead, Andre flung the basketball into the air again in an imaginary layup shot, rasping "Aaalll right!" as the ball sailed into an invisible basket four feet below the ceiling.

I attempted to begin the lesson anyway: a ten-minute lecture followed by problems for the students to work on at their desks. It was then, to write on the blackboard, that I made a mistake I vowed never to repeat: I turned my back on the class.

Whack! Something hard struck me in the head. The three rowdies broke into mocking laughter again, and I lurched around to see a small rock rolling on the floor behind my desk. *"Who threw that?"* I screamed. I wanted to snatch it up and fire it back. But I remembered that I was the teacher.

My left temple pulsed with pain. I wondered if it was bleeding. And my heart pounded in frustrated anger. I wondered if everyone knew which kid had thrown the rock. Were they all rooting for him? I wondered mostly what the kids thought of their new math teacher.

But no time for introspection. I had to rescue the rest of the class from anarchy. A group of girls were huddled by the wooden closets along one side of the room. There was a mirror on the inside of one of the closet doors; it was a particularly popular item. "Girls, take your seats," I pleaded, approaching them. "It's time for class to begin." Marlene, a heavy girl with eyes that never seemed to open all the way, scowled. The rest of the girls continued to ignore me in my vain dreams of giving a math lesson. One of them was describing an important date with a boy named Germaine. "We're getting down after school," she gushed, as the others admired the new contact lenses that gave her brown eyes a startling forest-green hue.

On the other side of the room, two boys sat quietly near the front, heads on their folded hands, their eyes shut. "Darling, class is about to begin," I said to one, gently lifting his chin. His skin was smooth and soft, his eyes bloodshot. "Wake up and get out your notebook." No reaction. I let go of the boy's chin and his head dropped like a dead weight onto his hands.

I stalked back to the front of the room, opened my three-ring plan book to the marker for 8-16, and tried once more to begin the lesson. "It's 9:18, and this class was supposed to start more than twenty-five minutes ago. We have only seventeen minutes left. You know where you're supposed to sit. You know what you're supposed to do. Now, let's get moving. *Now!*" I might as well have been talking to myself.

The sun was just starting to break through the dirty windows that lined one side of the room. Heavy metal grates barred the windows like a jail or psychiatric ward. The bulletin board at the back of the room was without decoration except for a smattering of graffiti. On either side of it were bookshelves with glass doors that locked, but the panes were all missing. Neither were there books in the empty cases. The kids' desks were a messy jumble all over the room and some of the plastic chair seats had been sliced in half.

Then, my eyes met Saheedra's. She was sitting quietly in the first seat in the fourth row, directly in front of me. Her notebook was open and she had faithfully copied the only words I had time to put on the board. "Date: Sept. 20, 1988. Class 8-16. Aim: How do we multiply two-digit numbers?" Her hair was black and cropped short. Like Marlene, she was a heavy-set girl, but her clothes were neat and freshly laundered, and I suspected from her earnest approach that she would prove to be one of my more diligent students. She looked so eager, so happy, so ready for a good year at school. So was I.

But it wasn't just Saheedra and me. There were seventeen other kids. And I didn't know what to do with any of them. I had run out of ideas. I stormed to the back of the room and threw the door open.

"Is anyone out here?" I called, expecting to find a teacher or a security guard, anyone who could help a new teacher whose class had gone out of control. The hall was empty.

I shut the door and stomped to the chalkboard again, trying to be dramatic. The basketball was still winging around in the back, and another group of boys was now playing a card game called Uno. "Your homework," I declared, "is to memorize the 8 facts. 8 times 1 is 8. 8 times 2 is 16. 8 times 3 is 24, and so on. I'm going to write them on the board. Copy them into your notebooks and learn them!" Hardly anyone listened.

I began writing the facts on the board, my body turned sideways so I could watch the class. Only Saheedra and a quiet boy on the right side of the room were copying the tables, and what difference did that make? They already knew them. A stocky boy sat silently in the midst of all the chaos. He was not copying the facts either, but he, at least, had done well on the first quiz.

The room was still a circus of activity. *"Didn't you hear what I said?"* I shouted again. "Write the times tables into your notebooks right now!"

Suddenly, Tameeka stood up. She wore plaid pants in a dozen shades of green and a red cotton sweater. She was so fat it was hard to tell where her bust line ended and her stomach began. She had a loud voice—she had erupted twice earlier in the week—and I was terrified that she would be the next one to challenge me with some caustic remark. She had yet to take out a notebook or a pen, and had spent the first half-hour of our class that morning pretending to sleep.

"Shut the fuck up and let the lady teach," she suddenly roared so loudly that one of the windowpanes shook.

Abruptly, the room fell silent. The kids were as stunned as I was.

But before I could take advantage of the silence, the bell rang, and the students stampeded for the door. Andre tucked the basketball under his armpit and blithely sauntered into the hallway, cruising past the assistant principal, who monitored the third floor corridor. The rest of the students rushed to the drinking fountain, or to the end of the hall, where a wide unsupervised stairwell beckoned.

I wearily gathered my books and my chalk and the gray satchel I carried everywhere. It was 9:35 A.M. One class down and four to go. The day at Walt Whitman Intermediate School in the Flatbush section of Brooklyn had barely begun.

Around the corner, down a long hall and around another corner I raced as fast as I could make my tired legs go. I had just turned the second corner when the late bell rang, and I scampered up the stairs to the fourth floor. As soon as I emerged from the dark stairwell, I saw that I was in for more trouble. Students from my 8-7 class were milling outside Room 402, the room that was supposed to be ours at 9:38 on Tuesday mornings. Another teacher was already ushering students—her students—inside. When I glanced in, I saw that many of her kids were already sitting quietly, ready for class. This teacher was actually going to get a chance to teach. I was jealous.

"Hi," I said, approaching her. "I'm Mrs. Sachar. I think this is supposed to be my classroom." I pulled out the official schedule I had been given the week before. Sure enough: third period on Tuesdays, Room 402.

"I don't think so," she countered. She didn't introduce herself.

"We're supposed to be in Room 402. And we're not moving. We've already met here once before."

I was in no mood for a fight. "Well, could you tell me what I should do about this? Who should I see?"

"Go to Program," she said.

"Program?" I asked. "What's that?"

"The program office. Third floor. I forget the number. You'll find it."

The 8-7 students mobbed in the hall could not have cared less that my lesson on "finding the pattern in a sequence" was side-tracked. A few of the boys were absorbed in whatever was pulsing from their Walkman headphones. Several girls were quietly talking in a corner. Two boys tried to flirt with the prettiest girl in the class.

"Don't move an inch," I insisted, realizing I was only addressing the two best-behaved kids in the class. "I have to go straighten this out." I knew I'd be breaking some rule if I just left the kids there, but I saw no alternative. There were no other adults around. Teachers were grabbing kids by the collar and hauling them into classrooms and slamming doors, and suddenly, at 9:40 that Tuesday, it was just me and my 8-7 kids stranded in the hallway without a room.

I deposited my stack of books on the floor and asked one of the students to guard them. Then I bolted down the stairwell to the third floor to find the assistant principal's office. When I finally located it, I blurted to the man inside, "I have this problem. Two of us were booked for the same room at the same time. I guess I need the program office."

The assistant principal showed me the way. "Can you fix Miss Sachar's program?" he asked the man in charge.

"Oh, no," came the response. "Another problem?"

I produced my program. "It seems two of us are scheduled for Room 402 at the same time." He stared at a large, handmade, poster-sized grid listing every class and period in the school. "8-7 should be in that room," he muttered, scanning the board. Then, "Oh, here's the problem." He paused. "Let me find you another room. This happens once in a while."

School had started the previous Wednesday and most every teacher had a different program with different rooms every period of every day. The program man remained calm. He'd obviously been through this before. But he was stumped.

"We've got a little problem here," he admitted. "There's not a single room in the school that's vacant."

That was fine with me. They could just cancel my 8-7 Tuesday class, give the kids an extra gym class and give me an extra preparation period. Besides, I was scheduled to have class 8-7 twice on Tuesdays; they wouldn't want me, let alone math, twice in one day.

"Guess we'll have to assign you to the cafeteria." He wrote Cafeteria onto my program card and told me to return to my kids. Back I tore around the first corner, down the front hall, around another corner, and up the stairs, only to find my 8-7s gone crazy in the fourth-floor corridor. Two girls were jumping rope. "First comes love, then comes marriage, then comes Marlon in a baby carriage. Right, Marlon?" The rope smacked loudly on the floor. One boy was tracing a Marvel comic. Another ran around pretending to shoot other kids with a ruler. "Okay, I'm Tyrone," he barked. "Cough up every dollar you got."

"Follow me now," I commanded no one in particular. *"We've got to get out of here."*

Off we went, the twenty-four kids and their teacher in a disorderly file down the four flights of stairs to the basement. As soon as we entered the cafeteria, we collided with other kids and teachers. Two other classes were already assigned to the cafeteria for what appeared to be dance or gymnastics. Some kids were jumping rope, others playing cards.

"This will be our classroom," I told my class, trying to seem enthusiastic about a room with no chalkboard, no desks, and windows so high on the wall that the only way to see out was with a ladder. "Please take seats at these three tables."

"We're not having school in *here*, are we?" one boy moaned.

"Well, it looks that way," I said. "Don't worry, we'll make it work."

Just then, Bob, the program man, came in. "I have good news," he announced. "We'll put you in Room 107. Not now, because we have to move the teacher who's in there. But next Tuesday, that's where you'll go. Don't worry. It's just your first week. It'll get better." Bob was also the school's union leader, and the week before he had warned me to put firm discipline policies in place the first week of school. I wondered how he thought I was doing.

"We have to make a change," I told the kids, "but it's better than being down here."

Anything would be better than this steamy cafeteria. "From now on, Tuesdays, third period, I want you to come to Room 107. Please mark that change onto your program cards." Most of the kids responded, and made the change while I walked around to help those who couldn't figure out what I was talking about. A few had already lost their program cards, the postcard-sized schedule of their class and room assignments for the year.

I didn't know what the change would mean to the kids, but I knew that for me it would be no fun. On Tuesdays I would start by teaching 8-16 on the third floor, southern wing, then, at the end of second period, I would have three minutes to dash to the first floor on the other side of the building. At the end of third period, I had to zip up to the fourth floor. What careful planning went into running Walt Whitman Intermediate School!

When the bell rang, I breathed a sigh of relief. I still had one more class to teach before lunch and I was already exhausted. Fortunately, that class was 8-1, the best I had. And we were going to do another lesson on rounding numbers, which the kids had found great fun the Friday before.

Up the four flights of stairs and around to the other side of the building to Room 402 I raced. This time, the room was empty but for a dozen of my own kids. I pulled out my Delaney attendance book and began marking students who were tardy.

"Sorry for being late, Mrs. Sachar," said one girl who walked in after the late bell. Frankly, I couldn't believe I made it on time myself.

"Just be on time tomorrow," I urged. "Within three minutes, every student had a notebook out and open while I filled the chalkboard with work. We had thirty-eight minutes to go, and I was determined to teach for every one of them.

"I like what I see in here today," I declared loudly. "Neat rows, quiet students, respect. That's what I want to see every day." A few kids smiled. Then, from the second row, Tiara stood up. "You don't have to yell, Mrs. Sachar. Mellow out, man!"

I put the Aim on the board: *How do we round large numbers?*

I put a Do Now on the board: *56,501. Round this to the nearest thousand.*

"Okay, let's go over the Do Now," I said after a few minutes, trying to speak quietly. "What are the rules for rounding numbers?"

More than half the kids shot hands into the air. I called on a girl near the front. "Put an X over the thousands place," she said.

"Yes. And then what?"

"Then, look to the right."

"Why?" I prodded.

"To see if it's 5 or bigger."

"And why do we care if it's 5 or bigger?"

" 'Cause 5 is the halfway mark between 0 and 10. If it's 5 or greater, we're more than halfway there, and we round up."

"Yes? And then . . ."

"Well, it's 5 or bigger, so we round the 6 to 7."

"And what happens with the rest of the numbers?"

"Everything to the right drops to 0."

"Great. Now, tell me why."

" 'Cause that's what rounding is. You want a lot of zeros at the end of the number."

"What do we call a rounded number? Someone else?"

"An estimate," another boy said when I called on him.

"Yes. So what is our final answer?"

"57,000," another boy replied.

"Great!" I wanted to clap. They were getting it! "Now, here are ten more. I'm going to time you. See how fast you can round these numbers." I put ten more numbers on the board. Walking briskly around the room, I checked the students' work. There were many correct answers.

The time with 8-1 passed quickly, like the Friday before. Just prior to the bell, I announced the first test of the term.

"Already?" one girl groaned. "We haven't even been here a week."

"That's true," I said. "But, on Friday, we're going to have a test." I listed the topics it would cover, as the students wrote. "Now, here is your extra-credit problem, also due on Friday: *In a class of 30 students, 17 have dogs as pets and 20 have fish as pets. What is the least number of students that can have both dogs and fish as pets?*"

Immediately, the students set to working. Half of them were drawing pictures, and I was delighted by their attempts to solve the problem. Then I posted the evening homework. All opened their notebooks and diligently copied the assignment.

At the bell, four students crowded around my desk. "If I bring in problems for the class to do, can I get extra credit?" one girl asked. "If I tutor a boy in the class, can I get extra credit?" another wanted to know. A third told me she would be absent the next day but wanted to give her homework to another student to hand in. A fourth offered to help me decorate my bulletin boards for extra credit. Kids this motivated wanted quick answers and rewards for everything, and I would have to come up with novel ways to keep them stimulated.

. . .

After the late bell, I remembered that a week earlier I had given a batch of five rexograph sheets for copying to my supervisor, Vikki Kowalski, a new assistant principal who was also head of the math department. I had expected them to be ready well before my Monday classes, but they weren't. Now we were going through the Tuesday schedule, and they still weren't ready. I had no clue whether they would be ready even by the end of the second week of school. Teachers weren't themselves allowed to use the rexograph, the machine that turned a single purple ditto master into multiple copies of a worksheet for the kids. I was at the mercy of the sweet, gray-haired lady on the first floor who ran the copying room. I still had no textbooks for my students. The word in the school was clear: You can't give out textbooks until the school has settled down, whatever that meant. I wondered when that would happen. Or if.

I located Miss Kowalski in her second-floor office. "Any chance I'll have that stuff I gave you for tomorrow?" I asked. "Don't know," she answered without looking up. I told her I had been spending $10 a day on copying at a store in my neighborhood. "Being a teacher has more than a few hidden costs, doesn't it?" I said in an attempt at humor. She did not smile.

That day only my lunch hour passed uneventfully. I spoke with a few of the teachers as we ate, for the second day in a row, the school's overcooked breaded chicken patties and tasteless boiled vegetables. The new item on the menu, hamburgers, looked too rubbery to chew. But at least the food was warm, and I had yet to see a roach or a mouse in the lunchroom. "That will come, in time," I was assured. I related to the teachers at the table my morning traumas—the basketball rumpus in 8-16, the double-booking of Room 402, the well-behaved and eager 8-1 full of kids clamoring for extra-credit work.

"Yeah, we know the routine," one nodded. "Just be grateful we have a four-day week coming up."

"A four-day week?" Only four days of work? That sounded wonderful.

"You'll *live* for those four-day weeks," he confided. "Usually, you don't get more than three five-day weeks in a row. But once in a while, the Jewish holidays in September fall on a weekend, and then you might have four five-day weeks. This year, we're lucky." I had never been so excited at the thought of a day off. At my other jobs, I had never even paid attention to when the holidays fell. Brooklyn Day, he explained, was one of our upcoming holidays. Whatever—whenever—I'd celebrate it.

The bell rang too soon, and I was off to my next class. It was 8-7 again, for the second time that day. This time I got there before most of the students. As they rushed in, I could see that they still had no intention of sitting in their assigned seats.

I decided to be nice. "Ryan," I said, walking over to one boy, "I'm sure you just forgot, but you're supposed to be sitting in the first row, third seat, right here."

"I remember fine," came the reply. "But I don't feel like sitting there. I want to sit by Kevin."

"No, Ryan, over here." I pointed to his desk, my voice calm and self-assured.

"No, Mrs. Sachar, over here," he rebutted, mimicking me.

"Over here, Ryan," I said, suddenly angry.

"No, Mrs. Sachar, here," he parried in a singsong tone.

Ryan had pulled this stunt once before, and I had lost my temper, just as I was starting to now. I backed off from this budding tug-of-war, and so did Ryan, remaining in the wrong seat. The rest of the kids were fooling around, and they looked wild, too. Once again, my lesson on sequences would have to wait. Sequences were just too boring for a restless class in the afternoon. What to do? In my satchel, I had a stack of menus from a carry-out Chinese restaurant. Tuesday would just have to be Chinese menu day—I would have the kids plan a banquet menu and calculate the cost—once I got them in their correct seats. That was critical, the teacher trainer had told me. "You've got to stick to your seating plan," she said. I didn't know why it was so important, but she was the expert.

Kids were still talking and nearly all were out of their assigned seats, which alternated boy-girl. So I announced, "Now, I'm going to turn my back and count to ten. When I turn around, I want to see every student in this room in the right chair. Let's see how fast you can do it."

I started to count and heard a few shuffles though not enough to indicate the kids were obeying. I was sure that when I turned around, most of the kids would not have budged. And then, what would I do? If I yelled, they would just laugh. If I cried, they would stare. If I did nothing, I would gain nothing. No matter what my response, what small kernel of respect I had earned would be gone.

"Eight . . . nine . . . ten." I spun around, grateful that no rock had been thrown at my head. The kids still had not scooted to their designated seats. More than half of them sat defiantly on the desks.

"You know," I scolded, "this is not particularly funny, and it is not particularly cute. You have a helluva lot to learn, and I have a helluva lot to teach you. We could have a great year. Or we can have a year of stupid games like this. Now, I am going to read the name of each student, and I am going to ask you to sit in your seat, and if you do not move, you will get a zero for the day. And if you don't keep your seat for the rest of the year, you will get a zero every day." Threatening thirteen- and fourteen-year-old kids with little red circles in my roll book seemed ridiculous. But if this was what they demanded, so be it. The teacher trainer had said that if giving 100s to the good kids didn't inspire the bad, then give zeros to the bad kids and terrify the good. What consistency! Try rewards. If that doesn't work, try punishment.

"First row, first seat, Terrence," I ordered. "Now move."

"I'm here. I'm here," Terrence protested. The kids chuckled: the joke was on me. Terrence was exactly where he was supposed to be.

"First row, second seat, Tanya." She was there, too.

I cruised through the rest of the room even as the kids laughed at me and my commands. Reluctantly, however, they moved to their proper seats. Six minutes before the bell was to ring, we finally had every student in the correct seat. I stood at the front of the room and smiled at this small triumph.

"Now, that's more like it," I said. "Tomorrow, I don't want to have to go through this again. You guys got it? Either we can have a great year, or I can treat you like babies." An interesting thought, considering that many of the boys had beards and the girls breasts.

I wrote out a simple homework assignment on the board. "On an index card, write three sequences, each of which can be solved by another student. Write the answers to each sequence on the back of the index cards. Make them as easy or as difficult as you like. Just make sure they work."

"What's an index card?" Kevin called out.

"Kevin, please raise your hand." In our three days of training in August, we had been told not to call on any student who spoke out of turn. Those rules had seemed so plausible in a classroom of adults, but here they seemed absurd and unenforceable.

The bell rang, and, to my relief, my program card said I could stay put. Both my Tuesday afternoon classes met in Room 225. But my relief was short-lived—my next class was the one I dreaded most, 8-12, twenty-eight kids who could barely read, or do math. I wondered how they would react when I passed back the first quizzes of the year. Passing was 65 percent. The average score had been 22 out of 100.

The first to enter the room was a sweet-natured boy named Sherwin who asked me where he was supposed to sit. "I can't remember with every day being a different room." I smiled because I knew just where he sat: third row, second seat. He was always there, beaming at me while I tried desperately to get the rest of the kids to pay attention.

If only the other kids coming into 8-12 were as cooperative. Five girls entered, jabbering about boys, and slouched against the windows. One of them suddenly hopped onto a desktop and perched on it. The rest of the kids, too, sat wherever they wanted. It was obvious that I would have to run through the same charade all over again.

"Okay, I'm going to read your names again, and if you don't sit down right away, you will get a zero. We're just not going to have this every day." A chorus of complaints erupted.

"What's her problem?"

"I thought you was going to be nice."

"You's a bitch like all the rest of 'em."

"I appreciate the compliment," I replied sarcastically. "I'd rather be a bitch than a wimp. Now let's get moving. Crystal, you will sit here, in front of me, the better to see you, my dear."

Crystal shuffled slowly to the front of the room and dropped her book bag onto the desk. "You bitch," she repeated.

"Germaine, you're next. Right behind Crystal."

"Now, you, Jarred. Here."

"Oh, come on, Mrs. Sachar. I have stuff to talk over with Junior."

"No. Work it out outside class. Next period. Or after school."

I turned to a group of girls, addressing the tallest and prettiest of them. "Diamond, you're here."

"Okay, Mrs. Sachar, you won't have no problems with me."

"Well, ain't she the cooperative one," Tawana said.

And on it went, until every kid was in the seat I had assigned the first day.

"Now, today, I am going to pass back the first quiz of the year. I have to tell you I was pretty unhappy with the results. I know you all can do better. We're going to go through the problems and the right answers one at a time."

"There she goes again, the bitch," I heard from the back of the room.

Among the thirteen boys, none scored higher than a 50. Four boys had gotten only one question right out of ten. Among the sixteen girls, there were two 70s, one 10, one 0. The rest were 20s, 30s and 40s. The hardest question was : *If you have to stack 200 sheets of paper in 8 equal piles, how many sheets will you put in each pile?* Only two students had the correct answer. Three had attempted to solve it and knew it required division, but could not figure out how to divide 200 by 8.

Standing beside my desk, I called each student in turn, handing back the papers. The first few eyed the score at the top of the paper and scowled, shoving the test papers in their notebooks. Then, I called Patrick Johnson. He had scored a 10.

"Fuck this class," he said when he saw the mark. "Watch this, teacher bitch." He took the paper, covered with my painstaking corrections, and ripped it down the middle. Then he put the two halves together, turned them 90 degrees, and ripped again. And again and again, until he made a handful of tiny flakes. He spat on them and tossed them into the air; they rained like confetti onto the floor.

"Well, that's great, Patrick. And how do you think you're going to learn, doing that?" I asked.

"I don't give a shit," he elaborated. "You be here. I be out making money, a lot more than you's ever gonna know."

"Patrick, you'll be nowhere without an education," I said, wishing I had a better reply. "Life on the streets will get scary real fast."

"Yeah? We'll see about that." He was a thin boy with a head of tight black fuzz, into which the shape of a zigzag had been shaved. He flaunted the same macho arrogance that had already made him a star of this unruly class.

The class was still. Everyone was waiting to see who would make the next move. Then—saved by the bell.

"What a year I am going to have," I thought. "What a year."

As I walked to my car after school, a load of books and papers piled in my arms to my chin, a woman approached me. Pointing over her shoulder to the school, she asked, "You teach in the hole?"

"That's what they call it? The hole? It seems okay to me," I said. "Some of the kids are a little wild, but not all of them. It's a decent place."

"I hear it's a dump, a good-for-nothing dump. I got my kids out before they had to go there." She wore a smart business suit, her hair tied tight in a bun. A young boy stood close to her, holding her hand.

"I guess I wouldn't really know," I told her. "I've only been here a week."

"So you're a rookie," she laughed. "That explains it."

As I walked away, I could still hear her laughing. I wondered uneasily just what the joke was.

2

Wanted: Almost Anyone

There are teachers coming into the system taking and passing exams who are close to illiterate. They are not stupid, but they can barely read and write. Why does this happen? Because the system is desperate for bodies. We have forsaken most standards.

—A former assistant principal at Walt Whitman Intermediate School who graded exams for the Board of Examiners, the teacher-testing agency for the New York City school system that was eliminated in January 1991.

In late May 1988, I walked through the heavy glass doors of the Board of Education personnel building in downtown Brooklyn seeking a license to teach in the New York City public school system.

I had wanted to teach for years, but had not until then found a way to do it without derailing my career as a newspaper reporter. In the previous two years, I had been covering the Board of Education and the city schools for *New York Newsday*. I spent hours interviewing and observing dozens of teachers in as many schools. More and more frequently, I found myself feeling jealous of the men and women at the front of the classrooms. I saw my own idealism reflected in so many of them, especially those new recruits who talked so passionately of "shaping young minds." I began to wonder whether I had the magic spark, and whatever else it took, to shape a mind.

Increasingly, I also had grown to dread my beat at *New York Newsday*. I dreaded the frequent press conferences of arrogant educator-bureaucrats who dodged my questions; I hated the agenda that governed my life. Anything of substance coming out of Board of Education headquarters was news, news that I not only must cover, but cover first, at least a day before the other three major dailies in town. Racing to beat the competition with the results of citywide reading and math tests or the next Board of Education personnel appointment put me on top of the world one day, when I got the scoop, and just as quickly pulled me down the next, when *The New York Times* or the *Daily News* beat me to it. My self-worth was entirely dependent on how many prizes I had won, how many front-page stories I had written, how many times my exclusives were picked up by the wire services or acknowledged by the competition.

So needy had I become for professional recognition—for splashy, front-page stories and nods of praise from senior editors—that I spent hours every day calling "sources," a word I hated, tracking down promising hints of scandal. "Got a hot tip?" I would beg from every disgruntled bureaucrat I could find. That single, aberrant teacher who talked dirty to his students or smacked then with a rod: those headlines would do more good for me—and my career—than reporting the real education story in New York City. By the spring of 1988, as the school year dragged to an end, the thought of yet another year of press conference double-talk, hyped hot tips, and the same stories about the appalling decline of test scores seemed too oppressive to bear. And, I was ashamed of my very pride in this game. It had so little to do with the real crisis of the schools, the crushing daily problems my stories revealed. Beneath the headlined scandals was an ongoing civic and human disaster.

What was actually going on in the classrooms in our city was a story more intriguing—and I suspected, more important—than any I had yet written. But covering it, reporting from the trenches of an inner-city school, would be almost impossible from the press gallery. Besides, I couldn't imagine any principal or teacher letting me sit in and watch the goings-on in a typical classroom. But what other way was there for a reporter to actually experience classroom life? There was only one. I would have to give up all those thrilling scoops that gave me clout in the newsroom and a top billing on the daily news budget. Maybe the inside story—the why, the reality of life in the city's 30,000 classrooms—could be mine, after all: if I got a job as a teacher. Maybe I would find a satisfying new career in teaching and not care if I ever made the front page again. I felt I was trading a vicarious existence for a desperately consequential one.

When I told my editors of my plan to get a teaching license, the city editor laughed. "It'll never happen. What school system would be foolish enough to allow a reporter into a school?"

"This one," I said.

If I came back, I could always write a series of articles for the paper. I had no such plans. I was going to become a teacher.

I did not, in fact, have the qualifications for a permanent teaching license in New York City. But neither did more than 12,000 people then teaching in the city's schools. I'd reported that story: they taught under temporary licenses granted to those who lacked education training and student-teaching experience, but did have a bachelor's degree. A bachelor's degree, I had.

Only five years earlier, I would not have been allowed to teach in New York at all. However, with the severe teaching shortages that developed in the mid-1980s, the Board of Education was forced to lower or eliminate virtually all prerequisites. Teachers had been retiring in record numbers while the number of new applicants had plummeted. Out went requirements for student-teaching experience and education degrees. Even these changes couldn't halt the shortfall. Additionally, every year since 1986, the Board of Ed had dispatched recruiters to Puerto Rico seeking Spanish-speaking teachers. And the schools still needed teachers for bilingual classes in Urdu and Albanian and people skilled in plumbing and electrical crafts for vocational high schools, where students who struggled academically could, theoretically, learn a trade. This same teacher shortage, which would open a spot for me, was expected to intensify by the mid-1990s, when another 40 percent of the city's 62,789 teachers would be eligible for their pensions.

Surely someone as eager as I was to fill a useful role could find one. For despite the aggressive recruiting efforts, there were still classrooms without permanent teachers on the first day of school. So serious was the situation that 10,000 teachers were assigned to teach unfamiliar subjects; they were "out of license," making their way through geometry when geography was their area of expertise, demonstrating shop techniques instead of declining Latin nouns. At many schools, traditional courses in sewing, ceramics, and art had to be eliminated altogether because teachers just could not be found to staff them. In this climate, anyone within reason—responsible, organized, and without visible defects of character and appearance —was in demand. Teaching skills, or lack thereof, were secondary.

If I could pass brief written and oral exams and a simple finger-print clearance ensuring that I had never been convicted of a felony, I could get the so-called TPD (temporary per diem) license. That, a single slip of paper, would qualify me for a job in one of the city's 965 public schools.

My first stop on the morning of May 25 was the Office of Recruit-ment and Counseling, a room the size of half a football field that spread out behind a heavy, windowless metal door on the first floor of 65 Court Street. The building lobby was attractive; on the wall opposite the imposing entrance was a huge mural painted by stu-dents from a Brooklyn junior high school showing happy kids of all races playing in a schoolyard. At a table in the middle of the hall sat a guard who pointed me in the direction of the Office of Recruiting. In the middle of that room was a cluster of student desks for appli-cants, while the perimeter was ringed with teachers' desks for the advisers. Here the Board of Education would determine the area of my temporary license.

At the information desk a harried young woman wordlessly slipped me a stack of forms while all four buttons on her rotary-dial telephone blinked insistently. "Recruitment, please hold. Recruit-ment, please hold. Recruitment, please hold," she rattled off between glances at me. She gestured at the student desks, where I sat with my bundle of documents to complete. Six times I listed my name and address, four times my education background: Stanford Univer-sity, California, B.S. in economics, 1980; Horton Watkins High School, St. Louis, Mo., diploma, 1976; public elementary and junior high schools in suburban St. Louis. Four times I detailed my work history—reporter, *Newsday* and *New York Newsday*, since 1982; re-porter, *The Home News*, New Brunswick, N.J., from 1980 to 1982. I searched for a request for personal and professional references, but found none. The paperwork finished, I thumbed through a brochure labeled "Professional Employment Opportunities in the New York City Public Schools." It was organized like a term paper outline: Section I, Part A, subparts 1 to 5. Some of the subparts had sub-subparts. And some of the sub-subparts had sub-sub-subparts. No table of contents. No index. Nor could I find any substantive information on what the life of New York City teachers was like, the basics and essentials like the number of hours in the workweek, specific responsibilities, job benefits. There was no list of job openings, nor any attempts to sketch the organization of the vast New York City school system itself. The most relevant information of all—how to find a job in this system of 972,000 students, 965 schools, and 32 local districts—was nowhere to be found. The booklet did have five maps, one of each borough. But the only schools on the maps were the city's 117 high schools. The elementary and junior high schools were nowhere to be seen.

The part of me that was still a journalist wondered if this massively useless document was an official hint of things to come. When I did at last locate my salary on a scale at the back—$23,000 a year —a man signaled me to his desk on the other side of the room. Mild-mannered, of medium build, with a tie hanging loosely about his neck, he wore no jacket and his shirt collar was stained with coffee. He gestured for me to hand him the forms I had just completed. He did not bother telling me his name or his function. So I was not even sure in what division of the Board of Ed he worked.

"So, you wanna teach?" he mumbled, scanning my college transcript.

"Yes, I do."

"Well, I have bad news," he responded without looking up. "It's common branches, or social studies, either junior high or high school. You're not qualified for anything else."

Common branches? What was that?

I had hoped to teach math or journalism, I told him. "I'm a reporter for *New York Newsday,* and I know of several high schools that have journalism programs."

"No license here to teach journalism," he interjected. "You mean English. Sorry. Won't work. You didn't take enough English in college."

"What do you mean?" I insisted, trying to decipher my transcript upside-down. All those literature courses I took had to be on there somewhere. I implored him to look again.

"I don't see a single lit course," he said.

"Oh, I know. See, I took them through the humanities department. That's how it works at Stanford."

"Doesn't count. Board of Examiners won't allow it. It's gotta say 'lit.' " I felt like Alice on her first day in Wonderland.

"That seems pretty absurd, doesn't it?" I asked. "I've worked as a reporter for eight years, read everything from Plato to Orwell in college. But I'm not qualified to teach English or journalism?"

"Nope."

The exchange only deepened my curiosity about the Board of Examiners, the teacher-testing agency for the New York City public school system. I had written newspaper articles about the examiners, and the Board of Ed's many unsuccessful efforts before the state legislature to have them eliminated and their function declared redundant. The board was finally abolished in January 1991, two years too late for me. It was common knowledge—closer to legend—that the Board of Ed and the literalists of the Board of Examiners were a nightmare to work with. But I had no idea that I would not be allowed to teach English simply because the examiners' requirements were so absolute and nonnegotiable.

"How about math, then?" I ventured. I had taken calculus in high school and scored a 4 out of 5 on the Advanced Placement Calculus Test. My transcript showed advanced calculus in college as well as a dozen economics courses that relied on calculus and more basic math. Certainly I knew enough math to teach any grade in New York's junior highs.

"Nope. Not enough math in college," my counselor said.

"I don't understand," I said, trying to sound calm. "You're telling me that if I took five math courses in college, even if they were basic math, that would be okay. But since I took almost all of my math in high school, I'm doomed, even though it was calculus."

He nodded.

"I've got an idea," I said. "Give me a math test, and I'll show you I know the material that's covered in junior high school math courses."

"We don't do that."

"So what am I supposed to do?"

"Take social studies. There're no jobs, of course, but you can get the license."

This was maddening. "No jobs? Then, what's the point?"

"You wanna get a license, miss?" I was beginning to wonder.

"Okay, make it social studies," I agreed.

After another ten minutes filling out still more forms, the counselor bundled them with the completed ones I had given him, and directed me across the hall to be fingerprinted. I left the Office of Recruitment and Counseling convinced that the Board of Education had no interest in recruiting me. As for counseling, I now needed some myself.

The heavy metal door I had opened two hours before slammed behind me as I walked across the hall into another room full of student desks. This one was busy, noisy with applicants for all sorts of jobs, from nurse and janitor to assistant principal. Everyone sat waiting to be fingerprinted. After turning in my paperwork, I listened to the many languages filling the air around me. Among the many, I could make out Spanish and German and what sounded like two different Asian dialects. Many others I didn't recognize.

Three hours later, my name was finally called by a man working at a stand in the middle of the room. He grabbed my right hand as if about to handcuff me, then pinched each of my fingers hard, rolling them one-by-one over a black ink pad and onto a white card. He then slapped a wet towelette in my palm. "Clean up," he commanded.

There was no bathroom or sink in which to clean my hands properly, so I just stood there lamely doing the best I could with the tiny square of moist paper. By the time I at last made it up to the examiners, it was nearly 3 P.M. I had been at the Personnel building for five hours. I was tired, hungry, annoyed, and depressed that I had nothing to offer that was wanted in the city school system. And now I was filthy, too, my fingers as black as a grease monkey's. The starched white suit that I had worn to impress had black smudges in the shape of half-moons all over it. I had wanted to look and sound professional, but I looked more like a coal miner than a teacher.

The gray-haired man who called my name after another hour's wait was courteous and friendly. He put his hand on my shoulder as he escorted me to his office, a small enclosure with a lone smoky window looking out on a brick building across the way. As I sat down, he shook my hand. "Sachar," he said, considering my application, "you know, that's a famous name." I smiled, relieved to be in the presence of someone who might treat me like a human being. "I guess so," I responded.

"The head of Brandeis University is a Sachar," he said. "You related?"

"Yes, my great-uncle." He smiled warmly.

"Well, what can I do for you?" he said.

"Get me a teaching job."

"We'd love to have you," he said. "What do you want to teach?" I sat back in my chair and tried to look dignified, crossing my legs and unzipping the leather envelope in which I carried my passport and transcript. He looked up quickly after scanning my application further.

"Why do you want to teach social studies?" he asked. "You'll never get a job."

"That's what they told me to say downstairs," I said.

"Don't you want to teach English?" he asked. "With the journalism background, that would make more sense." I couldn't believe what I was hearing. Didn't the first floor and the fourth floor talk to one another?

"I thought I couldn't teach English. That's what they told me downstairs. Or math either." I had actually leaned toward math because a teacher could quantify success and failure. Either the students learned to add and multiply or they didn't, and the standardized tests would clearly show it. I could see whether the kids had learned what I had taught.

"Well, now that I look over this transcript, I see that we can't get you a license for English or math after all," he said, "but we could get you a license for elementary school, and you could probably find a job in a junior high teaching one of these subjects."

The conversation was beginning to sound like Kafka. I couldn't get a license to teach math or English, but through some quirk of logic I might never figure out, I would be allowed to teach these subjects if I could get a license to teach elementary school, otherwise known as common branches. Why hadn't the man downstairs explained these wrinkles to me, and how many other people passed through this system without getting pointed in the right direction?

Exhausted, I confessed, "I don't understand."

"I know. Things don't make much sense around here," he said ruefully, shaking his head. "But if I were you, I'd get the common branches license, for elementary school, everything through Grade 8. Then you can look for a junior high that will hire you for math or English. Don't worry about a thing. I'll call downstairs and we'll switch your application from social studies to common branches."

He finished the paperwork and told me to return a week later for two exams, one written and one oral.

"Be on time and bring two pens. After the test, you'll be set," he said. "We need people like you."

I extended my hand, which he took in both of his. I prayed he wouldn't notice all the black ink dried on the tips of my fingers. "Let me know how you make out after your first year. I'm sure you'll do just fine."

. . .

The question seemed straightforward: *A group of second-graders is having trouble reading simple words. What would you do to help them?*

Around me sat thirty-four other applicants for all manner of teaching posts in the New York City school system, high school and junior high, special education and bilingual classes. We were given time to prepare our answers on paper before reciting them aloud in the oral exam. I scribbled two outlines, one for each question—the other one was about teaching a lesson on "community" to second-graders—and informed the proctor that I was ready. Quickly, she directed me to an adjoining office. Its only furniture was a table and two chairs, and the examiner, another nameless bureaucrat, instructed me to sit opposite him. Our conversation, he informed me, would be taped.

I started to explain that I was obtaining the elementary-ed license only so I could look for a job teaching math or English in a junior high, but he cut me off.

"Look, you're here for common branches," he said. "I am not interested in whether you can answer questions about junior high."

He switched on the tape and I began to speak. I would use flash cards, I said, with the kids who couldn't read. I didn't know if that was correct, but I remembered back to my own days in elementary school learning to read. Teaching "community" was tougher. I shied away from the pat answer—take the kids on a walk around a city neighborhood. Maps, I offered instead, would come in handy, and briefly told how I would use them.

I told the examiner I was done answering the questions.

"Maps with second-graders?" he boomed. "Why? Do you really think second-graders can understand maps?"

"Well, yes, I do," I said timidly. "If you bring it down to their level, by working with large maps of streets they know."

"And where are you going to get these maps?"

"I would assume the schools would have them. Or I could make them."

"Don't assume anything. Haven't you ever thought of taking them on a walk down a city street? Wouldn't that make more sense? We're talking about seven-year-olds, Miss Sachar. The only way maps would work is if you had them make one of their bedroom," he said. "Something they know."

"Maybe you're right," I responded, hoping I didn't sound as defensive as I felt.

"Now, Miss Sachar, tell me. What would you do if you had a kid in your class who couldn't see?"

I thought for a few moments.

"Miss Sachar, did you hear the question?"

"I'd inform the school nurse and send a letter home to the student's parents to have the child tested. Maybe if it was a really impoverished child, I could contact the neighborhood medical center and they could make arrangements."

"Most of our schools don't have school nurses. You're thinking of schools from years back." His impatient tone implied that he knew a lot more about this school system and these kids than I ever would.

"Well, then, the letter would have to do."

"Miss Sachar, what about just moving the child? Putting him in the front so he could see? How about a little common sense here?"

"I thought you meant that he literally couldn't see," I protested, "that he had a serious vision problem or was blind or something."

"Well, why don't you *ask* if you don't understand the question?" he retorted angrily. "Now, Miss Sachar, I have another question for you. Did you know that the flash card technique you suggested with the studying of consonant blends has a name?"

"No, I didn't," I said. "But it won't make much difference since I intend to teach in the junior highs, not in the elementary schools. And I don't intend to teach reading."

"That's not my concern. What is it called, when we ask students to work with consonant blends?"

I told him I didn't know. I had never asked students to work with consonant blends.

"It's phonics," he said, "and when you've taken your master's degree, you'll know that." He smiled. Did that comment mean I was going to pass?

Returning to the reading problem, he asked, "How about having the kids work in small groups? Wouldn't that work? Have the students who understand the reading concepts work with the ones who don't?"

"Maybe you should be teaching, not me," I said, trying to be light.

"I did teach, Miss Sachar. This interview is about you, not me."

There was a long silence while he finished filling out the testing form. As the minutes dragged on without a sign—a smile or nod of encouragement—that I had made it, I became convinced that perhaps I had failed, after all.

Finally, he said, "You know that since you have no teaching experience whatsoever, you'll have to take some courses?"

"Yes." All temporary-license teachers had to sign an agreement obligating them to acquire, in the next three years, at least twelve post-graduate education credits toward a master's degree in education.

Folding up the test papers, my examiner asked, "Well, do you have any questions?"

"No, well—I'd like to know how I did."

"You can't tell?" He turned off his tape recorder, then grabbed my hand firmly and shook it. "You'll hear from us within eight weeks."

On my return to the main room, the proctor, a stout middle-aged woman, greeted me with a warm smile. "Ready for the written exam?" She handed me a copy of the test question: How would I select books for a second-grade classroom? I wondered what the obsession with second grade was.

The proctor told me that the content of my essay was much less important than my grammar and spelling, though these, I discovered later, weren't terribly important either. An assistant principal who had spent years grading these exams for the Board of Examiners after school hours revealed that I could have made as many as five spelling and grammar mistakes per page and still passed. Many applicants wrote essays that were almost incoherent. But they would pass, "as long as they show a fairly basic understanding of the English language. The school system needs bodies."

In my essay I stressed the need to select books on a variety of subjects, with special sensitivity to the racial composition of the class. As I handed in my paper, the proctor told me I would have to be fingerprinted again. Back to the dreaded Fingerprinting unit, I thought. She smiled as though reading my mind.

"No, here," she said, taking my right hand. She gently took my fingers one by one and ran them over the pad of invisible ink. My hands came away clean, and I wondered why they hadn't heard about this more considerate system downstairs. Surely, no mere children could be this frustrating, no junior high this infuriating. These, after all, were experts—professionals at it. I would try anyway.

I left the large pink building and headed for the subway. By the middle of the summer, I would know whether I had passed the exams and whether I could begin to look for a job as a New York City schoolteacher.

3

At Last, a Job

Are you breathing? Do you have a pulse? Then you can teach in the New York City public schools.

—Henry Plotkin, a former math teacher at Walt Whitman Intermediate School.

Four tall and husky men walked down the sidewalk of Veronica Place, laughing and joking, knocking elbows like reunited college chums. They were just passing the corner of the beige-brick school that rose between blocks of attached two-story homes and auto-body repair shops, when I caught their attention. They stopped, obviously pegging me as an outsider in this neighborhood of largely immigrant black families.

"Is this the junior high?" I asked. The sign over the entrance said PS 246, designating an elementary school.

Smiling, the biggest of the four said, "Yeah, why?"

"I'm looking for a teaching job," I replied. The men guffawed. "Are you guys teachers here?" They wouldn't be parents, since they didn't have children in tow, and they didn't appear to be residents of this largely black enclave of Flatbush, Brooklyn.

Again, they found me somewhat amusing. "What's so funny?" I asked. I knew: they were laughing at the naiveté of this too-perky young woman dressed in a conservative suit, hair tied neatly in a ponytail, who assumed that teaching positions might still be available a week before the first day of school.

The burliest of them, a dark-haired fellow whose shirt popped open over his swelling belly, looked incredulous. "You *serious?* You want to teach *here?"*

"Why not? Is something wrong?"

"Don't worry. You'll get it. They don't turn *anyone* down here."

"Well, that's good news," I replied, "because I've been turned down almost everywhere else."

"That's the New York City school system for you," another said, putting a beefy hand on my shoulder. "Make you feel just great, don't they?"

My new companions showed me into a crowded lobby bustling with people getting reacquainted after the summer vacation. The chatter was of cruises and Disneyland and trips to Europe. And:

"How's the baby?"

"Where's your boy going to junior high this year?"

"You getting 9SP again?"

In my prim suit and faux pearls, I was overdressed. Jeans were the favored apparel for these veterans. A few women wore shorts, and I looked in vain for one man in suit and tie. Half the staff were black in a city where overall only about one fifth of the teachers were. There were a few teachers even younger than I, and some much older ones, too. French, Spanish, Yiddish swirled around my ears.

Although I did not go to school in New York, I felt a wave of nostalgia in the surroundings: next to the main entrance was the front office, and in the office, a long, elbow-high counter, like schools everywhere. I waited at that counter patiently for half an hour, hoping one of the secretaries just beyond would invite me in. I left my perch occasionally to pace back and forth and hopefully catch their eye. I had plenty of time to read all the notices on the two staff bulletin boards. On the wall, the time clock monotonously clicked off the minutes. Other teachers milled around the mailboxes, asking when the program office would open so they could pick up their teaching schedules. I told at least ten people that I was there to apply for a math teaching position. They smiled politely: none offered to help me locate the principal.

Finally, I ventured boldly behind the counter, declaring to anyone who would listen, "I was just sent here by the district office. I'm here for the math vacancy."

The clerk motioned me back to the visitor side of the counter. "You'll have to see the boss," she said. "Please wait there."

One of the secretaries was hunting for phone receivers, which had apparently been put away over the summer. Only one of the telephones was working. The others were missing their headpieces.

They rang and rang and rang, but the secretaries had no means to answer them. A second secretary was typing. A third guarded a closed door of an office marked PRINCIPAL.

When, at last, that door opened, out stepped the man I had first seen two weeks earlier at a job fair in Manhattan. He wore an open shirt with a colorful crocheted Islamic skullcap. He had been seeking teachers then, and today, only days before the students would arrive, he still had openings. Most schools were already fully staffed; this one wasn't. As much as I rejoiced, I also wondered why.

That job fair itself had been pure chaos, Room 464 at Martin Luther King, Jr., High School in Manhattan full to bursting with teachers and administrators. I recalled the deputy superintendent of District 17, hiring teachers like a busy bakery clerk filling orders. "You want French?" he would ask an applicant. "I got openings at 61, 246, 320, and 390." There were six junior highs in his district. When an applicant chose a school the deputy sent him off to meet the principal. A match was made every five minutes. That day, I had supposedly found a place, too—teaching math at IS 391, one of the better schools in District 17. But, three days later, I was informed by phone that this vacancy did not, in fact, exist. Back to the deputy superintendent I raced for another slot. "Go see Claude Winfield at IS 246," he had said. "He needs bodies." And here I was.

A middle-aged black man, about five-foot-ten, Claude Winfield wore sunglasses so dark I couldn't even see the outline of his eyebrows. The colorful crocheted cap fit snugly over his oval-shaped head. He was dressed in loafers, dark blue pants, and a jacket with the words "Whitman Basketball" imprinted across the left breast. "Have her meet with Miss Kowalski," he whispered to his secretary, glancing across the counter in my direction.

Hoping someone had gone to hunt down this Miss Kowalski, I waited in the front office for another twenty minutes.

"Haven't seen her," one teacher said when I asked. "Try on the second floor. That's her new office."

I was just about to go upstairs when I overheard a woman at the front door introducing herself to a parent. "May I help you?" she said. "I'm Miss Kowalski."

Vikki Kowalski wore a plaid skirt and a pumpkin-colored shirt. Her auburn hair, slightly frizzy, was shoulder-length and curly. Her fair-skinned face was bare of make-up. She was tall and wide-shouldered. She seemed strong, as though from carrying books, with muscled calves that suggested many years of climbing school staircases. She wore a brass-colored metal ring with dozens of keys like a bracelet around her wrist. It was so heavy that it left a dark pink imprint on her arm when she shifted it to the other hand.

"Excuse me," I said. "If you're Miss Kowalski, I think I'm supposed to see you. I'm here to apply for a math position."

She did not return my smile. In a strong voice, with stern demeanor, she ordered me to follow her up the stairs. She looked humorless, just as I expected an assistant principal to be. Her office on the second floor was but a cubbyhole cluttered with boxes, with three oversized lockers, a desk, and two tall metal cabinets. A yellowed shade blocked the lone window. The telephone atop her old wooden desk, like the phones downstairs, lacked a receiver, its base filthy with smudged fingerprints. She apologized for the mess; as a new assistant principal, she had yet to set up shop. Last year, she had been a teacher.

"How may I help you?" she asked, still cheerless and unsmiling.

"Well, I was told in the district office that you have a vacancy teaching eighth-grade math. I'm hoping you'll ——."

"Why should I hire you?" she snapped. It was the first time that anyone in the school system had asked me why I wanted to teach or why I thought I was suitable for the job. I decided not to take offense at the edge of sarcasm in Miss Kowalski's voice.

"I'm energetic, I know math, and I think I can do a good job for you," I answered.

She examined the packet of materials I had given her—a résumé, several reference letters, and a copy of my temporary teaching certificate. "Well, we do have two vacancies in the department, one teaching eighth-grade math and another teaching a corrective math program in the seventh grade." The teacher for this remedial program, she explained, would have about ten different classes a week, for two or three periods each. I envisioned hundreds of kids I would never get to know well.

"I'd prefer the eighth-grade position," I told her. "I don't really want to share my kids with other math teachers. I want to take credit for their successes and responsibility for their failures."

"You really think you can handle the eighth grade?" A hint of suspicion entered her voice. "You know, the eighth grade has a lot of paperwork." In addition to teaching five classes, I would have a homeroom class and thus also a great number of administrative chores connected with the students' high school applications.

"I think I can handle it."

"*Thinking* you can handle it is not good enough. Not when we're talking about deadlines."

"Well, okay, I *know* I can." I wanted to give it back: "Deadlines, lady? Try making the first edition with a breaking riot story!"

Then, she asked, "What's your discipline policy?"

I didn't have one. So I improvised: "A teacher who moves quickly, who gets going right away in the classroom—a teacher like that won't have discipline problems." Trying to sound upbeat and confident and anticipating her follow-up, I added, "But if I do, I will ask the child nicely to stop. If I get no response, I will send for help."

She was unconvinced. "I really think you should try the corrective math," she said. "This eighth-grade program—actually, it would have been my program—it's very tough."

"I think I can handle eighth-graders." I couldn't understand her reticence. Clearly, no other applicants were lined up at the door to fill the slot. And in just a week, the kids would arrive.

Trying the diplomatic approach, I said, "I bet it's hard seeing a new teacher come in to take your program. But I'll do it justice, I really will."

She relented. "You'll have to see Mr. Winfield."

"I have the job?"

"It's not up to me. But I'll tell him you have my okay."

Perhaps she had a curriculum guide I could study. No. A textbook? No. Any reference materials? Nothing would be available until the head of the math textbook inventory arrived, or until she had time to sort through the stack of unlabeled boxes that had recently been dumped in her new office. "Good teachers," she added helpfully, "don't need textbooks."

Principal Winfield was still in the front office and he invited me in. "Sit down," he said gently. The table between us was covered with papers. At one end of the table, a large window looked out on a residential street of several neatly kept attached houses. On the sidewalk were two junked cars missing all their wheels.

Winfield peered through his sunglasses at the materials I had just shown to Miss Kowalski and handed my résumé back to me. He put my completed application in a separate envelope and asked, "Why do you want to teach inner-city children?" It was awkward trying to talk with someone whose eyes I could not see. It felt like a power ploy.

"Well," I ventured, "the school is close to my home, and I've always wanted to teach." On the résumé he had handed back to me was my last job—newspaper reporter. If he noticed, he didn't say. I assumed it didn't bother him: he didn't worry, or didn't care.

"I like your enthusiasm," he told me. I didn't feel that I had been particularly enthusiastic, but I smiled. For fifteen minutes, he spoke about his school, his pride in its championship math team, their annual trips to foreign countries, including one several years earlier to Russia. Pictures from that tour decorated a bulletin board behind his desk. This year, he said, the school would sponsor a trip to Africa. "We're doing things here that are so inventive they're not even being attempted elsewhere in the country."

I decided not to probe, but if the school was so inventive, I wondered, why was it ranked in the bottom sixth of all junior highs in the city? The most recent reading ranks report had it 149th out of 179.

"It sounds like a school where I'd like to try my hand," I said. "I hope I'll have the chance."

"You will. And, by the way, I run the school the way I've run this interview—informally."

"So, I have the job?"

"I said you'd have the chance, didn't I?" he responded, suddenly smiling.

As I gathered my things, I thanked him warmly and made small talk with professional inquiries.

"How many students do you have here, anyway?"

"Two thousand, three hundred," he replied matter-of-factly.

"Really?" I asked. That was more than had been enrolled in my entire college freshman class. I was incredulous: the school building looked too small to hold them all.

Winfield caught my surprise. "Yeah, we should have 900. It's supposed to be an elementary school." Which explained the narrow corridors and stairwells, and that PS 246 sign over the front door. The place looked chaotic already, and those 2,300 students had yet to arrive.

When I left Winfield's office, I remembered the map question at the Board of Examiners. I took the advice to heart and decided to explore my new neighborhood on foot. So I set out down the halls, to learn the layout. The building was arranged in that classic mid-century plan familiar to any former urban school child: a four-story, U-shaped structure surrounding a courtyard—classrooms in the arms, auditorium and gymnasiums in the middle, and student and teacher cafeterias in the basement. The outdoor space was an asphalt playground and assembly area, surrounded by cyclone fencing with huge gaps. It had two basketball hoops, a few game boards, and more graffiti than I'd ever seen in one place at one time. Odd-numbered rooms were on the streetside walls, even-numbered rooms facing the yard. The indoor gyms seemed only big enough to handle about 100 kids at a time and had no locker rooms or showers. There were also no student lounges, and no hall lockers for the kids to store books and coats.

On the first floor was the bathroom for women staff members. It was truly filthy: water and urine covered the floor and no stalls had toilet paper. Doors and walls were covered in graffiti. "Teachers is fucked up," one scrawl advised. Beside an overflowing trash can, paper towels littered the floor. The cold-water spigot was missing, and the hot water was scalding. There was no soap. I shuddered to imagine what the student bathrooms were like. Once school started, the principal was supposed to distribute teachers' bathroom keys and, presumably, someone might even clean the bathroom.

The classrooms looked a bit better. Some freshly painted in bright colors—orange and several shades of blue—seemed cheerful and welcoming. But the new coat had been slapped right on top of old, chipping paint, and it was already uneven and scabby, beginning to peel.

The first official faculty meeting started fifteen minutes late in an auditorium plainly too small even to seat an entire grade at once, let alone the whole school. I counted 480 seats. With dreary, pasty orange walls and broken chair backs gaping in the otherwise orderly rows, it was not an inviting place. A curtain was drawn across the stage with black construction-paper letters pasted in a crooked line near the top: "SUMUS UNUM," they read. "We Are One."

I sat three rows back, alongside another rookie just hired to teach French. When Winfield finally arrived, he strode to the mike at center stage to welcome us back.

"We're going to have a wonderful year," he declared. The first in a series of announcements he made drew immediate applause: Eighth-graders would now lunch during eighth period. It meant nothing to me, until the man behind me said, "Thank God, they'll be out of the school early." The next announcement also provoked cheers. There would be five lunch periods instead of six. "We're trying to eliminate unnecessary chaos," Winfield explained. He had removed his crocheted cap, but the dark sunglasses remained.

Winfield then dropped a bomb: teachers and students were

being organized into clusters, which "would travel together." There would be three or four clusters per grade, each cluster to include four or five classes. At the time, neither I nor the teachers around me understood any of it. "Teachers, not students, will be traveling. We'll have a lot of kids again this year," he continued, as the crowd groaned. "And to comply with Chancellor Green's request, we will move as quickly as possible to eliminate the time clock." Like factory hands, teachers were required to punch in and out every day. A few applauded their union's small victory, but most were silent.

Then Winfield outlined his goals for the year. "In language arts," he said, "we've been at 48, 49 percent on the reading test. I'd like to see us get to 50." This was odd. According to the Board of Ed, less than a quarter of the students in this school had scored at or above the national average on the previous year's standardized reading test. Winfield seemed to be using an inflated statistic, perhaps citing a different test, to put his school in the best possible light. Administrators often fudged the numbers, especially for the press.

"We want writing in the content area," he continued. "Even math." Since he did not elaborate, I could only guess how kids should write about math.

Apparently, math was a real sore spot. "It's so in need of improvement. We have a lot of work to do. We're not looking to penalize. We're looking to improve teaching at IS 246." Winfield paused for a moment. After glancing at his notes, he said, "I'll be in the building more this year. Last year my goal was to be out of the building." Teachers roared with laughter. I assumed he must have been visiting other schools, trying to learn how to improve his own. No, teachers around me explained, that wasn't it. "The guy would just vanish," said one. "He's a joke," whispered another, "never around." A third told me Winfield made himself the math department supervisor the year before but rarely visited teachers to make the mandated observation reports. "Was he sick?" I asked in a whisper. "There've been rumors," came the reply. "But if he was, he should have gotten someone else to take over, and he never did."

As assistant principals distributed a three-page handout, Winfield talked us through it, item by item. He actually pleaded with the staff about attendance and punctuality. Most teachers showed up every day from September through November, he said, but by January, "way too many of you are calling in sick." Substitute teachers only "throw the school into chaos." I was beginning to get the feeling that this school was often in chaos, a feeling confirmed by Winfield's next remarks. A new public address system being installed, he said proudly, would soon allow teachers to stick a key into a special box in their rooms and radio the front office that "you're having trouble and you're panicking." The staff loved this and broke up like an out-of-control class. Actually, the thought of it was pretty funny, all of these grown men and women radioing distress calls. "I'm panicking. Send HELP!"

"What happens then?" a teacher yelled out. More laughter.

"I haven't finished." Winfield was smiling. But his audience was laughing so loud that it was hard to catch his reply. "You ask for help and you'll get it." When would I use my panic key? A rape? A robbery? A knifing? A kid who won't hand in his homework? A lot of things could make me panic, I thought.

Since we had just been told we would be moving from room to room, someone asked where we should leave these handy panic keys. "We'll have to come up with a system," Winfield replied. "We can't leave them in the rooms because of the inquisiteness of our students." *Inquisiteness?* I was sure I had heard him correctly. "He often makes mistakes like that," whispered a veteran English teacher beside me. "Even if he said it right," another added, "it's the wrong word. He means criminal mischief."

Next was Teachers' Choice, a Board of Ed program through which every teacher could order $227 in supplies. The catalog was the size of the Manhattan Yellow Pages.

"Anything being done to track down the items we didn't get last year?" a man wearing a yarmulke called out.

"Absolutely not," Winfield answered. More laughter. And, oh yes: this year, we should not order mimeograph paper through the catalog. The school would have enough to get things copied. This immense good news was met with silence.

"Any questions?" Winfield asked. A woman reported that her staff bathroom key no longer worked. Winfield explained that the locks had been changed and teachers would have to get new keys. "When?" she asked. "Eventually," he answered. The meeting had lasted an hour.

It was time to pick up keys to my classrooms. The set an assistant principal gave me had five unmarked keys on it. My homeroom didn't need one; the door was wide open.

The floor had been swept, but the rest of the room was in disarray. The wooden coat closets in the back were coated with graffiti. One window shade was ripped and dangled like an unwanted dress falling off a junk shop hanger. Leaning like an abstract sculpture on the floor in the front of the room was my desk, missing one pair of legs. The two blackboards, one in front, one at the side, were dilapidated. One was missing its chalk ledge. I saw no chalk or erasers anywhere. The wooden floor was warped and scratched, sorely in need of a fresh coat of varnish. I hadn't counted on the bright and cheery rooms of my St. Louis junior high school, but this was even worse than I expected. The only decorations were cutouts from *National Geographic*, taped over the front blackboard. I counted the chairs and panicked when I tallied thirty-seven: the thought of so many kids in one room! My room.

I tried the door, just to make sure it locked easily. Lock? It didn't even close. The painters who slapped a coat of turquoise haphazardly all over the room had painted the door, too, and now it stuck. When I found the janitor, he followed me back to the room. Heaving all of his 180 pounds against the door, he was barely able to ram it shut. "Seems to work okay to me," he said as he walked off.

The four buddies I met that morning stopped by my room when the bell rang and invited me to lunch at a Kentucky Fried Chicken on Flatbush Avenue. Along the way, they regaled the newcomer with what a crazy place IS 246 was, insulting the principal, their colleagues, and each other with glee and gusto, making me laugh until I hurt. One asked with a knowing smile, "So, how hard was it to get the job?" He was right; IS 246 was not exactly a highly selective institution.

Departmental meetings began after lunch, and Miss Kowalski produced a textbook for me. I was flattered that she had remembered my request. Now, she was warm and gentle, a considerable change from our interview. She also clarified Winfield's "writing in the content area" remark, suggesting we give the students a project each marking period. "Have them write on the origins of the ruler or the Pythagorean theorem."

When the meeting ended, I tucked the textbook into my gray satchel, a bulging bag I was beginning to regard as my lifeline. Erasers, we learned, must be carried from room to room so the kids don't steal them or use them as weapons. Same with chalk. All my pens and chalk and erasers would have to go in the satchel. With the cluster traveling routine, I would be moving almost every period. A human bookmobile, I would have no room to call my own.

Having picked up my schedule and the rosters of my five classes,

I prepared to leave at 2:30. I had been at the school since 8 A.M. That evening, too, I knew, would be spent on schoolwork, reviewing my program and the rosters, filling in my grade book, and beginning to construct lesson plans for the textbook I had just received.

"I think I'll be heading home," I told Miss Kowalski.

"No, you won't," she snapped. "You may not leave until the bell rings at three o'clock."

I felt chastened and angry at being treated like a child. "So they really take this clocking out time literally?" I asked mildly.

"Sure do," she said. "You got work to do? Take a seat in your homeroom and do it." I retreated up the stairs to my empty classroom, feeling every inch the novice. It was true—I had a lot to do and a lot to learn.

4

You Don't Have to Love Them . . .

You are going into classrooms where you're going to be facing enormous problems because our children have enormous problems. So many of them are living in a terribly brutal, new kind of poverty. School is the only thing in the world that provides them with some hope. As rich as is our school system's history, there is so much to do to recover from years of neglect. We have physical plant problems that are a national disgrace. And the security problems, too—if one teacher or one child isn't safe, then none of us is safe. I'll tell you, teaching is physically, emotionally, intellectually draining. But it is also a job where you can see yourself making a difference to individual flesh-and-blood human beings. You are the future, and the future is in your hands. Good Luck.

—Sandra Feldman, president of the United Federation of Teachers, to 2,000 first-time New York City teachers, the Felt Forum, August 25, 1988.

The few days before the students arrived passed quickly. "It's always great," one teacher confided, "when the kids aren't around."

But I couldn't wait to meet the kids. Alone, I stood at the blackboard and practiced speaking to imaginary students in the empty seats. In downtown Brooklyn, I visited a school supply store for teachers, spending several hundred dollars on workbooks. Every free moment I read up on pedagogy—books on child psychology, discipline, teaching principles and methods. After I heard from other teachers that junior high kids like stickers on everything, from tests and term papers to homework assignments and report cards, I bought stickers in dozens of varieties. If they liked them, I would have them.

Despite the plentiful talk about how tough kids were at this school, I was confident that if my classroom was an exciting place, my kids would quickly fall into line. So I mapped out a kind of stock market game for the kids to play and arranged for several friends who worked in finance to come speak to my classes about how banks worked. What I lacked in experience, I would make up in enthusiasm, ingenuity, and resourcefulness. The anticipation was exhilarating.

As eager as I was to begin, I still had to master the intricacies of the paperwork. And I still needed to meet my new colleagues. One graciously offered to explain the procedures of the Red Roll Book, a citywide attendance record so important that a seven-page memo would soon arrive with precise instructions on how to complete it. With his help, I cracked the code; with the memo alone, I'd still be scratching my head.

From the woman who ran the mimeograph room, I learned that Miss Kowalski's permission was necessary before anything could be copied. We were absolutely not allowed to mimeograph our own materials, and would have to give the copy room at least one or two days' prior notice. The mimeo lady was the principal source of copied work for 130 teachers and she worked only half a day, from 8 A.M. to noon. Because of these restrictions and the district's desire to conserve paper, she said I would be limited to one class set from any rexomaster, as the worksheets were called. Textbooks would not be given out until the end of September after the kids had "settled down," so I visited the copy room and asked for six sets of 100 copies each, figuring I would need other materials to get me through the first weeks of school.

"Not enough paper for all these rexos," the mimeo-room lady said sympathetically, putting her arm around me. A veteran told me how to cope. "Just hand out the thirty copies and collect them at the end of the period." And then what?

"Use them again the next period."

"But what if you want to use them as homework and let the kids write on them?" I asked. "Oh, you don't let the papers leave the school. Kids aren't allowed to write on rexos. If you want to use the rexo as homework, copy the problems onto the board and tell the kids to copy it down. That can take the whole period, and then you don't have to teach as much."

The photocopying machine in the front office was already "out of order," as was the machine in the attendance secretary's office. When I watched my supervisor copy something on her machine, she turned each page over to copy again on the other side rather than use new sheets of paper. Unable to count on regular use of the school's equipment or even its paper supply, I struck a private deal for the year with the owner of a copying store near my home. It cost me over $40 each week, but at least I got what I needed without a hassle.

The woman who ran the mimeo room had a husband: he handed out school supplies. His chalk was rationed, a box at a time. Nor apparently could I get at the several hundred reams of notebook paper in his storeroom closet. "We might run out if I give it out," he explained. Scissors and staplers had to be ordered from my $227 supply allotment, or borrowed from another teacher, or bought with my own money. The crayons, boxes and boxes of them, were not for student use. And, until he got an okay from higher-ups, not for our use either. I was allocated a stack of red construction paper to decorate my bulletin boards, one roll of Scotch tape, one eraser, and a single marking book to record my grades.

In the course of this dismal introduction to the economic realities at IS 246—we don't have it, and if we do, you probably can't use it—I did meet a few of the other teachers. One afternoon, while I was in the front office, a social studies teacher asked me how to spell *copying*. He knew how to spell *copy*, he said, but could never remember when to change the *y* to an *i*. After I explained the rule, *copier* still seemed to stump him. "I'm a terrible speller," he sighed, "which is why I went for social studies instead of language arts." Another teacher was helping her friend to spell *preferred*. "P-e-r-f-e-r-e-d," she said.

I had imagined the teachers' lounges—one on the second floor and one on the fourth—would be comfortable havens for staff revitalization. Instead, they were tiny, carpetless rooms the size of walk-in closets, stuffed with tables and lockers.

Winfield called a meeting for the new teachers at which he explained more administrative details and passed on a few words of philosophy. "You don't have to love kids to teach," he told us. "You just have to respect kids." Teaching at Whitman, he told us, "can be very rough; it can also be easy." When he visited classrooms—and his class visits had already been scheduled, he said—he looked "not for silence, but for teaching." A good thing, as other teachers guaranteed that the kids would rarely be quiet for long.

The last day before the students were due to arrive, Winfield wore a red-and-white gingham shirt with an open collar, his crocheted cap, dark sunglasses, blue pants, white Reeboks, and a red sweater with two white stripes across the breast. "I dress this way so the parents don't think I'm the principal," he said. He wasn't kidding. Earlier that morning, parents flooded in, trying to transfer their kids in or out of the school. Incognito, Winfield went silently and anonymously past them down the corridor.

His parting words to rookie teachers that morning were an admonishment. "I don't like complaints with no purpose," he declared, relating the tale of a teacher who had complained to him earlier that week about her class schedule. She thought it a poor program because she was assigned to teach computer science, a subject she knew little about. "The kids know more than I do," she protested. "Now, I have a response to that," Winfield said. "Are the kids always supposed to be the dumbest persons in the room?" In spite of his refreshingly liberal attitude, I clung to the hope that I would know more math than the kids in my classes.

New teachers were also required to attend a workshop as part of Project Basics, a program created to help two dozen troubled schools in New York. In addition to being a Project Basics school, because our reading scores and attendance were below state standards, we were supposedly an SUR school (School Under Review). We had three years to improve, or the Board of Ed had said we would be shut down. But the board often delivered empty threats about closing schools to scare administrators and teachers; in our drastically overcrowded school district, an outright shutdown seemed a particularly foolhardy and unlikely possibility. The board had nowhere to send all the displaced kids.

Our workshop, called "Getting Started," was run by Barry Kantrowitz, often described as one of the liveliest teachers at Whitman. "If you're a shouter, shout! If you're a pacer, pace. Watch the best, but adapt your own style," Kantrowitz advised, after telling us what a shy and insecure guy he was. He paced back and forth across the room, then stopped suddenly with a question. "A kid shouts out the answer, and it's right. Do we acknowledge him?" I raised my hand. Sure, I would acknowledge him, I said, but I would ask him to raise his hand the next time. "Wrong!" said Kantrowitz. "Kids who call out, ignore them." Difficult to do, he admitted, but we must try. "Praise! Praise! Praise," he added, "give lots of it."

He also warned, "Be careful: the year before, a teacher was assaulted after opening his classroom door to a student passing by. Close and lock the door always." (And if your door didn't close?)

To students who ask, "Does it count?" we should answer, "Everything counts." Collect everything, and put some sort of mark on every student paper. Our grading policies must be clear. "How you grade is up to you. But state your policies and stick to them."

For help on public speaking: watch Jesse Jackson, or Mr. Rogers of children's public-television fame. "Jackson is dramatic, inspired. Rogers is an expert at the conservation of language."

What to do with a kid who constantly asks to go to the bathroom? "You know who's full of crap and who's telling the truth," said Kantrowitz. But avoid confrontations. "In every confrontation, you lose. And the kid is a hero to the class."

And one more thing: "The problem doesn't exist unless you have written it down. That's the Board of Ed." That meant if a student misbehaved, we should take note on a Blue Card. If we phoned a parent, that should be recorded on an index card. A paper trail had to be assembled of every provocation by every recalcitrant student and every action we took in response; otherwise, the presumption of angelhood prevailed.

Then Kantrowitz, a social studies teacher, gave us a social studies lesson: about the kids who actually attended Walt Whitman. It was the first time anyone had bothered. "We are not dealing with motivated college graduates here. We are dealing with lazy children. If this was such a wonderful job, you wouldn't have gotten it. Do you know that we still have four vacancies in this building one day before school starts? You have to realize that cops don't scare these kids— don't think you're going to. If you're really in a pickle, invoke God's name. It's illegal, dishonest. But it's tremendous. The kids love it."

When he finished his lecture, I asked what he thought of my supervisor, Vikki Kowalski. "The smartest woman in the school," he averred. A Whitman math teacher for ten years until her recent promotion, she had just won a $1,000 prize from the New York Alliance of the Public Schools for teaching excellence. She spent it on a party for the staff. "A real salt-of-the-earth person. Use her. Tap her. Get to know her."

Kantrowitz genuinely loved being a teacher. As we were getting ready to leave, he offered, "Remember. What we do is subtle, mystical, magical. We can be kind, gentle, soft, but not confused."

. . .

Between the rules of the classroom and the rules of the school, there was much to learn. There was a strange protocol, almost a pecking order, related to even the simplest things. Teachers, for instance, were to use the pay telephone in the cafeteria rather than the phones in the front office or in the offices of the assistant principals. Administrators were to be addressed by their last names: Miss Kowalski, Mr. Newman, Mr. Novins, Mr. Berkowitz, Mr. Winfield. We had to remain in school until the dismissal bell rang, even without a last-period class. And we were to clock in before the opening bell, even if we were free first period. However, there was no dress code. Many teachers wore jeans, and those who dressed more formally stood out.

Students were tracked in classes by numerical designations, 8-1 the top class of the eighth grade, and 8-16 the bottom one. All kids knew the number of their class and exactly what the designations meant. It was a public statement of their intellectual ability—an evaluation, a prediction, and practically a self-fulfilling guarantee. Incredibly, with the exception of a single section handpicked for math ability, students were tracked solely on the basis of their reading scores from the previous year. Translated, this meant that the students in each class took *all* of their academic classes together, as if a good reader was inevitably also gifted in math, social studies, and science. Only for electives like foreign language, shop, and gym were classes ever split up or combined. This unilateral tracking system seemed to serve no child's interests and could have devastating effects. And I knew from years of reporting on standardized test scores that barely two-thirds of the time was there a close relationship between a student's reading and math scores. Surely there had to be some terrific readers tracked into 8-1 who lagged behind in math, and poor readers with real math aptitude sitting frustrated among the 8-16 castoffs. I was going to be teaching both 8-1 and 8-16. I was curious to find what other complications would unfold.

I expected to have each of my five classes the same time every day, five days a week, as school was sensibly arranged in my era of junior high. But, except for one class, I taught each class only four times a week, for forty-three minutes each. The head of the programming office explained that state regulations require sex education, foreign language, shop, and phys ed, with the result that "a lot of the academics have to go." So, my schedule was incredibly complicated and impossible to remember. Every day, I followed a different routine in different rooms with different kids. I even taught one class, 8-7, six times a week. When I asked why, the program head shrugged. "That's just how it worked out. No particular reason." Programming was done for the school's benefit, not for the students'. Still, in a school that ultimately would enroll nearly 2,000 students for the 1988–89 year, it was an enormous task—to do it all, let alone well—especially without a computer.

Since many of my classes met in Room 327, it would have made sense for that to be my homeroom. But, Room 327 belonged to a language arts teacher, and from the first days of school, I felt tension between us. I asked her if I could use one of the bulletin boards in her room to show off the good work of my students. No; she planned to use all of them herself. Three weeks into the school year, however, they still had not been decorated, so I asked again to use just one. "Stop bugging me," was her reply. Since I never taught class in my own homeroom, there was no convenient place to post my students' work so they could see their accomplishments on display.

The need for something as simple as a bulletin board brought one point home early on—I had no place of my own. Even when I wanted to relax alone, there was nowhere to go except perhaps a stall in the bathroom or a seat in the windowless roach-infested teachers' cafeteria. The teachers' lounges were often noisy and crowded; sometimes, it was hard to find a seat in them. My homeroom, though spacious, was mine in name only, in use by others almost every period of the day. I did not feel comfortable sitting in the back of the room during another teacher's lesson, and it was not my prerogative to do so uninvited.

I walked through my schedule several times before the kids arrived; I would be teaching in ten different classrooms. Tuesdays looked especially bad. I would teach that 8-7 class twice and have only one free period all day in which to prepare. I already knew I would need that time badly. I quickly realized that going out after work would be impossible; I would probably need a nap.

More than learning the ropes, I was absorbed those first days with the students whom I had yet to meet. But the only information I could come up with on the 141 kids I would teach was their reading and math scores from the prior year. For some, I did not even have that, and so set out to gather the information myself, working student by student through a printout as thick as a dictionary. Locating and copying each score took five hours. No one bothered to tell me that there was a folder for every student with this information right in the first-floor office.

The scores I copied into my book stunned and worried me. In my top class, 8-1, several students had scored above the 90th percentile on the citywide math test the previous spring, meaning that out of every 100 students taking the test, only ten had done better. That was the encouraging news. But a few in 8-1 were down at the 33rd percentile. Here was that tracking fallacy in human terms—good readers in the top class of the eighth grade who were at least one year behind in math. All for the convenience of scheduling.

In 8-7, supposedly a middle-level class, the scores were dramatically lower. One student, Jimmy, had scored in the 8th percentile. Ninety-two out of a hundred students in his grade had done better. The average was somewhere around the 40th percentile; yet this was my second-best class. My other classes, 8-12, 8-13, and 8-16, had many students at the 20th percentile or lower. Fully one third of this group scored in single digits. The news got worse and worse—one child, Shereeza, had scored in the 1st percentile: out of 100 students taking the test, all had done better than she. Her reading score was similar, and I wondered if she was functionally illiterate, one of those kids I had written so much about but never met, much less attempted to teach.

"Don't expect miracles here," one teacher told me. "Especially with those bottom classes." I was just beginning to grasp the scope of the problem. While several teachers had warned that my program looked a bit more difficult than most, with so many classes at the bottom of the grade, there were some consolations. One was 8-13, a handpicked section composed of students who were sweet, well-intentioned, and even academically able, many emerging from bilingual or English-as-a-Second-Language classes where they were nurtured in small groups by special teachers. In my toughest class, 8-16, only twenty-four students were on the register, a fifth less than usual. Naively, I believed that the small size would compensate for the fierce reputation of some of the kids. Rose-Ann, for one, was returning to Whitman Intermediate School for a fifth year. She was already sixteen years old, the age of most high school juniors. She would make my life miserable, my colleagues assured me.

Without biographical details on most of the kids—partly because I didn't know who their former teachers were—I pored over the names. Many of Whitman's students were first- or second-generation West Indian immigrants. Additionally, more than 10 percent of the school's students spoke a language other than English at home —either Haitian Creole, Spanish, or Chinese.

Since its days in the 1950s as the neighborhood elementary school for highly stable middle-class Jewish and Irish families, the school had changed radically. More than half of the students received a free lunch and another 15 percent paid a reduced price; an even greater number, although eligible, did not apply, apparently unwilling to be stigmatized as poor. For many students, the school was a revolving door. Only 58 percent of those who entered finished their eighth-grade year there; the rest transferred, usually because their families had moved. The typical class section would be assigned at least five or six new kids during the year and lose the same number.

I was also still trying to figure out what I would teach. The textbook worried me; I had never seen one so incomprehensible. There were entire passages I could not understand unless I worked through them word by word. To say nothing of a document called the Scope and Sequence that was a bare-bones course outline of what I was required to teach.

Miss Kowalski gave me the Scope and Sequence on Thursday of opening week, and I spent most of that day trying to match up the "performance objectives" with the relevant lessons and problem sets in the textbook. For all my insistence that I was completely capable of teaching junior high math, whole topics in the Scope and Sequence were new to me. "Performance objective 8.12.02.01A," for example, said students would be able to "read, interpret and make a histogram." I had no idea what a histogram was, much less how to "make a frequency polygon from a histogram," the next objective. What was a frequency polygon?

Then there was objective 8.12.03.01A. It commanded me to teach kids to "determine a permutation of n things taken r at a time where $r \leq n$." I would also be expected to teach the kids negative exponents as well as scientific notation, a mathematical shorthand for writing very large and very small numbers. It was hard to imagine a use for these topics in the lives of most people. And with 10th percentile reading and math scores, would the students I was about to teach be even remotely ready to understand them?

Looking over the outline was a dismaying task. If I was to cover the entire document by year-end, there were several other theoretical topics that I was supposed to teach as early as the fourth week of school. For instance, performance objective 8.08.02.05A said that kids would know how to "raise an integer to a given power, e.g.,$(-11)^2 = (-11) \times (-11) = 121$." That was just the second power. Fine. How would I explain $(-9)^9$, which was also on my course outline?

Anything could be taught, I told myself, with a good plan and a good textbook. So I set to comb the 561-page tome. I wanted to start with percents, also one of the first topics in the Scope and Sequence. I had some ideas for challenging and engaging assignments, like having the kids clip mortgage ads so we could talk about something real—loans and interest—and how they affected the cost of buying a house.

But first, I would have to review fractions, and show the kids how to convert a fraction to a percent and vice versa. How did the textbook explain that, I wondered.

A teachers' edition of the book was "unavailable." The Scope and Sequence offered no help whatsoever, and all I got were strange looks when I asked if anyone had ever collected teaching materials, games, exercises, or problems relating to the eighth-grade math curriculum.

Turning to page 160 in the textbook, I found "Percents as Decimal Fractions." "The % symbol represents two decimal places," it began. "When it is removed there should be two more decimal places than in the original numeral. To express a percent as a numeral for a decimal fraction, we rewrite the digits of the given percent but drop the percent symbol. Then we move the decimal point two places to the left. A decimal point is understood after the ones digit in a numeral naming a whole number."

This was gobbledygook, word soup! I could convert a percent to a decimal fraction in my sleep, but this explanation was so convoluted, so dependent on a vocabulary I was sure the kids did not possess, that I decided I would do better on my own. I turned to another section and another. Here were the textbook's explanations:

"To subtract any rational number from another rational number, we add to the minuend the opposite or additive inverse of the rational number which is to be subtracted."

"An algebraic expression or algebraic phrase may be a numerical expression . . . or an expression containing one or more variables joined by operational symbols."

"To find what percent one number is of another, we find what fractional part one number is of the other expressed in lowest terms. Then we change this fraction to a percent, using the percent equivalent if it is known, otherwise we change the fraction first to a two-place decimal, then to a percent."

I looked at the problem sets in the percent section, and found this: "Ms. Lee bought an oil burner for $900. She paid 30% cash. If the balance is to be paid in 18 equal monthly installments, how much must she pay each month?" First, my kids would have to figure out how much Ms. Lee paid for the burner, then how much was left to pay, then divide that amount by 18. This was a three-step problem. How would kids in the 10th and 20th percentile in math approach this? How could I help them?

Even when I looked at the topics that were supposed to be easy, like how to add and subtract negative and positive integers, I knew the kids would be stumped. Neither well-designed nor colorful, the book was obviously behind the times, completely unlike the books I had seen at progressive schools. There were no illustrations, no vivid graphics. The Board of Ed was supposed to allocate $25 per child per year to purchase textbooks, which should mean new up-to-date math books at least once every four or five years. Yet the book I held in my hand was written in 1964 and purchased in 1979, nine years before. It was ratty, missing pages, and the back cover was partially destroyed, altogether a dubious message to the kids. For a moment, I wanted to be a journalist again, so I could call the City Desk. This was a scandal: someone might go to jail over the Missing Book Fund. Whitman had to replace several dozen lost math texts every year; I wondered why they weren't buying something more interesting. Instead, Miss Kowalski told me, they kept reordering the same books, year after year.

Sizing up my teaching arsenal, I found: I had no experience, no how-to-manual, and no packet of lesson plans. What I did have was an antiquated textbook I could follow only with painstaking attention and a course outline that seemed opaque and irrelevant. I had no formal training, except a three-day crash course given by the Board of Ed in the summer, where I saw a good number of weary and cynical veteran teachers, including one assistant principal who told the new recruits, "The students are the enemy, but time is an even bigger enemy." Even at that staff development program, we spent most of our time filling out forms and learning how to get the kids to fill out forms. We certainly did not roll up our sleeves to tackle the questions of what to teach or the more difficult one of how. I had to get help. I had to find Miss Kowalski.

"I don't see there being any problem with this book," she told me. "You have to learn to pick and choose. You will find many useful problems and many useful explanations."

"Really?" I asked in wonder. "The kids can do this stuff?" I pointed to a problem that told kids to "express 7.66½ as a numeral naming a mixed number."

"If it's taught properly, they can," she replied. "They can do anything if you teach it the right way."

All weekend, before the students arrived, I thought about Miss Kowalski's words. Kowalski, it was said, *could* teach anything. She had taken kids from the bottom classes and turned them into national math champions, and she had won that $1,000 award for doing it.

"If it's taught properly," she had said, "the kids can do anything."

If it's taught properly . . .

Energy and common sense would have to carry me a long way. And first, I would have to find a way to win the kids over. Somehow . . .

5

Day One, and Counting

The first year in teaching is always the hardest. You have so much energy and you want so badly to succeed. But you have to get broken in. And that can be devastating.

—Bob Moore, teacher of mathematics, Walt Whitman Intermediate School, and chapter chairman, United Federation of Teachers, two weeks into the 1988–89 school year.

I stood on my toes and held the placard as high as I could over my head. As the courtyard filled with teachers, students, and parents, one fact of my new life as a New York City schoolteacher in the heart of Brooklyn hit me hard. I was in the minority; I was white. For the first time in my adult life, I would be living and working every day in a place where black adults and children far outnumbered those of any other ethnic group. In this school, to be precise, the principal, an assistant principal, several guidance counselors, 3 deans, and 72 teachers were African-American, representing 55 percent of the faculty; 43 percent were white, and the remainder Hispanic or Asian. Of the 1,711 students, 89 percent were black and another 8 percent were Hispanic. Just three students were listed as white on the school's student census, but of those only one immediately stood out. He was the son of the head of the Parent-Teachers Association; I had already met her, and I spotted her shy, slight boy in the play yard that first day of school. He looked as conspicuous as I did. I had never been among so many black people at once. I was secretly embarrassed at paying so much attention to this obvious situation; after all, the business world from which I had come probably looked no less segregated to the typical black person. But I couldn't help myself. I felt like an intruder—not because I might be considered a reporter, but because of the color of my skin. And I was no less aware of the vast disparity that existed economically between me and the kids. A great many of them were poor, and I was not. Like the vast majority of my white colleagues, I knew almost nothing at first hand of black life or the poor in America.

The bleakness of Walt Whitman Intermediate School also struck me forcibly. As a reporter, I had visited many such schools, but none had been my working home. This one, with its graffiti-caked brick walls, was where I would now spend most of my waking hours. No grass surrounded the building, only the concrete and the cyclone fencing, cut through countless times, that supposedly marked the school's boundaries. The netless basketball hoops stood forlornly at one end of the concrete patch, which was uneven with cracks and holes. Only a few fading lines where four-square and hopscotch could be played were visible.

"Anyone for 8-5?" I yelled into the mass of kids, most of whom towered over me. Kids were throwing basketballs, showing off new hightops, or painting on one last coat of crimson nail polish. A few of the boys, their hands caressing the buttocks of young girls, were obviously trying to act a summer older. Others, whose parents were escorting them, looked like they wanted to flee. Every time the arm of one mother rested on her son's shoulder, he wiggled uneasily aside. "Mama," he moaned, "stop."

Vibrant in the early-morning sun, new graffiti danced like neon all over the outside walls of the school—shiny black, red, and blue lines on the beige bricks that had been erected fifty years before.

A beefy boy with a big grin and arms too long for his body walked over to my post at the side of the building and offered to hold the placard. He was at least a foot taller than I. "You're too short, lady," he said. "How you gonna get them kids to listen to you?"

The same thought was beginning to cross my mind. Some of these kids were huge. Supposedly sixth-, seventh-, and eighth-graders, from eleven to thirteen years old, several looked mature enough to be in the last years of high school. It wasn't just their height, though a few were six-footers, but an air of bravado and toughness that most preteens don't yet understand, much less flaunt. Some of the boys had mustaches; a few others were muscled and brawny. A number of the girls looked well into puberty and proud of it; they pushed their breasts out and winked at the boys they coveted.

I stood with the other homeroom teachers, waiting in the courtyard in my designated spot for all the students of 8-5 to arrive. I tried to make small talk with the kids who were gathering around me and with Tyrone, the boy who had offered to hold my placard. I was supposed to have twenty-nine students. With ten minutes to go before the 9 A.M. bell, I counted only twelve.

"Have a good summer?" I asked a few kids. "Yeah," one replied. "What did you do?" I was eager for conversation. "Nothin'," he said. "Hung out," said another.

I looked around at the placards announcing 8-1, 8-7, 8-12, 8-13, and 8-16, the classes I would be teaching. At first glance, I didn't see many differences in the kids from one class to another. Almost all the girls were well-dressed, many in tight-fitting jeans that hugged their bodies. The earrings on some girls were extravagant, large gold hoops and other shapes that tugged at their ear lobes. Many of the boys wore gold, too, around their necks and wrists.

Just as one of the assistant principals, a balding, thin man in charge of this courtyard lineup, signaled that I should head upstairs, a woman tugged at my shoulder. "You Winston's teacher?" She was middle-aged, dressed for work, with a smart leather handbag over her shoulder and dark green eye shadow on her lids.

"Well, I'm his homeroom teacher." I extended my hand. "I'm Mrs. Sachar."

"I just don't know what to do with my boy," she said, tears welling in her eyes. "He started out in 7-1 last year, but he just fell apart. The grades was terrible. Right, Winston? And now he's sunk down to 8-5. No good, this boy." Winston, a short, light-skinned black boy, shifted about uneasily, looking like he wanted to disappear into the ground. "I just hope he'll do better this year. I got such high hopes for him." Winston's mother showed no signs of leaving, and, like her nervous son, I, too, wished she would. I felt sorry for him, surrounded by new members of his class who were, to his dismay, learning about his past at Walt Whitman.

I patted his shoulder. "I'm sure he'll do just fine," I said, turning to the rest of the kids and hoping she would get the message. "Now, I want to know exactly what he does today," she said. "I'll be calling you, okay?"

I turned to the twelve kids around me. "Is everyone ready to go upstairs?" I was hoping for a loud and enthusiastic "Yes!" No one said a thing. "Okay, then," I added, trying to smile, "let's go."

Inside, as I had feared, I had to bang open the door to Room 315 with my hip. At least, the key worked. I had organized the seats in neat rows and, several days earlier, had even fixed the teacher's desk with my own screwdriver after three repair requests were ignored. The desk still wobbled if I leaned against it, but at least it would hold my books and satchel. Because I had no desk key, I could not leave anything inside it. The much-heralded PA system with the "panic" keys still wasn't fully installed.

"Welcome back to Walt Whitman," I began, trying to sound like a veteran, as the kids shuffled into the seats. "We're going to have a terrific year."

After some minor adjustments in the seating the kids assigned themselves, with only a few groans when I broke up best friends, the homeroom period went smoothly. Monitors collected the index cards I had passed out for biographical information, and two kids eagerly set to the task of decorating the bulletin boards, gingerly tacking up sheets of blank construction paper over the corkboard. I asked another student to go find out when homeroom period would end, and he left the room and returned quickly with the answer. I even memorized a few of the names, meeting Suk-Ma, who sat in front, and Mary, a chubby, buxom child who kept her head buried in a Harlequin romance. Ricky, three rows back, told me he was Amerasian; his father had fought in Phnom Penh, which accounted for his Asian face and American name. Both his parents lived here now. Of the children who ultimately dribbled into the 8-5 class that morning, twenty were black and two were Asian.

When the bell rang, I dismissed 8-5 into the packed hallway of the third floor. "Have a great first day," I called out to no one in particular. "You, too," a girl replied. We smiled at each other, and I felt the emotions I imagined teachers all over New York City were feeling on this first day of the new school year—hope that all would go well, desire to tackle the job ahead, and relief that we were finally off and running.

That first Monday morning I walked into Room 327 looking for Shereeza, the student who had scored lowest in the entire eighth grade—in the single digits on both reading and math tests the previous year. I wondered if our first meeting would somehow shed light on her dismal performance. How was it possible to spend eight years in school and still be unable to read or write? What was life like for such a child?

Many of the students in 8-16, my first math class that day, were already seated in the room when I arrived, and I didn't want to embarrass Shereeza by asking for her by name. I asked two boys playing a hand-held video game in the back of the room to sit down. They did; I felt wonderful, in control of the class.

I passed out the Delaney cards, the ancient seating-chart system used throughout the city, and index cards for birth dates, phone numbers, and other personal information. The room was quiet. On the blackboard, I showed how the cards should be filled out, and then I went from desk to desk watching the kids at work on their first task. The intense concentration on their faces impressed me; they looked so diligent and serious. But the work they were producing was appalling.

Jordene could barely write. She clutched her fist around her pen as if it were a dagger, and her handwriting roamed all over the card like a preschooler's. She wrote that she lived at 3505 Foster BrooklyNewYok. Kenneth Thomas misspelled both his first and last names. "Kenth Thomoias," he wrote, the "K" backward. It took him twenty-five minutes to finish. For his birth date, he wrote "193 17." I had asked for a parent's name followed by a phone number. Kenneth wrote "CrSoane Go" followed by a six-digit phone number. He gave as his home address 208 20 ave D8923. None of it made sense so I asked him to tell me the information instead. "Don't know," he said, when I asked his birth date. "Don't know," he said, when I asked his address. "Not sure," he said, when I asked his phone number. I had suspected from Kenneth's 16th percentile reading score that he was at least three years below grade level. Now I wondered if he could read at all.

I had also asked the students to indicate their gender, since some of the names on the rosters—Sheniqu, Clemente, Germaine—were unfamiliar to me. "Female—look and see," wrote Rose-Ann, a physically mature sixteen-year-old. Her hair was dyed a Day-Glo red down to an inch above the black roots. Her card, at least, was legible, with all the information I had asked for.

As I observed the busy students, one girl in the first row caught my eye. Her hair was neatly tied in two long, black pigtails, the perfect part down the back of her head framing lovely mocha skin beneath. She had dark brown eyes, but the left one was big and wide, the right one lazy, the lid drooping, half-closed. She was sitting so close to the blackboard that, with the sun beating in from the windows on the opposite side of the room, she would not be able to read anything on it because of the intense glare. And there was no room to pass in front of her even to write on the board in the first place. When I asked her to move one seat back so I could get to the board and she could see better, she shyly complied. It was then that I also noticed she limped heavily, dragging her right leg. She was no more than five feet tall and wore a pink skirt that was missing a hook-and-eye at the waistband. The zipper was broken, too, so that her underwear showed. She looked near tears. I watched over her shoulder as she painstakingly wrote: Shereeza Moodan.

Her handwriting, like that of so many of her classmates, was abysmal, like a first-grader's, the words on her index card disorganized and misspelled. Brooklyn was spelled "Brookln," with capital letters for the *B*, *R*, *L*, and *N*, and she didn't know how to punctuate. Later that day, when I dialed the home phone number she put on the index card, a recording said the number was no longer in service.

I wanted to sit down with Shereeza and talk to her, but there were twenty other kids and little time for chats. All I could do to show I was on her side just then was extend a smile, and Shereeza returned it sweetly.

I wanted to evaluate the kids' readiness for the year's curriculum, but the mimeo-room lady still hadn't prepared any of the materials I had requested the previous week. So I passed out my private stock: a sheet asking for answers to the multiplication tables. It was from a workbook for third graders. Ten minutes would be enough, I thought, and from there, we could discuss the year's curriculum. But as I walked around the room, I saw that less than half the class understood the simple times tables. One boy, Chetwyn, was trying to figure out the answer to the problem 6×9 by adding 18 and 18 and 18. That actually showed some pretty complex thinking, yet he simply did not know that $6 \times 9 = 54$. When I asked the students to pass in their sheets, many groaned. "Just two more minutes," one girl pleaded. I relented, but the mood was no better four minutes later, when I again called for the sheets.

With the fifteen minutes we had left, I decided to try a rote drill of the "9 facts"—$9 \times 2 = 18$, $9 \times 3 = 27$, $9 \times 4 = 36$, and so on. Previewing the year's curriculum—scientific notation and simple interest and permutations and probability—was definitely out. I imagined that other teachers were handing down classroom rules, not yet attempting academic work. Another new teacher in the math department had written out thirty-four classroom rules on three separate sheets of paper and planned to spend the first week on nothing but her rules. I wanted my kids to perceive me as lively and relaxed, as well as serious about academics.

"Okay, today we're going to learn the nines." I put my chalk away and told the class to clear their desks. Some of the kids looked relieved, and I wondered for a second whether they might welcome a teacher who had no preconceptions or illusions about their knowledge, perhaps even praying for one who wouldn't fault them for what they didn't yet know. But many of the students were indignant. "That's second-grade stuff," said a girl who had a good grasp of the tables. Another, studiously bored, pulled a mirror from her bag. I was just as frustrated at this further proof of the one-parameter tracking fallacy. Still, most of these kids needed to learn the tables. How else could we begin to convert fractions and percents? The times tables were the basis of everything in math—they needed to be second nature, acquired by repeated rote-drill and reinforced by practice.

"Now, repeat after me," I said, walking down the first aisle. "It's really simple. 9 times 1 is 9, 9 times 2 is 18." I pronounced the numbers precisely, in a staccato voice. "All together—" From the students: only silence.

"Again: 9 times 1 is 9. 9 times 2 is 18." A few kids picked up the chant. The thought of doing this for so many different facts, and in every area of their missing basics, suddenly seemed daunting, but I went on.

"Louder," I boomed. *"9 times 2 is 18."* I couldn't tell if it was anger, intimidation, interest, or hostility, but more of the kids started to chime in.

"Now, let's really go for it," I coaxed. "9 times 2 is 18." I was rewarded with a half-hearted recitation. This shtick had little charm, and the kids had little patience for it.

I glanced over at Tameeka, a tall, overweight girl of fourteen whose squinted eyes gave her a continually angry and challenging look. She never seemed to be relaxed. Her bust was one huge, swollen mass, straining open her button-down shirt; she could not close the snap on her pants. Her upper arms, too, were ballooned with fat. Her hair was tied in two short, tight pigtails that stuck straight out from her head like spikes.

"9 times 2 is 18!" The class tolerance was waning fast, and I looked straight at Tameeka, who sat mute.

Approaching her desk, I urged, "You too!" Her face was cocked to one side, her body slumped in the chair. "Say it!" I bent closer. "You're one of the ones who doesn't know it. 9 times 2 is 18."

"Cuntface," she whispered, looking straight into my eyes, and then lay her head on her hands to feign sleep. I lost it.

"What did you just call me?" I exploded, my lips an inch from the top of her head. My face felt flushed with impotent fury. She didn't even look up, but just pretended to snore. Not a half-hour into the first day, and already I was under siege.

Sitting alone in the last row, Rose-Ann started to laugh. The other students turned in their seats to watch her act. She had sauntered in twenty minutes late, shouted out that she was bored, and immediately pleaded to go to the bathroom. "I have to go," she had announced, theatrically grabbing her crotch. I had managed to ignore her disruptions, but her ridicule now, when I was obviously losing my composure and authority, might get the whole class going.

"Quiet!" I insisted. She laughed even louder.

Stalking to the back of the room, I said, "Miss Mason, could you please zip your lip?" I drew my fingers across my mouth.

"Mrs. Sucker," she spat back, "could you please fuck off?" I was reeling. What had made these two girls so vicious? How could I retain control?

Among the other teachers, Rose-Ann was as famous for her lip as for her age. "She's supposed to be out of here," one teacher said, "she's already been here four years." Another told me that I was not apt to see much of Rose-Ann anyway. "She only comes to school when the weather's bad. When it's nice, she hangs out with her druggie friends." Rose-Ann had once declared her one goal in life—to be "the woman of a crack dealer." What was I supposed to do with her? She knew a lot more about controlling me than I did about controlling her. And for now, that was all that would matter in class 8-16— control.

I had greatly overestimated my talents as a teacher. I did not, as I had imagined, have a way with the kids. My enthusiasm was returned with contempt; my empathy was unwelcome. Indeed, many of them seemed to hate me. Only in 8-1, my top class, did I feel confidence in what I was doing, but even there my control was fragile. If I let up for a minute, if I made even one mistake—at the blackboard or in talking through a problem, even in following the unfamiliar classroom rituals—my credibility was up for grabs.

I had also greatly underestimated the problems of the school and what they might mean for me. Simple bureaucratic details devoured the little free time I had. Arranging to pick up textbooks, three weeks into the term, took hours. Without a home base, I ended up carting the 150 books to my homeroom and then running back and forth all day to distribute them in each of the ten classrooms I used. It was an organizational nightmare, and, until all the books were distributed, I was constantly disrupting other teachers' lessons to get another stack of books out of my homeroom. I had to beg to get some closet doors repaired before they crashed down on the students. Too late: one door did fall off its hinges during a class, and banged to the floor, leaving a big bruise on a forehead—mine.

I taught classes of twenty-eight kids with desks for only twenty-three. Kids sat on radiators and on windowsills. In Room 402, a third of the desks did not have tops and a third of the chairs were cracked in half—by student vandalism. The second week, I gave a quiz to my largest class, and six students had to write bent over at the window ledge. After three written complaints, seven more desks arrived, three weeks into the term and, finally, every student could sit down in math class.

For the first three weeks, I also had no key to any of the three teachers' bathrooms and would have had to use a filthy toilet at an auto-repair shop across the street were it not for the kind security guard at the school's front door. She took pity on my plight, and during the second week of school, agreed to slip me a key to the nurse's bathroom, which was blessedly clean and well-stocked.

Mostly, I was lonely. The 140 kids I expected to keep me company were far from companions. If any of them wanted a closer relationship, I couldn't read it from their actions. Perhaps most depressing was the realization that I had no teaching philosophy, no point of view, in the classroom.

The other teachers were not my friends, either. The more time I spent in the second-floor teachers' lounge, the more uncomfortable I felt. It seemed that other teachers pulled away from me when I spoke about bad kids or lousy days. Most of their conversation centered on their own families; I was obsessed with what went on in class. Only a few teachers who spent time there were white, and I was often the only one—at which times a great distance seemed to be evident. Apparently I was slow to get the message! A place of my own—even a desk in the back of another teacher's room—would have meant a great deal to me, but I had nowhere to go. I sometimes retreated to the basement teachers' cafeteria to grade papers and prepare for lessons, but it was a logistical ordeal. I would just settle down to work when the forty-three minutes were up and I had to rush off to a class on the third or fourth floor.

Rose-Ann, the Day One Terror of 8-16, soon stopped coming to school altogether, just as the veteran teachers had predicted. But two others, twice as challenging and twice as big, replaced her. The rosters of my other classes kept changing, too, and I reorganized seating plans time and time again. I felt disorganized and confused, uncertain what to teach or how to teach it. I was staying up past midnight every night just to write lesson plans and grade papers.

The first quizzes, given after Miss Kowalski's suggestion that I find out the level at which the kids were functioning, showed many to be years behind. The Scope and Sequence I was there to teach seemed hopelessly beyond these students' abilities. I did not know where to start or whom to ask for help. Everyone else on the faculty looked so busy and self-assured. I felt I had to keep my own humiliation at the chaos in my classroom locked inside me. So I smiled and told everyone that things were going great. But things were not great; they were grim.

Some of the kids were a delight—well-behaved and attentive. Upon arriving in class, they'd quickly open their notebooks and immediately begin copying the work on the board. But those were the exceptions, and most of my classes were dominated by the troublemakers. There were so many of them.

On only the third day of school, Keith Thompson turned 8-12 upside down. The period started smoothly enough, reseating the students who had forgotten their assigned places. Keith was the last student I came to in my travels up and down the six rows of seats. "And you are here, Keith," I indicated, pointing to the last seat in the last row.

"Shut up," he said, looking at me.

"What?" I wasn't challenging him: I was sure I hadn't heard him correctly. "Shut up," he repeated calmly.

I tried not to appear upset. "Keith," I said mildly, "please sit down."

Suddenly, he spat at me. I felt the saliva running down my nose. My voice became tight and strained. "Keith, sit down now," I demanded, wiping my face.

He bolted toward the front of the room and hurled his books at the chalkboard, then ran back to the far corner and stood with his arms taut across his chest.

"Come here. Now," I said, quietly walking to the door of the classroom. He didn't follow. *"Keith, come here now,"* I yelled, throwing open the door, hoping to spot an administrator or a security guard. The halls were empty, all the other classroom doors shut, and, I was certain, locked. I could not leave my room. Oh, for the magic panic button! Still not operable.

Several of the other students stood on their seats, enjoying every second of the showdown. I stalked over to Keith and grabbed his hand. "You will have to leave this class," I ordered, my voice growing louder. He yanked his hand away, hard, and a gold ring on his finger ripped my palm. It began to bleed.

"Fuck off!" he snarled. "Get away from me."

I marched back to the door, shaking, praying in vain that someone would magically appear to remove him from the room. We were on the third floor, two flights up from the security guards downstairs. There was supposed to be a teacher on patrol. I saw none. I decided that this was an emergency.

"I need help. I need a security guard," I shouted into the empty corridor. *"Mr. Newman! Miss Kowalski! I need help."* No one.

Finally, a teacher in a white lab coat came around the corner, and I passed Keith over to him urgently. "This child is disrupting my class," I sputtered. The man in the white lab coat remained cool; he led Keith away without incident. Still livid, I continued, "This student does not know how to behave. He doesn't belong in school. Get him out of here!" Suddenly Mr. Newman, an assistant principal, appeared and took over custody of Keith.

Fully aware that I had been put to a trial by fire, I returned to my room, wondering what the students thought. Had I won in their eyes by taking on a rough kid and getting him out of the room? Or lost because I got rattled, and panicked, only prevailing when someone else arrived to solve my problem? Unsure whether I was victim or victor, I paced around the room lecturing, in an attempt to reassert my control. "Students who behave like that are not welcome in my class," I said, wagging my finger at Tessa Francis. "You are here to learn." Then down the side aisle: "And you, Lyndon, you are here to learn. So are you," pointing to another student. "And you. And you." A boy raised his hand. "And me, too?" he asked meekly, so sincere I wanted to hug him. "Every last one of you," I said, sweeping my hand in a circle to include them all. "And students who behave like that will not be allowed in this room. They will not keep me from teaching this class." As I spoke these brave words, I wondered where Keith Thompson had gone; and when he would be back. In the silent room, I turned to the blackboard and put down some simple problems for the students to copy.

After the bell, I sought out Mr. Newman to ask about Keith. He knew Keith from summer school, where the boy's father had dropped him off one day without explanation, except, "I don't know what to do with him anymore." That was the last they saw of Keith's dad. Newman sighed and said, "If parents feel that way, what are *we* supposed to do in six hours and twenty minutes?"

After my last class that first harrowing week I sought out Vikki Kowalski, who was not only my math department supervisor but also the assistant principal in charge of even-numbered eighth-grade sections. In both respects, Keith Thompson was thus her responsibility. As she dangled her heavy key ring, I confessed I was afraid to teach 8-12 with Keith in it. I could not deal with the sort of disruptions he had posed every day so far. "What do I do?" I beseeched, my voice breaking with emotion.

"Call his parents," she said. "And keep a card on him. Write everything down." I vowed I would, and began rehearsing what I would say to his parents. "Your son is a juvenile delinquent." No, too cruel and imprecise. "Your kid ruined my life today." Too emotional. I would have to come up with something reasonable, but definitive—specific enough to be shocking.

As soon as I arrived home that afternoon, I dialed Keith's home. "Mr. Thompson," I began, "I'm sorry to bother you on a Friday afternoon, but your son caused terrible problems in my class today." I related the entire story, complete with the spitting incident, the book-throwing, the "shut up" and "fuck off" outbursts, omitting only the bleeding palm. I could hear Mr. Thompson breathing heavily, but he did not interrupt. "Keith may not want to learn, but other students do," I continued. "I am sure you can understand that behavior like Keith's can destroy the atmosphere in a class." I was unsure what to say next.

After a long pause. Richard Thompson spoke. He and Keith's mother had split up five years before, he said. There was another son, well-behaved. Keith, though, had been in and out of various schools, suspended every few months. The man had hoped that Whitman would solve his son's problems.

His wife, he added, was a manic depressive. He believed Keith might have inherited a tendency to the same disorder, and so had brought him to a psychologist several years earlier. But when Keith spit in his face, the doctor summarily refused to continue seeing the boy and his father did not seek out another doctor. "I don't know what to do with him anymore," Mr. Thompson said. Equally at a loss, I asked if he ever discussed his son's future with him. "He just wants to deal drugs," Mr. Thompson said. "This is what I'm up against." I asked whether Keith had less troubled moments. I wanted his father to keep talking. "Is he calmer in the morning?" "Mornings are terrible. I have to wake him for school, and he says the same things to me that you heard him say in school. The words out of that boy's mouth are something, aren't they?" Mr. Thompson was both articulate in his concern and despairing. "Well, let's work on it," I finally said. "If we're both on Keith's side, maybe he'll get the message that someone cares about him." Mr. Thompson sighed. "Yeah," he said, "thanks for calling." I sensed he had already heard all these platitudes. Now here they were again, from yet another school without answers.

In the comfortable surroundings of my den, I sat at my desk and considered the future. For every student I confronted those first few days, I encountered another troubling story. I wondered how many more I was going to wrestle with as a teacher at Walt Whitman.

On the one hand, there was some satisfaction in hearing an explanation, however grim, of the roots of the problems—the beleaguering disorder, pain and rage of inner-city lives. On the other hand, I was terrified. These children would bring their problems to me every day of the year for the next ten months. How was I going to cope?

Planning to read through chapters 4 and 5 of the eighth-grade textbook, I crawled into bed and promptly fell asleep. When I awoke, still exhausted three hours later, it was dark outside. A weekend lay before me.

6

Two Students

You remind me of the shepherd who's lost one sheep. You should thank God for the hundreds of sheep you have left. You worry about the one that's gone.

—Victoria Kowalski, assistant principal, Walt Whitman Intermediate School, after an October 1988 staff meeting when I described how overwhelmed I felt by teaching.

Shereeza was so far down the hall that I could not make out her face, but I could see her limp. Ever since our first 8-16 class five days before, I had wanted to talk with her alone.

It was now confirmed that Shereeza did not know basic arithmetic. I decided that if we could start with memorization of some simple facts—$9 + 8 = 17, 9 \times 8 = 72$—she might be able to improve her dismal performance. Of course, there were indications that other problems beyond my reach might also be involved—the limp and the lazy eye, for instance, suggested neurological problems. But her ignorance of elementary addition and multiplication seemed like a difficulty I could remedy.

"Shereeza, you know that work we did the other day, on the times tables?" I asked when I met up with her in the front hallway. "Well, I want to help you learn them." I put my hand on her shoulder. I had begun to wonder if she and my other students from the bottom classes even grasped the concepts of addition and multiplication, if they knew why the basics of math mattered—that, by learning the times tables, they could solve simple problems in life, make change, and acquire the tools to proceed with fractions, percents, and decimals. I assumed they knew that much; these, after all, were topics for the second and third grades. But, it was quickly obvious how little the kids understood, and how much explaining I needed to do.

Although it was a warm September day, Shereeza wore a heavy winter coat. The blue nylon was ripped at the shoulder, and the coat was so long she nearly tripped on it as she walked. Shereeza was silent, her head bowed. "You know what I mean about the tables?" I asked, hoping for some response. "Like, 6 times 9 is 54, and 7 times 9 is 63. Those are the times tables. Do you think your mom can help you learn them?"

When she spoke, Shereeza's words were both thickly accented and so slurred that I could barely understand. "Momma's not here," I thought she said.

"Where is she, your mom?" I asked. Shereeza didn't answer. After a long pause, she said with great effort, "I live with brother."

"Well, could he help? You see, I have an idea." I was not sure she was following, but I tried anyway. "I brought some flash cards." I pulled them out of my satchel and showed her. "And I was hoping that your brother or your mom or someone at home could review them with you and teach you the tables. I think it would make math a lot easier for you."

Shereeza did not reach for the cards. Awkwardly, I placed my books and satchel on the floor, to show her how the cards worked. "See, it's really easy. The problem is on one side and the answer's on the other. Like here, it says 6 times 6, and then the answer, 36, is on this side." I flipped the card over to show her. "If you go over them enough times, you'll remember them, I just know you will. Could · your brother do these with you?"

"Brother works late."

"Well, then, how about if you stay after school and I help you?"

"I have to cook," Shereeza said.

"You have to cook?" I asked. "For whom?"

"For building." I was still not sure I heard her correctly, but decided not to press.

She did not seem to understand why these times tables mattered. And, maybe, in her world, they *were* completely useless. My solution—a few once-overs with flash cards—obviously was not going to fly. I had assumed that foundations could be relaid in a neat, orderly progression. The kids would learn the tables, then go on to some basic work with fractions; that accomplished, we'd tackle percentages. We would thus be able finally to stack the blocks of basic arithmetic and get to that nagging Scope and Sequence. I had not considered that to reach these kids might require means far more heroic than I could muster.

I picked up my things and began walking down the front hallway, with Shereeza beside me, careful to keep the pace slow, so she could keep up. Maybe she was just nervous, I thought, as some students get when teachers single them out for personal attention.

We stopped in front of the drinking fountain, one of but two in the school that worked. "Shereeza," I asked, holding the knob for her to drink, "I'm just curious. Do you know which number is larger—30 or 300?"

She wrinkled her forehead and looked up at me, for the first time all year.

In the tiniest frightened voice, she responded, "30?"

"It's okay," I whispered. "We'll figure something out."

If my problems those early weeks had been limited to slow, quiet children, for whom a simple dose of affection was sufficient antidote, I might not have been so worried. But the slow students became an obsession precisely because I did not know how to help them. Veteran teachers warned that referring eighth-grade students for special education was a fruitless exercise; the kids would be passed on to high school anyway and they'd stay in my class all year. Yet the thought of Shereeza sitting through my classes completely baffled day after day, for the next ten months, seemed desperately unfair— to her and to me.

Then again, quiet students, however slow, were a welcome relief from the disruptive ones who aimed to destroy my classes. I had only a few easy days, when the students found seats fairly quickly, took notes, and turned in some homework, before the atmosphere deteriorated. Just to get them to sit down began to take fifteen minutes, and was followed by a constant battle to teach. Students threw paper airplanes, played radios, or sat gabbing with their friends, ignoring me completely. Screaming left me hoarse; lecturing on the need for "decorum" provoked taunts. One day, I even staged a crying scene, curiously hopeful I could provoke a little sympathy. For a day, the kids were awed or shamed into quiet, but by the end of the week, it was bedlam again. If I was able to teach twenty minutes out of any forty-three-minute period, I considered it success.

Some of the students, like Keith Thompson, were headaches one day and absent the next. I soon looked forward to those few days each week when they cut school. But other disruptive students promised to be chronic problems. These students, like Jimmy of 8-7, were consistently and predictably rude, arriving with great fanfare late every day, then misbehaving for what little time remained. Of my five classes, three—8-7, 8-12, and 8-16—had students for whom school was a personal carnival, providing a captive audience for their antics. I felt guilty for resenting them, certain that I was the only teacher so impatient, or harboring such anger toward students who were still children. Acting up, I tried to remember, was just a terribly troubled kid, "acting out."

The trouble with Jimmy began the first week of school. He refused to take his seat, so I allowed him to sit where he pleased. Bending the rules was always my first maneuver—a foolish one, veteran teachers cautioned, for the kids who are the least disciplined need rules the most. But I so badly wanted the kids to like me those first weeks that I tried to accommodate whenever I could.

My problems with Jimmy promptly worsened. By the third week, he had a ritual prank—raising his hand constantly to pose questions that had nothing to do with class work. I fell for the bait every time. His questions were tame enough at first. "Mrs. Sachar, could I get a drink? I'm gagging in my throat," or "Mrs. Sachar, how about a night of no homework?" Their innocent tone did not last long. One day after waving his hand frantically, Jimmy asked, "Mrs. Sachar, where do babies come from?" Calmly I told him to ask his health instructor. Another day he tried, "Mrs. Sachar, do you like sex?" I refused to call on him again, but the next day, while I was explaining how to add positive and negative numbers, his hand shot up and he called out, "Mrs. Sachar, is it true that blacks have longer dicks than whites?" I lost my temper and sent him off to the dean. Five minutes later, he was back with a note. "This is not a discipline problem," the dean had written. "Please readmit to class and call his parents." I was furious, but I had no recourse. If the dean was not going to back me up, I would have to cope myself.

Over the course of the next month, I kept detailed notes on Jimmy, recording many of his inappropriate questions, among them:

"What is an orgasm?"

"Do you have orgasms, Mrs. Sachar?"

"Do you think Mrs. —— is a racist?"

"Why does you always pick on the kids who ask questions?"

"Who taught you to teach, 'cause you ain't a very good teacher."

"Do girls masturbate as much as boys?"

"Do you masturbate, Mrs. Sachar?"

Unprepared as I was for many of the situations confronting me at Whitman, with Jimmy I was totally at a loss. He was a mystery. He was thirteen, short and less developed than the other boys in his class. His voice was just beginning to crack, and I noticed a few times that he had tried to shave, in hopes, I think, of helping along a mustache. His aptitude scores were uneven, the 8th percentile in math, but at the 58th percentile in reading—hence his placement in 8-7, supposedly an above-average class. In math, he lagged as much as my worst students, without a comprehension of some of the most basic concepts. His attention span was shorter than a toddler's; more than half of each class, he was out of his seat.

Yet, he seemed to care. One day after class, he asked if I would help him before school. We had been working on sequences: 1, 4, 7, 10 . . . ?, and he got every problem on the test wrong. When we met for twenty minutes the next morning, he was polite, actually affecting in his attempts to ingratiate. "You have beautiful green eyes," he said. "And you're really a great teacher."

"Maybe you can work harder in class, then."

"I just do all that stuff for attention, you know. I just want the kids to look at me."

"Well, I think this is a better way to get attention," I said quickly, turning abruptly to the tutoring problems, hoping to avoid one of his very personal questions.

In the hallways, Jimmy always said hello, and often, after misbehaving in class, approached my desk to apologize. "I was really bad today, wasn't I?" he'd say after a real debacle.

"Yes, Jimmy, you were rude and disruptive."

"I'm going to be better tomorrow. I really am."

I wanted so much to believe him. He seemed sincere, looking me straight in the eye as he spoke. And when he left the room, he always said, "Bye, Mrs. Sachar. Have a nice day."

Yet, his one-on-one kindness was evanescent. Once back with the other students, Jimmy was raring to perform. I just assumed he

could not resist until I visited the 8-7 English class and saw that
Jimmy's English teacher had no problem keeping him in check. I felt
betrayed; he had solicited my sympathy and repaid it with treachery.

Then, one afternoon, he went too far. It was an unusually hot
day, the bright sunlight beating relentlessly into the room, unfiltered
by our broken window shades. The students finally settled into their
seats, and I began to put some work on the board. Then I heard a rap
at the door. It was Jimmy, fifteen minutes late.

"Yes?" I was not sure whether I should let him in. He tried to
sneak past me, but I blocked his way.

"Geez," he said, disgusted. "Let me in!"

"You're late, Jimmy. You'll have to get a pass."

"Oh, come on. I'm just a little late." He was bouncing up and
down on tiptoes. For a second, I wavered, but held firm.

"I'm sorry, Jimmy. Just go get a pass and I'll let you in."

His face turned fierce with anger, his eyes flaring with rage. "You
bitch," he snarled and spat at me.

I slammed the door. I was fuming and embarrassed, sure that
the other students had taken in the entire scene.

Quickly, I put ten problems on the board—enough work to keep
everyone busy while I figured out what to do when Jimmy returned.
I perched on my desk, my arms taut with tension.

After a relatively quiet five minutes I heard another rap at the
door. Jimmy was back, his pass once again signed by the eighth-
grade dean as if nothing had happened. "Well, Jimmy, welcome
back," I said. "Come in and take your seat."

"I don't feel like sitting down," he declared, sticking his right
hand out in a perfectly timed maneuver. "I feel like dancing." He
shot out his arm, bent at the elbow, and pivoted gracefully, in the
opening moves of a rap routine. As he danced, humming as he moved,
a few students started to laugh. I couldn't help watching in admira-
tion. He was good.

"Jimmy, sit down now. You have no right to ruin this class."

"Yes, I do," he said. "I have to pee." More students became
caught up in the act. Attempting next to ignore him, I turned to the
board to write answers to the remaining problems.

"Who has an answer to number four?" I called.

"Mrs. Whatever-your-name-is, I have to pee," Jimmy interjected. "I mean it. I'm going to go right here." He reached down and
put his hand on his crotch. First, spitting and now, crotch-grabbing;
it was becoming a trend. "Jimmy. Sit down. Now."

Nearly everyone in the room was giggling. Jimmy had stopped

his dance; instead he began jumping up and down like a gymnast on a pogo stick. "I mean it. I have to pee," he repeated. "I have to pee. I have to peeeeeeee!"

Room 225 resounded like a comedy club. I had a horrible vision of my supervisor, Miss Kowalski, walking in at that moment. Her office was just across the hall. Then again, I *wanted* her to walk in. I had told her how disruptive Jimmy could be. Perhaps, if she saw for herself, she would get me some special help.

"You will have to wait, Jimmy." There was a school rule that boys could only use the restrooms between classes. Nervous and angry, I turned to the board. Jimmy had ruined my Tuesday class, and I had an awful premonition that he would try it again on Wednesday and Thursday, and maybe every day for the rest of the year. The thought terrified me.

Abandoning my lesson, I wrote a homework assignment on the board, purposely lengthening it so the kids had to spend the rest of the period copying it. At the sound of the bell the class tore out. There was no question that in the twenty-nine minutes he had been in the room, Jimmy had made the class his. I was far more furious than I let on, frustrated that I did not understand the boy's problem. But his problem was now my problem, and I was determined to get to the bottom of it.

I began obsessing about Jimmy day and night, asking myself what I was doing wrong. Perhaps my rigid conception of a teacher's role was to blame. Why couldn't I just go with the flow? Loosen up? Mellow out? Be cool? Maybe if I didn't look as if I cared so much, if I laughed along with Jimmy, he wouldn't need to put up such a fight. Then again, I kept remembering images of my favorite junior high teachers; there was no question who was in charge and even if we hadn't learned, we behaved. The more I thought about it, the more I just wanted to get Jimmy out of 8-7, like other students I had seen transferred from class to class.

So, I wrote a letter to the two assistant principals in charge of the eighth grade, Mr. Newman and Miss Kowalski, requesting Jimmy's transfer. I did not mention his bad behavior although I had earlier discussed his shenanigans with Miss Kowalski. Rather, I based my recommendation entirely on his poor mathematics abilities. He was far behind the rest of the class, I pointed out, as evidenced by his standardized math score.

I wished I had the tools, the expertise, whatever I needed to cope with Jimmy; I felt conscience-stricken and selfish for giving up on him. But if I didn't, the rest of the class would suffer. I had enough working against me. I was a new teacher with three bottom-level classes, more than my share. The dean seemed utterly uninterested in helping out. When I sent him discipline problems—kids who threw pencils, who used profanity, or who cheated right in front of me—he had one all-purpose response. "This is not a discipline problem. Readmit to class."

When, after a week, no reply came to my letter about transferring Jimmy, I wrote another—this one urging a special-education referral. I placed it in the mailbox of the woman in charge of guidance for the eighth grade, and waited for her response. Again, I heard nothing.

Two weeks later, however, when Miss Kowalski met with me to review my lesson plans, I asked, "Is anything being done about Jimmy?" "Oh, yes," she said, "I talked with Mr. Newman, and he thinks the class placement is entirely justified based on the student's indicators."

"What indicators do you mean? His math score is in the eighth percentile."

"You'll have to ask Mr. Newman, but I think you can assume that Jimmy will be staying put. Just keep doing what you've been doing—meeting with him before and after school and giving him a lot of remediation." I felt like saying it didn't seem to be working, that I was tired and frustrated and offended by the school's passivity. But I held my tongue and nodded weakly, saying, "Okay, I'll keep trying."

And I did. I talked to other teachers about possible solutions. I figured someone must have an approach that would work with Jimmy. I described his behavior to every eighth-grade teacher I met. One told me calling parents never works as well as talking to the kid directly. Another told me to ignore the student in school but harass his parents. "Make life so unbearable for them," he said, "that they beat the hell out of the kid." I did not know if either method would work—one seemed extreme, the other ineffectual—so I talked to Jimmy at school once again, intending at all costs to avoid involving his parents.

With no improvement through the early weeks of October, I had no recourse but to call his home. The woman who answered the phone, Mary Sanchez, promised me that Jimmy would improve. "I know the boy is awful," she said. "I hate him as much as you do." "I don't hate him," I replied. "I just dislike his behavior in my math class. And I know he can do better." Jimmy told me the next day that Mary Sanchez was not his mother, but his aunt. His mother and father, he told me, lived in England. "No use calling her anymore, is there?" Jimmy sneered. "She's not even my mama."

The records were not clear on whether Mrs. Sanchez was a parent or a guardian, and the other teachers were not sure either. As much as I wanted to find out what strange, sad situation had this boy living across the ocean from his parents, I didn't know how to go about it. Besides, there was so much else to do: stacks of papers to grade, lessons to plan, attendance sheets and high school applications for my homeroom. There were workshops to attend and textbooks to review. And without a little time for myself, I was going to fall apart.

7

Reaching for the Court of Supreme

My main goal in life is dream (hope) is to be a good lawyer for Crimmnal Justice in the Court of Supreme. [sic]

—Jimmy, a student in 8-7, Walt Whitman Intermediate School, 1988–89.

I ended my first month of teaching with a test in every class. In 8-13, I added an impromptu extra-credit problem: "In a paragraph, describe five uses for mathematics in your daily life."

It was a last-minute device—I saw that the students were finishing early, and I wanted to keep them occupied until the bell—but the exercise had some unexpected results.

Many of the students in 8-13 had spent the previous year in the cozy environment of small bilingual classes or in English-as-a-Second-Language classes, where the students' native languages were spoken most of the day. However, once their score reached the 20th percentile on a Board of Ed reading test in English, they were moved into large English-only classes like 8-13, some full to the legal maximum of thirty students. Controversy had raged for years about that 20 percent threshold score, which many parents felt was unfairly low. Their children, they said, still did not know English well enough to join the mainstream. But others had successfully argued in court that kids would learn English best in an all-English classroom environment.

In New York, where some school districts were operating at 140 percent of capacity—with classes crammed into bathrooms, large closets, gymnasiums, and cafeterias—it was simply a question of space. An English-as-a-Second-Language or bilingual class, often limited to fifteen students, usually took up the same space as a regular, thirty-one-student class. So 8-13 had been created by Newman, one of Whitman's most sensitive administrators; he thought that kids just emerging from small, bilingual classes would feel and do better grouped together.

Many of these students spoke Spanish among themselves and their writing abilities suffered accordingly. Only eight out of thirty students in 8-13 turned in answers to my last-minute extra-credit essay problem. Their pens moved slowly across their test papers; they were concentrating intently.

Anita, one of the top students, handed in her paper first:

> *1. we need the mathematics because if we go to the supermarket and they said the is something in this is not true and if we dont no math they gone take us money of.*
> *2. to know the sum*
> *3. to know how, add, seustraction, divution, multiplication*
> *4. It important for writing in our lives.*

Jerine's paper came in next:

> *1. the reason why we take math is because we have to pass the math test in april.*
> *2. we need math also to get a job.*
> *3. to help you to be good in telling time*

Raji, a recent Guyanese immigrant who was one of the brightest in the class and one of my favorites, wrote:

> *mathematics always help me with numbers. also with fractors, money, and also help everyone with add + subtracting and to do math that, why I am good with math. so I always think what math can learn you.*

Susana, a native Spanish speaker, wrote:

> *1. we need to know mathematics because if we go to a*
> *supermarket and they give you the wrong amount and you*
> *don't know math they are going to trick you*
> *2. to know the sum*
> *3. to know how to add to divide and multiply subtraction*
> *4. everybody needs math.*

Su Nam, who had recently emigrated from China, sighed when she handed me her paper. "I no good at writing," said the tall, deliberate girl with a real talent for my subject. "I try, but it no good." She had written:

> *the 5 mathematic was adding subtracting, multiply, negative and positive Integers. that will help you solve the problem by adding or multiplying the number of positive and negative these five mathematic will help you understand.*

Natasha's paper came in last. She wrote:

> *One uses of mathematics is money which we need to know how to handle. We also need to know mathematics for reading numbers. To known all about math is to you have to know math in all your subject is one of the greater known subjects besides reading.*

The kids' writings gave me useful new clues. For although these brief essays were a jumble of ideas, fragmented sentences, almost nonexistent punctuation, and dreadful spelling, the kids had clearly tried hard to put their ideas on paper; obviously, they wanted to communicate with me and had much to say.

I wanted to ask about their lives, their hopes for the future, their feelings about school. How would Shereeza express herself, and what would Jimmy say? What would come from Reginald of 8-16, who was a strong math student assigned to the bottom class only because of his grave reading problems? What could I expect from Pedro of 8-13, who had already told me that if his father did not wake him, he would "forget" to come to school?

As a math teacher, however, I couldn't justify an essay about drugs and other urban tragedies when I was supposed to be teaching 8.12×10^{23}. Instead, I decided to look through the cumulative record folders, which I had discovered in a file cabinet on the first floor. Perhaps other teachers in previous years had asked the very questions to which I sought answers. What were the kids' parents like?

What did they want to be when they grew up? What had their lives been like so far? What motivated them? How did they like to learn? I spent every free moment I had for the next two weeks scouring the records for clues. Some of my kids had been in this school system since kindergarten or first grade, and had taken writing tests along the way, which were slipped into the cumulative record folders. I read a few of them.

Clement Curtis, a tall, lanky boy of fifteen who had twice brought a basketball to 8-16 and who often cursed me and other teachers, had used his mother for the focus of a 1985 essay on "a special person." Clement was twelve when he wrote:

> *she is allaway special to me. one bay I ask my Mother to by me a bick for Me. she sed yes ond when whe To by the Bick she ask. me Which one I wont she bort it for Me and the next bay I went to the store and bort her a gift for her. And my Mother allway be specal. One bay she Told me to do someting for her and I forgot to it and she was made. but I hade to do someting to repay her. one bay I did all the work in the house she was proud of me. I know she is allway special one bay whe was going to the park. she got me ice care and whe went to the zoo, and ting was going find i allway was special to my mother And my father is special. all my family is special too.*

"How I learned How to write" was the subject of Terrence's essay in sixth grade. Terrence, a quiet boy whose only obvious problems seemed to be too little sleep and a sloppy appearance, had many prior troubles in school. A letter from his elementary school said he did no homework. His essay read:

> *when I was five years old I was learning How to write a sentence and when I got to first grade I had learn how to write a compsetion when I rote a composition I got a bike for my self I learned how to do my math*
> *and my addition and melluption tabeles and I got what ever I wanted and I acted like my brother untill. I got older and when I was eight years old. I was in third grade when I was in that grade. I was being pick on and Then I went to Kareley school and I learned how to fight and I was filling god and when the person keep botheeriing me we had a fight and I got and he god saspended and I come up to my reading level.*
> *the end.*

Other essays showed how much these kids had seen in their short lives. Renee of 8-7 had written an essay in fifth grade about being New York City's mayor for a day. She said:

> *When I was the mayor for one day it was very eciting But hard.*
> *I had a big office in city hall and also a secritary. I helped the*
> *poor people fine jobs and I hiered people to clean up the streets*
> *like taking graffeedee off the walls. . . .*
>
> *I helped the homeless people to find knew homes and thier*
> *facess looked very happy. I made the people feel very happy that*
> *I'm their mayor.*
>
> *Being the mayor for one day was not very easy but at lease*
> *I help the city and made them very happy.*

Marlon's folder did not contain an essay, but, as with a number of the others, it had something almost as interesting: a "Personal Inventory for Self-Evaluation." Marlon, a poor student who was repeating the eighth grade, had written that he wanted to be a lawyer, a computer programmer, or a basketball player, because "you get pay a lot of money." Marlon said that his parents wanted him to be a doctor. Under "educational plans," Marlon wrote that he "would like to go to Howard University or Harvard to learn a lot." On the citywide test in 1988, when he was a seventh grader, he had scored in the 17th percentile in math and 58th percentile in reading. He failed every class that year.

As the vast majority of my students were recently arrived immigrants, their record folders were empty. At Whitman, the only other information about each student was the attendance record, the quarterly grades and citizenship marks, and the yearly test scores. At no point during the three years students attended Whitman did their teachers prepare written evaluations, nor were student writings or class assignments a part of their records. The standardized writing test that each eighth-grader took in January was not included either. If I wanted to know about my kids, I would have to find out for myself.

I decided to start with 8-7, a class supposedly slightly above average for Whitman. Many of the students in this section were struggling with basic math, as one showed by asking how to divide 344 by 8, a fifth-grade task. Their language arts teacher had complained at lunch one day about how poor their skills were. "They don't even know what a verb or a noun is. Many of them can't write a complete sentence." Yet, they were supposedly well above the national average in reading. Their writing, I imagined, should be above average as well.

I asked my 8-7 students to write an essay of about 250 words about themselves: "What are your goals in life? What is your favorite part of school? Describe your life at home. What is good about it? What is not good about it?"

No sooner had I written the assignment on the board than five or six hands shot up. *"What's a goal?"* one boy shouted. I looked around the room hoping another student would offer the answer. One did: "It's like something you want," she answered. "Oh, like a dream, like," another girl said.

Working together, we composed a definition on the board. The kids looked more alert and enthused than usual. A few even began working before the bell rang to mark the end of Friday classes and the start of the weekend.

On Monday, nearly everyone turned in the project—far more than the handful that usually did their homework. As I read over the papers, I saw modest goals and grandiose plans. Several students said they had never before written about their hopes for the future and one admitted she had never even thought about such an idea before. Two students wrote notes thanking me for giving the assignment. I felt, for the first time, that I reached class 8-7.

Darrell, a bright but obstreperous child who was to leave school without explanation midway through the year, turned his paper in first. "My main goal in life is to be a baseketball player. My favorite part of school is Gym. At home, get to watch TV. What is not good about? too much work."

Jimmy's paper was next. "My main goal in life is dream (hope) is to be a good lawyer for Crimmnal Justice in the Court of Supreme. My favorite part of school is social studies. describe your life at home Boring. no kids to play with"

Lakeesha, writing in both cursive and block lettering, had composed one of the lengthier answers. She was one of the most well-behaved and attentive students in class, and also one of the most courageous. One day, when Jimmy stood up and yelled, "She don't know how to teach," Lakeesha shot back, "It ain't her. You don't know how to learn." I considered her an ally.

"My main goal in life," Lakeesha wrote, "is to graduate from college. 1. My favorite part of school: I like L.A. [Language Arts] because I like to read. 2. Describe your life at home. What is good about it, and what is not good about it? Good—almost everything. Bad—get blamed for things you didn't." At the bottom of the paper, she added, "My goal in life is to graduate from college so I can go on to be A veternarium. I lik Language Arts because I love to read."

Renee, the quiet girl who had written so movingly of being mayor for a day, wrote this: "My main goal in life is to be a laywer. My favorite part of school is language arts. What is not good about life at home? It is boring." More than half the kids, in fact, wrote of "boring" home lives.

I had asked for an essay, but nearly all of the students had turned in three- or four-line answers. Many had numbered the four questions, though I had not. They had little idea of what an essay was or how to organize one. And it troubled me that some of them described goals completely inconsistent with their progress in school. The would-be lawyers and doctors were already functioning several years below grade level in reading or math. Would they somehow magically catch up?

And what did these kids really know and understand of a doctor's or a lawyer's life? If only we could have a discussion about what a lawyer does, what a doctor does, maybe they would begin to see how much harder they needed to work. I wished that I could take the kids to a law firm, to meet the lawyers and paralegals, and to a hospital, too, where a doctor and nurse could speak to them about the academic preparation needed for medical work. But I could not imagine how I would arrange such field trips. Altogether, I taught nearly 150 students. How could I take them all on a trip at once? And how would I justify a visit to a lawyer's office while I was teaching math? Though this might be a direct, tangible way to make a connection between math and medicine or law, I was sure teachers would not be permitted to do something so far from the Scope and Sequence. I went back to reading the essays.

Saheedra, a small, quiet child who was always well-behaved, had clearly put a lot of thought into the assignment.

My main goal in life is to be a star like Whitney Houston. My favorite part of school is that some teachers are willing to learn the childrens but some of the childrens are not willing to learn and some do not appreciates what the teachers are doing for them. I thank Math, and Language Arts teacher for helping in my school work because I really need it and I am very greatful to them and I like them alot and that's all I have to say about my favorite part of school. The think I like about my house is that we respect each other, we care for each other when any think happens to one of us, we love each other very much and we obey each other and we have manners to elder people. The think I do not like about my family is that they talk too much, play too much and work too much that's what I don't like about my family.

The warmth of Saheedra's writing encouraged me. Her show business fantasy was surprising, because she seemed painfully shy. She never volunteered in class, and, when I stood beside her desk to try to give her individual help, she never met my eyes. But something was hiding inside, perhaps a need to lose herself in the limelight or even a wonderful voice.

Next on the pile was Kevin's response. Kevin had disrupted my class numerous times, most recently by leading a group of students in a noisy prank one Friday afternoon. Whenever I had turned to face the board, the kids began to violently rattle their desks. As soon as I turned to face the class, the racket stopped. It had infuriated me, and Kevin knew it. I suspected it would not be long before he would come up with a new stunt. Kevin turned in a three-line answer to the assignment. "My main goal in life is have a good job and have a repectful house whole. My favorite part of schools is gym. What is good about life at home my family what is not good about no pets"

The kids who posed the most severe discipline problems seemed to take this assignment lightly. Maybe, I thought, they were out of touch with how they felt about school and life in general, their repressed emotions only expressable by rude behavior. The inability to express themselves in writing might be a symptom. Yet the scraps of writing they did produce hinted at so much more: intelligent, vibrant souls itching for release.

I moved on to Tasheema's essay, and chuckled.

My main goal in life is to be a Fashion Designer and attend the high school of Fashion Industries and make dresses for my family and friend. After I make the best of my clothing, Then I will go out and open my own shop called "Fashions from Tasheema."

The good part about my life is that I have tuff sisters and I have a stepfather that loves me and my sister and help my mom with the bills and other things. Theres some promblems but he's always there for me. The bad part is that, my mother and father are separated but I still handle my self better. I'm am not doing so well in school. But I am trying to strive to do well.

Sometimes, I had a hard time liking Tasheema. She was a big girl who got into screaming fights—often in my room or in the hallways. She was coarse and immodest and irresponsible. At least once a week, I caught her in lies. One time, explaining why she had not done her homework, she said her house had been broken into and her mother was in the hospital after a pistol whipping by the robber. When I called to check on how things were going, her mother told me Tasheema concocted the entire story. Most days, though, I liked her. She was bright, even if she rarely applied herself to schoolwork. After I read her essay, I saw a more dreamy side to her personality that piqued my interest. What could I do in math class to help her make her store a reality?

Not surprisingly, some of the students who were doing best in my class wrote that their parents were involved in their education. At home, Carlia said, "I recieve support and love from my family. I always have to do chores, alaways get lectures about reading more, get better grades, and what they expect of me."

In many of the kids, I saw a spark of spirit and hope. If only I could find ways to kindle it.

8

Pi and Octopi

Mrs. Sachar, if you's gonna teach 8-1, you's gotta know how to do it. You don't let the girls sit by the boys. You don't call on kids whose hands ain't raised. You don't let kids be turning in work late. And you teach us stuff for the citywide. [sic]

—Tiara, a student in 8-1, Walt Whitman Intermediate School, after the second class of the 1988–89 school year.

With 8-1, my top class, I did not want to make any more mistakes. I already had my hands full, just surviving the other classes. If I lost control of my best, I would have no other job description than full-time lion tamer, and little hope of teaching anyone anything. So I made a point of always arriving to class early, with my lesson organized, typed and highlighted in a yellow marker. I knew just what I was going to say.

My first encounter with 8-1 had been a disaster. I arrived in Room 323 with high anticipation—thrilled with the sunny, spacious room. Marvel of marvels, enough desks and a clean blackboard. I was determined to set a tone of good humor in the class and plunge right away into real math. On that first day of school, I came armed with a series of problems I had devised the night before, to tickle the kids' interest with a little unusual-for-school eccentricity. We would be co-conspirators against the deadly B of E syndrome: Bored of Education.

So there were many problems like these:

Take the number of ounces in a pound of hamburger.
Divide by the number of tentacles on an octopus.
Multiply by the number of hooves on a horse.
And add the length of a foot in inches.

I had expected the students to revel in these odd problems and warm to a new teacher who bucked tradition, who trusted them to behave, didn't hector them about stuffy classroom conduct rules. They would reward my faith with excellent performance.

Things did not go exactly as planned. So caught up in my own starry-eyed visions was I that I allowed the kids to sit where they pleased as long as they behaved. It was an instant disaster: The ten boys clustered together in the back of the room, while the girls, all twenty-one of them, clumped into cliques around the room. Nor did they quickly take seats and pull out their notebooks; they spent fifteen minutes jumping back and forth, and the balance of the period yelling, joking, and sauntering about, while I futilely screamed for order. The cute little problems I had invented for them only provoked mockery. "This is soooo dumb," one boy moaned. I wanted to crawl under my desk. Couldn't I do anything right?

I vowed to myself that I would set the record straight. And soon. From class 8-1, I expected perfection or close to it and I would tell them so. We had too much to do, and too little time—forty-three minutes four times a week. We had to get cracking. There were integers, fractions, and percents to master, geometry and pre-algebra to be introduced, and concepts like pi and square root to explore. The thirty-one students of 8-1 would have to be on time, homework out and ready for review the moment the bell rang. Calling out, interrupting, rudeness—*verboten*. Class notes must be clearly written for me to review each month, and they would sit where I assigned them for the rest of the year. No more Mrs. Patsy Nice Gal.

It was not an easy sale. I could tell they smelled fear the instant they walked into the room that second day, the smile on my face discarded. I did not tell them that my own peace of mind and self-confidence hinged on them, that if I could not count on my best class, how could I deal with any of the others in this tough school? My face was expressionless as I stood in front of the chalkboard, outlining my expectations and conditions. They moaned, but surprisingly, they listened.

Lecture complete, I called for questions and hearing none, turned to the chalkboard to draft a problem. No sooner did I begin to write than a shout came from the second row. "Where's the Aim?" the skinny girl named Tiara demanded. "The aim, the aim, the aim," I groped to recall. "What are the rules about the aim?"

"This is 8-1, Mrs. Sachar," Tiara taunted in a nasal singsong. "Don't you know you're supposed to put the Aim on the board first?" I had forgotten.

"Be patient, Tiara. It's coming. And please raise your hand if you have something to say."

"AIM," I wrote, "to understand sequences." I assumed I could go on in peace, but I heard another groan of disgust—Tiara again. "Geez, is she new or what?" she stage-whispered loudly to her friends. "Doesn't she know it's supposed to be in the form of a question? What a ditz!" It was like "Jeopardy." I rewrote it as a question.

"Sequences?" Tiara whined. "That's so boring. We did that in fifth grade."

"Well, we're going to do it again in the eighth," I snapped. Actually, this was supposed to be the new material, but I quickly jotted down some trickier sequences that might stump even Tiara, in case I ran through my lesson plan too fast. At least her complaints were legitimate.

After putting some simple sequence problems on the board for the kids to solve, I walked around the room, checking their work. Stopping by Tiara's desk, I thanked her for her help. I was tempted to let her in on my secret—that I was a novice. But I decided against it—she and everyone else in 8-1 had probably already figured it out.

"You know, Mrs. Sachar," Tiara said as I stood by her desk, "you's probably heard about me. I'm smart. Very, very smart. Last year, I be getting the highest of all the girls on the citywide. And I be doing it again this year." It was true. Of the five students in 8-1 who had scored above the 90th percentile, Tiara was highest, at the 97th.

"Well, that's great, Tiara."

"You know about the citywide, don't you?" she asked. "Well, you've got to teach us stuff for the test." The year had hardly begun but Tiara was already thinking about the standardized April exam.

Returning to the board, I ran through my lesson, trying a whole series of sequences: $A, D, G, J, \ldots$; $2, 5, 8, 11, \ldots$; $10,000$; $1,000$; 100; $10, \ldots$; $1, 2, 3, 5, 8, \ldots$; $2, 4, 8, 16, 32, \ldots$.

Though I had expected the lesson to take thirty minutes, we sped through it in half the time, just as Tiara had predicted. To my surprise and delight, the kids were eager, intelligent, even impatient. Surveying my class happily, I saw the kids working in an atmosphere of quiet, intense concentration.

My only worry suddenly was a new one: finding enough work to keep them busy. What to do next? I pulled out the sequence I had added to my notes at the last minute and put the numbers on the board: *1,4,9,16,25, . . .*

"This is tougher, but I know you can do it. What's the next number and what is the rule?" I asked, hoping to stretch this one into a fifteen-minute exercise.

No hands. I waited. "Keep looking at the numbers," I said. "What do they have in common?"

"Oh, oh, oh! Call on me, Mrs. Sachar. I got it," Tiara blurted. I wished there were another volunteer, with perhaps a shade more modesty. But, there were no other hands and Tiara continued to wave frantically.

"Come on, 8-1," I coaxed. Tiara wagged her hand even more urgently. No other takers.

"Okay, Tiara."

"No, I don't want to say it. I want to show it on the board." Up she popped and skipped to the board. Her shirt and pants were tight over her twiglike body; her chest was flat, her hips indistinguishable from her waist. Her hair was arranged in six small ponytails, each tied with a different-colored barrette. Her features were not beautiful, but with her clear, smooth skin and big, round eyes, there was something utterly appealing about Tiara.

"36, 49, 64, 81, 100, 121," she wrote on the board. "And the rule is that you get these numbers by multiplying some number times itself. Like 3 times 3 is 9." So she hadn't used the terminology "perfect squares." She understood the concept.

"You may sit down now, Tiara," I said, a bit exasperated despite myself. A few students laughed in sympathy. Having been in class with Tiara for the past three years, they certainly knew that she could get under a teacher's skin. One child in the back of the room grinned at me, rolling her eyes as Tiara strutted back to her seat. I put the homework assignment on the board and told the students to copy it. A few moments before the bell, Tiara raised her hand.

"Mrs. Sachar, you know the lesson was too short."

"Yes, I know, Tiara," I said in the calmest, quietest voice I could manage. "I'll work on it."

. . .

Eventually, Tiara did settle down and slowly so did 8-1, the whole class taking on a personality richer and more rewarding than I ever dared hope. Two students in the school band asked me to watch them perform after school, another student prepared math problems for me to tackle so that she could then grade me. I would intentionally make mistakes, just to offer her the adventure of correcting my errors with her red pen. Nearly all attempted extra-credit problems, which I permitted them to work on as teams. They began to compete to be the best and to finish first. Their enthusiasm both thrilled me, and inspired me to show how much I appreciated their efforts. I also wanted to know the secret of what inspired them so, to help my other classes, which seemed so lacking in motivation.

Though 8-1 were the stars of Whitman, in many other junior high schools they would have been considered only slightly above average. A number of them just barely broke through the 50th percentile in math, while fully one quarter had scored between the 50th and 70th percentile in reading.

When I reviewed essays written by 8-1 students, I saw evidence of writing skills well below the eighth-grade standards I once knew. On one assignment—to find a use of percents in the daily newspaper and write an essay about it—only two students did not commit elementary errors in spelling, punctuation, or grammar. Even allowing for street talk—"the ain't factor," as one teacher called it—the papers were still riddled with mistakes.

Hoping to get more personal insight into my 8-1 students, I gave a test in December with an extra-credit exercise: to complete the statement, "My main goal in life is . . ."

Patrick, an overeager boy in the front row who wanted to answer every question, gave this response: "My main goal in life is to become a scientist and study space and other planets, because I'm a person who wants to know every thing."

"My goal in the future is to become a great architect, who will want to help the unfortunate," wrote Gary, a quiet, studious boy.

I plan to become as powerful as Donald Trump. I also plan to become one of the world's greatest architect, and would also want to go to other countries and design great buildings, so I would have myself notice around the whole world.

Stacey, who struggled hard with math, wrote: "My main goal is to be a Famos lawyer Because I want to be a lawyer it was my Dream for many years and Have a nice Home in L.A."

From Tessie, a shy, hardworking girl:

My main goal in life is to becom a perfecianol dancer. I love to dance because it is my way of expressing strong feelings. I am now taking dance in school. Hopefully I am planning on study- ing at the Dance Teather of Harlem.

Judith, one of the most popular kids in the class, wrote:

My goals in life is to become a nurse. When I referred to a nurse, I meant a secretarial nurse. A kind of nurse who work at the desk. Tell people information. But I never know in the future I might change my mind. I find being a nurse is a helpful occupation but also interesting.

Winston, a sweet, endearing child, wrote:

My main goal in life is to become a pilot. I will like to own my own airline so that I would help get people who have to travel far to go to work. I don't like to see the highway stopped up and people are stuck on the highway.

Clifford was a playful kid who, in the wrong class, would be nothing but trouble. He wrote:

My main goal in life is to be a scientist because I would find medicine that I can use the help sick people with diseases. Because I love to expierement with with things it influence to be a scientist. I love to become that specific type because I have a feeling that I should be one. I know you can make a lot of money from it. And my little brother also want to be one.

Tiara's response was unpredictable.

My main goal is to become an actress be rich having a acting/ Dancing school for the poor, black & talented girls and boys. I want to have my own charity function. I want to be rich and famous. I want to be a very, very successful actress.

The essays made clear that 8-1 was full of eager, capable kids who wanted to do well, who wanted to learn, and who understood the relationship between working hard today and achieving a dream tomorrow.

They attacked their classwork with a vengeance, delighting in puzzles and problems, even those with a purpose they didn't see right away. Hungry for more than mere information, they wanted to learn the real stuff of secrets: how to think and analyze. As long as I gave them ample opportunity to try their hand at the techniques and concepts I demonstrated, they even enjoyed my lectures. One day, to begin a unit on permutations and combinations, a topic far more theoretical than practical, I brought a bag of colored tiles to class and separated the kids into small working groups. They had to determine how many different ways three tiles of different colors could be arranged. Quickly, the teams determined that there were six combinations possible for a red, blue, and yellow tile. Two groups arrived at their solution by trial and error, but four groups solved the problem by insightful method and efficient means: first setting down a blue tile, then a yellow, then a red.

Yet, it was not obvious why one method was preferable or more efficient until I added a green tile and asked the students to solve the same problem with four tiles, then gave them an orange tile for permutations of five. Their homework was to extrapolate results for combinations up to ten tiles. When the students turned in their work the following day, I was surprised and delighted at the care they had taken with their presentations. One group had worked the problem on poster board, and the group leader asked to demonstrate the solution to the class. Another group typed its answer, with color-coded explanations. A third, after having solved the tile problem, offered five similar exercises for the class, supplying their own visual aids.

The range in approaches varied tremendously. Two groups actually succeeded in deriving the formula, one student proudly explaining that the general solution to such problems as $10 \times 9 \times 8 \times 7 \times 6 \times 5 \times 4 \times 3 \times 2 \times 1$ had a name, 10! or 10 Factorial. Others actually tried to work out all 3,628,800 combinations, deserving at least an accolade for persistence, though they gave up after wearying of the attempts. Even the teams that failed were not entirely discouraged; each explained in writing why they had reached an impasse. Only one group neglected to turn in the project, and they sheepishly requested more time, promising to have an answer by the end of the week.

That the problem was not posed as a real-life exercise clearly had not bothered them. The challenge to think was sufficient reason to tackle it. Later in the week, we turned the topic to practical problems: scheduling a basketball season, organizing outfits for a limited wardrobe, planning a school schedule—the kids were absorbed and enthralled. I was completely captivated. The more work we did, the more I wanted to stimulate them. Combing through Miss Kowalski's vast resource cabinets, I found workbooks on permutations and combinations and probability, and together we chewed through dozens of projects. We estimated the cost of a banquet using French menus, discussed the odds of a woman bearing five female babies in a row, used rulers and graph paper to map out our classroom. We had great talks—about how the science of probability shows the foolishness of playing the lottery and how a small change in interest rates can make a huge difference in the monthly payments on a loan.

So successful were these projects with 8-1 that I was eager to share them with my other classes. However, when I came into 8-12 one morning with the colored-tile project, the students only groaned. "Who cares about a bunch of colored tiles?" one kid yelled. "Bring checkers next time." Within minutes, the project deteriorated into tile-throwing, tile-stacking, and tile-twiddling. The few students who showed initial interest soon gave up. They worked eagerly with the three tiles, but when I added the fourth, they wanted to know immediately whether they had found all the possible combinations. "It's nine, isn't it?" Yolanda asked. When I told her to keep going, she uttered a noise of disgust. About fifteen seconds later, she called, "Okay, I've got it. It's ten." But when I urged her to continue, she hurled the tiles into her desk. "Shove it with your stupid tiles." I suggested tackling the problem methodically by putting the green tile first and working from there, but that, she said, was "too stupid."

It was much the same with 8-13 and 8-16. Even in 8-7, the students had a difficult time progressing from the three tiles to four, a process requiring making the leap from exhaustive trial and error to a methodical approach based on some insight into theory. I soon discovered that even if a majority of the kids were interested, a small, rowdy minority of, say, six might turn the room upside down in minutes. The top class, 8-1, was fundamentally different, deriving as much satisfaction from the process, and what they apprehended from it, as in the actual solution. No less important, because they believed in themselves, in me, and in the fruits of a calculated technique, they could be patient.

The longer I taught the students of 8-1, the more I liked them, and the more impressed I became with the depth and breadth of their talents. Hardly a day passed when one of them did not suggest an easier way to attack a problem. As my own confidence grew, I welcomed their suggestions.

One student gave me an exercise she had devised. "Take any even number," she wrote, "and, for each operation—subtraction, multiplication, division, and addition—do that operation by two. Taking 8, you will get: 8 times 2 cquals 16; 8 divided by 2 equals 4; 8 plus 2 equals 10; and 8 minus 2 equals 6. Then add these answers, 16 + 4 + 10 + 6, and you will always get a number divisible by 9. In this case: 36." Her mother wrote me proudly, "Ariel has always considered herself adept at math, but never has she considered herself a mathematician." I wasn't sure what theory the exercise proved except the most important one—kids want to learn and want to show what they know.

The kids in 8-1 had a passion for knowledge, even for some of the more dry and difficult topics in the curriculum—negative exponents, means and extremes of ratios, absolute values of numbers, irrational numbers. Curious about the Pythagorean theorem, we researched the question and I taught a class on the history of its derivation. I did the same with the origins of pi and the metric system. Sometimes, the kids asked questions I couldn't answer. One day, one of the boys said he knew of a way to calculate square roots with long division, without a calculator. There was such a method, one long forgotten from my own junior high days, so I told him I would have to look it up. It was okay with 8-1 not to have all the answers all the time, as long as I could quickly get the information they wanted.

By the end of the first marking period, another interesting dynamic had developed in 8-1—peer pressure—contributing, more than any of my efforts, to my success with them. My authority really rested as much on the kids' need for their classmates' approval as on their need for my acceptance. One day midway through the year, a new student was assigned to 8-1. Without knocking he barged into class and yelled out, "Hey, lady, where do I sit?" He was looking straight at me, a challenge in his voice and posture. "Excuse me," I said. "Do you see that I am in the middle of a lesson? If you think behavior like that will work in this class, you are wrong. These kids will not allow it." The words came spontaneously, but they were true. I was able to teach 8-1 because the students had accepted and endorsed my right to teach. Kids who acted up in 8-1 would be ostracized, not glorified, by their classmates.

In my other classes, I did not have that authority. Many teachers said that the kids in the bottom classes did not care, but the problem seemed not so simple. Those kids cared, too, perhaps even more passionately than the kids in 8-1. But their academic successes were so few, and their emotional and social problems so overwhelming, that school long ago stopped being a place to learn. It was, first and foremost, a place to act out—to explode, to play and shout and rant, to vent all their anger and confusion about life at home and the world around them. There seemed to be a tragic cycle of deprivation, pain, emotional immaturity and scholastic failure that no amount of need, desire, or effort could break.

One boy in 8-12 told me that his mother was a drug addict and had recently begun demanding that he help her shoot up. I asked if he wanted me to help find him a good foster home. If I tried, he warned, he would deny everything he told me. He would not leave his mother; they needed each other. It was unreasonable to expect him to be as abstractly devoted to colored tiles as the kids who went home to a warm dinner, a stable home life, and a cozy bed.

Disparities between classes showed up in other ways as well. In 8-1, for instance, a failing mark on a test was a mark of shame, invariably followed by attempts to prove where I had made a mistake in scoring. An 8-1 student would take what he got wrong and learn from his mistakes. The student in 8-12 who got a failing mark either tore up his test or turned it into a paper airplane. Both students may have cared, but one had failed so often he no longer believed in trying.

The peer pressure in 8-1 did have one insidious effect on the class —students who needed help often seemed embarrassed to ask. While a certain degree of competitive tension was healthy, I did not want the kids to feel intimidated. I worried I might be fostering too much competition in 8-1.

To help those students who were struggling the hardest, I began to run one-on-one tutoring sessions during the Friday assembly periods. While the rest of the eighth-graders watched *Princess Bride* or Michael Jackson's *Thriller*—a baby-sitting mechanism to contend with our overcrowded school—I sat in the back of the auditorium reviewing problems and trying to fill in gaps left from earlier years with those who lagged behind. Vikki Kowalski, in charge of the eighth-grade assembly, condoned what I was doing—at least tacitly

—by pretending to ignore it. After a few months, such extra attention helped even more than I had hoped. Not only did struggling kids get needed special treatment, but the others saw that their math teacher was not partial to the brightest kids in the class.

From time to time, 8-1 students would pass me useful tips on teaching. Tiara said I wasn't giving enough quizzes and suggested lengthening the homework assignments. Look for patterns in the students' homework, she told me, to figure out who was cheating. Two different sets of girls were sharing homework, and we curbed the problem before it had affected their grades.

Another student suggested a buddy system so that the kids who were struggling could get help from those who already understood the material. All were vocal if I wrote on the board either too much or not enough. Tiara always let me know when the topics were already familiar, or when I needed to move more slowly through new material.

Of course, Tiara was careful to offer assistance only when her friends weren't looking. Clearly, she was playing both sides of the street, sassing me in front of the class to show off to her friends, yet advising me confidentially afterward to gain favor. She had enough respect for me not to push insolence too far, but she was not about to risk her reputation with her pals, either. When she razzed me in class, it was just a reminder of where her real allegiances lay.

She was never easy to fathom. Brilliant but erratic, sometimes belligerent but equally concerned that class go well, she was the brightest kid in the class, not only by the measure of her test scores. When I presented a particularly challenging problem, Tiara was often the first, and sometimes only, student to understand it. Yet, she could also be lazy, and occasionally more arrogant than her ability justified. The afternoon before the final test of the first marking period, she cut class to hang out with friends on Flatbush Avenue. And after eking out a barely passing 70 on that test because she had missed the detailed review, she nearly failed the next one, too.

Some days, she merely came late, but often she neglected to do the homework. As a result, her grades suffered. When she was in class, she was usually attentive, although sometimes she fell asleep and snored loudly. Many of the students, teachers said, did not get enough sleep at night—they were required to take care of younger siblings or cousins, wash dishes, or do laundry. So I let Tiara nap, and hoped that her competitive instincts would awaken before it was too late. Disdaining her intellectual peers, she chose her friends mostly from the slower classes and from the bottom of our 8-1 class,

perhaps admiring them because they were more physically and emotionally mature.

Tiara's humor, which took the form of pranks, won her "Class
Clown" honors in the superlatives contest at the end of every year.
One day, my back turned, she replaced my math text with a Spanish
book. When I told the kids to turn to page 102, discussions of Roberto
going to the *tienda* filled the page, rather than Mary calculating the
interest on her 6½ percent car loan. It was a classic Tiara trick.
Annoyed though I could be at such moments, I secretly loved the
sillier tricks from Tiara, my genius goof-off showing off.

But she also had a cruel streak, which many other kids at her
level seemed to have outgrown. One afternoon I caught her poking
fun at one of the sweetest students in 8-1, a girl recently arrived from
the Dominican Republic who had spent the previous year in the
warm confines of a bilingual class. Mara possessed everything Tiara
lacked—a curvaceous adolescent figure, a mild, demure personality,
and an intense desire, far more serious than Tiara's, to do well in all
aspects of school, not just on standardized tests. Mara was so keen
on mastering her schoolwork that she did five times as many problems as I assigned each night and would then ask me to grade her
extra work the next day.

One winter afternoon, I heard Tiara's voice echoing down the
hall. Tiara was taunting Mara, dogging her steps and hurling her
sour words. When I heard what she was saying, I ran after her.
"Teacher's pet, teacher's pet, you little Haitian. Go back where you
came from, Haitian girl." That was considered the worst putdown of
them all, more cutting than any curse word, and often leveled by
American blacks at the blacks from the West Indies. Mara burst into
tears and dropped her head. She had no friends in 8-1 and had lost
touch with many of her buddies from the bilingual classes of the
previous year. Tiara, never one to admit errors in judgment, exulted
in her victory.

I escorted both girls to Mr. Newman, holding Tiara tightly by
the arm. She had a way of darting away the minute she saw trouble,
but didn't attempt to escape when I grabbed her. "I ain't doing
nothing," Tiara said defensively. "No? Tell it to Mr. Newman."

At moments like that, I wondered why I liked her so much.

In every class I tried to find a rhythm that would work, but only
in 8-1 had that rhythm come to me early enough in the year to

establish firm control. First, I would write the Aim on the board, then the Do Now problem, and quickly review the previous day's lesson to get the kids working as soon as they arrived. After going over the homework, I gave a brief lecture on new material in the remaining time, with the major portion spent doing problems. The students were as demanding of me as I was of them. They wanted not only to know whether they got the right answers, but whether the way they reached each answer was correct. I had to race up and down the aisles, checking the work of every student. Demanding though these kids were, I was always invigorated when I left 8-1. They were the single dependable bright spot of my day. Most of my other classes were a daily struggle of shouting and nagging just to win a few minutes for actual teaching.

The more confident I became of my ability to make the class enjoyable while retaining control—that dangerous and critical balance—the more fun we had. On the best days, I could not have felt more alive, more important, or more exhilarated to be a teacher. I told the kids I loved them, and they shone. In the reflected light of their praise and support, I found myself warming up even more.

Once a week, because the kids adored it, I taught the class in rhyme:

> *Now let's buckle down and get in the groove.*
> *Your teacher's here, and she wants to move.*
> *What kind of math shall it be today?*
> *I say Circles and Squares is the game we'll play.*
>
> *Now a circle here has no sides at all.*
> *On Stacey-woman I'm about to call.*
> *Tell me now, Stacey, what's the formula*
> *That we give for the circle's area?*

I also acted out silly skits and drew loony diagrams on the board. One day, while I was teaching a lesson on the circumference of a circle, I decided to pretend to be a child on a Ferris wheel. I asked the kids to figure out how many yards the Ferris wheel traveled in 12 revolutions if its diameter was 30 yards. I set my arms and feet in motion and giggled like a kid at his first carnival. The students were in stitches.

Another day, to introduce a unit on probability, I asked the kids to think of a real-life situation in which people took chances. I put on a wig and pretended to be a grandmother. "Let's see," I asked in a high, quavering voice. "My shoe size is 6 and my rent check is due on the 15th and my car has 4 tires and I was born on the 29th of the second month and I have 14 grandchildren. And that's my six numbers—6, 15, 4, 29, 2, 14. What game am I playing?"

"Lotto! Lotto!" the kids yelled in unison. "And tell me, how is probability involved in the lottery?" Soon, they were talking about how everyone who plays lotto takes a chance, that the probability of actually winning is minuscule. A few insisted on convincing their parents to stop playing the numbers. The exercise was confirmation both that they knew the limits, and that we could therefore have an open, exciting classroom.

Inevitably, because I took risks at their urging, I occasionally bombed. One day I tried to teach the kids how to compute compound interest without calculators, a topic on the Scope and Sequence. My lesson quickly bogged down in a quagmire of numbers, finally sinking altogether. The kids were bored to tears, and the next day I had to admit to them that I had screwed up; calculators and computers were the obvious tools to do this task. Happily, rough days were usually followed by good ones.

"Okay, this is the swimming pool," I said one day, after I drew a large rectangle on the board. I added a few ripples for waves. And then I drew another rectangle inside the swimming pool. "Now, this is a raft."

Tiara was already rolling her eyes. "Here she goes again, with one of her dumb stories," she whispered loudly to a friend. I plowed ahead, drawing a stick figure lying on the raft and assigning lengths and widths to the objects I had just drawn.

"Now, this is a naked man. And what do you think he's doing?" I realized I'd better not let them answer. "Of course! He's soaking up some rays." The class laughed. "Now, here is your problem," I said. "Find the surface area of the water that is not occupied by the raft."

The kids eagerly began work on the naked-man-on-a-raft problem. I walked quickly around the room, checking their work and results. Nearly everyone had it right, laughing and comparing notes.

"Shhh," I urged the kids. "What if the principal hears us?"

"Don't worry," said Ariel, Tiara's nearest competitor for good grades. "We'll tell him not to fire you." The kids then set to calculating the area of the island surrounding the inner tube. On days like that, I was on top of the world.

Yet, despite 8-1's success, the nagging problem remained—how to bring the good times to my other classes, too. Succeeding with the top class was to be expected. I was doing nothing extraordinary by controlling them and teaching them the Scope and Sequence. The real challenge, the real mark of an excellent teacher, as my supervisor told me when she heard of my success with 8-1, was to stimulate a class like 8-16. And so, as ever, I set out to try.

9

Separate and Trying to Be Equal

There is nothing you should know about me eccept for math is my favoret suject Becaus I know it very well the other suject is all right But math is my favoriet.

I think every one should be split apat in diffrenc math grup so that I could learn more and the other could learn. We are not learning anthing if other kids dont want to learn. [sic]

—Reginald, 8-16, draft of an essay, found in the waste can of Room 327 at Walt Whitman Intermediate School, October 21, 1989.

Reginald always sat in the back of class, ready with a notebook and a pencil. He was one of the few students in 8-16 who sat still, even in the midst of chaos. One morning, even as three boys dribbled a basketball around him, Reginald sat patiently, making no attempt to move from his assigned seat although it was directly beneath the imaginary hoop. His eyes still fixed on me, he waited for the lesson to begin despite the uproar around him.

Kids might be playing cards, fiddling with Nintendo games, or break dancing, but that didn't faze Reginald. He had nerves of steel. Nothing seemed to rattle him.

He was no goody-goody, though. On my drive to school in the morning, I occasionally noticed him sitting in front of his apartment building, three blocks from the school, a smoking twist of paper in his hand. Although he later told me it was incense—he said he liked to let the smell soak into his face before he came to school—it could well have been a marijuana joint. In class, his eyes sometimes had a glassy aspect, and he hung on the periphery of a bad crowd. Two of his "associates," as he called them, carried beepers, practically the badge of drug dealers; one had been arrested at fifteen for auto theft. But if Reginald was involved in the drug culture that invaded Flatbush years before and was even now touching our school, there were no certain signs. Still, nothing about Reginald would have surprised me. He was an enigma.

He was a big, heavy boy with a deep voice and a commanding presence, but a childish face, round and cherubic. His hair was cropped short, and, in the current adolescent fashion, amid his tight black curls, a pair of zigzag lines was cut, like a pair of lightning bolts. Above that cartoonish zap!, etched into the fuzz was the outline of a cloud.

Reginald showed early on that he was far above the rest of his classmates in math. While many of them needed a half hour to complete a simple times table quiz, he took only three minutes and did not miss a single problem. During the first weeks of school, while the class reviewed basics from second and third grade (adding columns of three-digit numbers, for instance), Reginald finished the twenty problems I put on the board before most students had tackled the first. He never said he was bored, but I knew he was.

I asked Miss Kowalski about moving Reginald to another class. Actually, I did not want to lose him as my student—I was grateful, albeit selfishly, for any child who both behaved and seemed motivated to learn. But he might be less bored in my more advanced 8-7 class. The administrators told me, though, that Reginald could not be moved: his reading score, at the 17th percentile nationally, indicated he would be at sea in all the other 8-7 classes. They said it was just too bad if he was more adept in math. A tracking system based solely on reading scores was primitive, they acknowledged, and sometimes, kids like Reginald with widely disparate reading and math abilities fell through the cracks. But they refused to change his class.

Miss Kowalski recognized the system's arbitrariness and did have one suggestion. "Let him reinforce his own skills by tutoring the other students," she said. "Surely, he could help some of the other kids you've been worrying about." From a teacher or administrator's standpoint, it had the ring of a good idea. But Reginald had just as much right to work through a math curriculum appropriate to his abilities as the rest of 8-16 had to a year of remedial math. To enlist him in tutoring Shereeza might help her and might even boost his self-esteem, but was it really fair? I was struck by the sheer dumb injustice of the system. Reading ability, Board of Ed testing experts would tell me later, had a strong correlation with math skills less than 75 percent of the time. Reginald was clearly one of those kids for whom the relationship was imperfect, at best. And in case no one at Whitman had noticed, a well-developed set of math skills would have real survival value in the world Reginald would face after school.

Of course, the path of least resistance was well trod at Whitman. Administrators often opted for the easiest choice, the least complicated solution, if it meant less work for them. The kids at Whitman and their parents rarely complained about the inequities wrought by the school; most probably did not know enough to object, and those who did often felt they had no right in such matters. Reginald's mother imparted her philosophy of uncomplaining forbearance to her two children: don't complain about being a victim, just suck it up and work harder. Reginald was unlikely to whine about the bad deal he had gotten in math classes. Even if he did, she was not likely to charge into school demanding a different class placement. Many parents did know about the wretched conditions at the school—rats and roaches, the decrepit graffiti-covered physical plant, the cartoon videos shown once a week for want of any academic resources to fill an empty time slot. Yet they rarely said anything about it. In a school of nearly 2,000 children, PTA meetings seldom drew more than two dozen parents.

Like a Potemkin village, whenever the parents came for scheduled visits, the administration was careful to present the school in its best possible light. Two weeks before the first Open School afternoon and evening, in late November, teachers received assignments for decorating bulletin boards in an exquisite coincidence of timing. All the floors were waxed for these visiting days, all the bathrooms made to shine; the school never looked so clean as when parents were expected. The parents came and went, but policy issues like the unilateral tracking system—of somewhat more consequence to their children's lives than well-buffed linoleum—remained an arcane secret. There was a tragic irony in the situation. The point of "local control," institutionalized in New York City in 1979 with the carving up of the city school system into thirty-two local districts, was supposed to be that parents would pressure schools into delivering tangible results; in practice, the district boards in the poorest neighborhoods, where the schools also faced the most daunting social burdens, often fell into the hands of political activists and educational charlatans. Parents were often too busy working or managing broken homes; many were too socially insecure to make waves or organize, let alone shape policy. The result: corruption at the top, corrosion at the bottom, catastrophe in the middle.

If Reginald was to make any progress in math, I would have to devise a personal program for him. Yet I was coming into the situation cold, with few notions of how to tailor a curriculum to the special needs of one student. The textbook was totally inadequate and I had no idea what self-teaching materials Whitman might have. Were puzzle books available? More helpful textbooks?

I was soon on a mission—looking everywhere for materials to use with Reginald. Finally, one day in October, the teacher trainer located a puzzle book for me. Each of the twenty-five puzzles would probably entertain Reginald for a good portion of the class period. In the first puzzle, he'd have to solve a series of math problems, then locate each correct answer from an alphabetic list of choices. When organized in the correct order, the letters spelled a simple phrase. The ability to solve math problems and place the letters in the right spots might have the bonus effect of encouraging him to sound out the words of the phrase. When I handed him the book the next morning, Reginald looked delighted, and quickly set to work.

For the first time in 8-16, I felt I'd accomplished something meaningful. Two different activities were going on in my room, and, however primitively, I had allowed children of different abilities to seek their own level. Reginald worked independently, while I taught the rest of the class, my own reward in seeing him bent over the puzzles in concentration, excited for the first time.

It was still a rough period. 8-16 usually was. In one corner, three boys insisted on playing Uno, the card game, and ignored all demands to stop. Angelie, a big, loud girl who seemed to detest everyone in school, shouted at Tameeka to "stick your head up your ass." To which Tameeka responded that Angelie was "the biggest cuntface in the school." Shereeza, as ever, sat quietly, looking entirely vacant. Every few minutes, Kenneth jumped up and paced around the room, his head bobbing up and down, shouting "Olé!" Then he would sit down again and pretend to sleep. Undisturbed, Saheedra remained hard at work on the day's problems, which, like reducing common fractions such as $2/4$ to $1/2$, should not have given an elementary school student panic. Most of the other students, however, were lost. I felt awful.

All of the students except for Reginald filed out of the room when
the bell rang. I was relieved that the period was finally over; we had
not made it past two problems before the place erupted with kids
shouting that they were bored and hated my class.

"Baby work," one boy had sneered. That it was—but on their
level, all the same.

Reginald though, seemed unaware of the whole ruckus. The
other kids gone, he slowly approached my desk, carrying the puzzle
sheet I had given him forty minutes before. The answers to the puzzle, he told me, spelled out a phrase. "That's great, Reginald." I
extended my hand toward the paper. "I'll look it over and give it
back tomorrow."

But instead of surrendering it, he began to read aloud. "Th . . .
Th . . . Th . . . Th . . . Ro . . . Rone."

I looked over his solutions. "T-H-R-O-W-N D-O-W-N," the puzzle phrase began. He solved every math problem perfectly and put
every letter in the right place, but could not read the words the
letters formed. His breathing grew heavy with effort. I couldn't walk
away. "Thrown . . . thrown dow, dow. Thrown Down. Thrown down
by . . ." He paused and tried again. It took him three more minutes
to finish. "Thrown down by an earthquake, the broken pieces remained about one thousand years." Two of the words—*pieces* and
remained—he could not read at all, though he made an attempt at
every one. "There," he sighed at last, more exhausted than elated.

I did not know what to say. Reginald was so big, a foot taller
than me, and twice as wide. Even so, I wanted to hug him. He had
tried so hard. I was close to tears as he stood there—this persevering
man-child who performed complex three-step math computations,
yet couldn't read a simple English sentence. Reginald's world, I realized, was at every turn a place of daily personal defeats. Despite
three extra periods a week of small-group reading instruction, it was
a humbling struggle just to read aloud, and a brave effort to try. His
courage deserved support.

"I'll find you another puzzle," I promised as I gathered my
books.

"Yeah, okay," he replied, and we left the room together.

In subsequent weeks, I brought more puzzles for Reginald. Each
took an hour to prepare and get copied onto a worksheet, but this
was my private project. Some days I was lucky, finding a puzzle
relevant to the unit my other classes were studying, and so I gave
them the same puzzle I had created for Reginald. It was an imperfect
system, as I still had no time to work with Reginald alone or to go

beyond the basics of those puzzles into really new material. And although the puzzles were challenging, they did no more than keep him busy, failing to stretch his mind or cover the Scope and Sequence topics for the eighth grade. Even his questions had to go unanswered during class since I did not want to call attention to our arrangement. To conduct parallel lessons with separate worksheets for different levels required energies and expertise I did not have. And how fair would it be to refuse other kids who also wanted to work independently?

I really needed an aide to help out in 8-16, but there was no way to get one. In the 1960s and 1970s, such low-rank classes as 8-16 had a limit of twenty-two students, but the cap on class size was eliminated in 1979, during the city's fiscal crisis. Now, every regular-education class, whether composed of highly motivated students like those in 8-1 or students with serious learning problems like those in 8-16, could legally have thirty students. And, at Whitman, almost every class did; there were no aides available for even the toughest classes.

A work-at-your-own-pace approach in 8-16 seemed an idea whose time had come; still, the kids at the bottom of this bottom class needed individual attention. Some did not know even the basic arithmetic needed to work simple problems. Others could do the arithmetic, but could not untangle a verbal problem into the set of facts needed to solve it; they could not do any practical reasoning or analysis.

Some of the students, I was astonished to discover, did not understand the concept of division. One day, I asked the kids to take a pile of 10 cards and divide it by 2. Other than Reginald, not a single 8-16 student could sort the ten cards into two equal piles. When I asked the kids how we might use toothpicks to demonstrate that 6 times 8 made 48, they simply could not grasp the concept, no matter how I rephrased the question.

As the weeks passed, the two-tier system began to create its own predictable problems. Some of the students realized that Reginald was getting special work and wanted the same privilege, insisting that they, too, could solve the puzzles. Marlene, who earlier in the week asked me how to multiply 34 × 6, had declared she could solve one complex exercise involving long division and reducing fractions. What a fraction was, let alone how to put one in simplest terms, was a mystery to her. The puzzle could only lead to more frustrated failure, but I felt I had to let her try.

Pondering the whole mess one night, I realized I was sending the wrong signal to 8-16: Reginald's problem could be treated separately, while their academic problems, however unique, would be dealt with en masse. Reginald's situation had been the first I had noticed and felt capable of dealing with quickly and efficiently. After all, he was a good math student. These kids so often got the message that they were worthless, the stupid ones at the bottom of the grade. And I was reinforcing it yet again.

Meanwhile, there were so many whose problems were more severe than boredom. For instance, there was Kenneth. In addition to shouting Olé every six or seven minutes, he was nearly illiterate, incapable of writing his own name. Usually somber, every now and then while staring out the window, he would suddenly begin to laugh uncontrollably. He did no homework and steadfastly refused to take notes in class. The entire year, I never heard him speak a complete sentence, and when he did utter a word or two, it was unintelligible. Seemingly intellectually arrested and emotionally disturbed, he probably should not have been in a regular public school to begin with.

Jordene's records claimed her reading score was at the 19th percentile, but her previous reading teacher insisted that rank was too high: indeed, Jordene could not read at all. Her math score, like Kenneth's, was in the 3rd percentile. She had just repeated the seventh grade, entering eighth grade as a sixteen-year-old. She had so many problems that I utterly missed the most comprehensive one until quite late in the year, when I gave an exercise in point-plotting. On a piece of graph paper, each student drew two axes, horizontal and vertical. They were to plot a series of points and then connect the dots to form a picture. In the first of these puzzles, the completed picture was to be a horse's head. Riddled with errors, Jordene's drawing resembled a mangled star. I learned why during a lesson on probability. I gave each student a single cube from a pair of dice and asked how many sides it had. "Ten," said Jordene. When I next asked how many spots were on top, she counted one of its two dots three times, and said the side had five dots. Obviously, her learning disabilities were rooted in some sort of neurological problems that made her misperceive the very forms and shapes of the real world.

Not until the school year was over did I discover that Jordene lived with eight siblings, a crippled, frail mother, and an unemployed father in a decaying high-rise apartment building overrun with rats, roaches, and the nauseating reek of chemicals. Every few minutes during my visit, Jordene's mother, perched on the edge of a couch whose springs were popping out, jumped up and sprayed a can of Raid into the air.

There were many students, like Shereeza, whose true medical condition—cerebral palsy? mental retardation? I had no way of knowing yet—seemed to be implicated in every academic problem. With many, I had no grasp of what they were coping with, or what impact it had on their abilities to learn, let alone how to get them screened or treated. Their medical records, usually no more than a scant list of immunization dates, seldom included useful information notes. Nor did the record folders contain write-ups from previous teachers. Yet it was obvious that vision and hearing problems had to impair reading and writing abilities, that nervous tics and emotional outbursts had to be relevant to so many of the students' learning problems.

Not all the students in 8-16 were physically or emotionally troubled. Saheedra arrived punctually every day, worked diligently, and mastered much of the material. Robert, a boy assigned to 8-16 midway through the year, also had excellent work habits and a genuine interest in school; he, too, did very well. But these students were the exception; I often thought they as well as Reginald should be moved to a class in which real math could be taught.

It finally dawned on me that 8-16 was the dumping ground for intensely needy, overage children thrown together with no expectation of improvement and few clues to teachers about their special needs. The lowest sections often got the newest teachers, the most inexperienced and the least able to help them. Nonetheless, these kids would be pushed on to the ninth grade, regardless of how they performed in eighth grade, because they were simply too old to remain in junior high school. The administration's message, unstated but irrefutable, was that disorder and failure were tolerable in 8-16 because, after all, it was an impossible class. As long as the door was closed, the problems in my room and the rooms of so many other struggling teachers did not exist.

Only on Tuesdays was 8-16 easy because I taught the class early in the day, second period. Most of the kids failed to make it to school in time for the 7:50 A.M. start of first period, so, on Tuesdays, my class was their first. That meant few had yet erupted. Many students detested each other, and chivalry had no place in their world—boys had no qualms about punching girls, and girls socked each other at will. If I got them before the first fights broke out, there was a chance to teach.

But one Tuesday morning I arrived in Room 327, to a sight unlike any I had ever seen in a school. A small boy had a bloody nose and was weeping alone by the windows. Six or seven desks were turned upside down. Marlene, as tall as most of the boys and stronger than many, held a desk over her head, about to throw it. Half the kids were screaming, almost every word out of their mouths malevolent or obscene.

It began as what was called a "he said-she said" fight—not over provocative actions or disputed ideas but about insulted egos. Tasha apparently told Marlene that Tonqua said something nasty about her, so Marlene enlisted her friends to trounce the slanderer. Usually, fights like these were provoked for reasons so trifling as to be ludicrous—but the results could be bloody. To these kids, a rumor was as solid as fact; a friend's betrayal justification for a battle.

"There's a fight going on in here," I yelled over the hallway din. Between classes, it was always frantic on the third floor as students shoved and pushed their way down narrow corridors built to accommodate the elementary school kids years before. No one came to my rescue. Loath as I was to enter the fray, I had no choice. I was shorter and slighter than almost every student in 8-16, and my voice no match for their angry shouts. "Please sit down," did not carry much weight over "Shut the fuck up, cuntface!" or "Who asked you, you Haitian piece of fuck dirt?" But there I was, and the fight was escalating fast.

Marlene, desk over her head, seemed the most dangerous, and I ordered everyone around her to move away. For a moment, her attention was drawn elsewhere and I grabbed her wrist as hard as I could, my fingernails digging into her skin. The desk tumbled to the floor in a clattering crash. Just then, I noticed that Tameeka was set to hurl her notebook across the room. I caught her chin in my hand and boomed, *"Sit down. Now!"* She was startled. *"You heard me,"* I yelled. *"Get in your seat and be quiet!"* "Cuntface," she retorted. I hollered to two girls in the back of the room to find someone, anyone, to help. Luckily, just as Marlene was bending down to try to lift her desk again, seventh-grade dean Bob Rich arrived.

Rich, standing six-feet-four, had a cherubic face but a thunderous voice. He was universally liked by the kids, and his appearance in the doorway of a classroom usually compelled order; the kids would shuffle quietly into their seats even after a vicious brawl.

"Pick up the desks," Rich roared, and the kids scrambled to put

the desks in order. When everything was quiet—a matter of seconds —Rich turned to me and nodded. *"That's better,"* he barked, his voice still resounding with authority. "Let me know, Mrs. Sachar, if these kids cause any more problems."

On such days, I could not help making comparisons to 8-1. In 8-16, I was always on edge, even when not attempting to stop a fight. I wasn't merely paranoid; the kids often were plotting nasty surprises. It might be a paper airplane barrage or a chalk-throwing nightmare. Although I longed to appear calm and measured, I was no such thing. I was worried, anxious, at times plain terrified. I did not trust the kids in 8-16, and they probably did not trust or respect me. I wanted to establish a rapport, as with 8-1, but I could find no interests the students shared with each other and none they shared with me. A few did want to learn, but they were a minority. The rest were interested only in the distraction of the moment—settling scores, listening to new tunes on a boom box, banging a basketball around the room, or, amid the tumult, simply sleeping. They craved instant thrills. The litany of study—learn—earn was no sale to them; they thought they knew better. Several asked me why it was better to go to school than to sell drugs. "If you ever want to get into it, Mrs. Sachar," offered one boy, "I can help you. Knowing what you be knowing about math, you could be making a lot of money for your family."

One afternoon just before Christmas break, I asked the students in 8-16 to gather in a circle so we could discuss their plans for the future. Six of the poorest students, including two who could not read, said they wanted to be doctors; two others hoped to be lawyers. Five saw themselves as future engineers, although they did not know basic addition or how to multiply two numbers. Told that they would have to go to college and graduate school to attain their goals, they looked genuinely shocked. "All of you can do it, but you've got to begin to work today," I explained. "You have to act as if today is the first day of the rest of your life." They did good work that day, but the next day we were back to their normal rioting.

The differences between parents of the 8-1 and 8-16 students were as strongly defined as those between their children. The 8-1 families tended to be lower middle class; most of the parents had finished high school and held responsible jobs. Whereas 8-16 was composed mainly of the children of recent immigrants, parents of the 8-1 kids had typically lived in the United States more than ten years. Already largely acculturated, all expressed discrete hopes for their children and had thought about how to help. They insisted that homework be done and used incentives to motivate their kids. On Open School nights, they came to retrieve their children's report cards, and they wanted to know how their kids could do better. They openly demonstrated their love, and were not afraid to back it with discipline.

In 8-16, on the other hand, the most troubled children came from desperately impoverished families. Some were on welfare; others, newly arrived immigrants; many, here illegally, could not obtain public assistance. Ghastly as were the physical conditions at Whitman, they seemed luxurious compared to the homes in which some 8-16 students lived. For many of these families, the chief issue of the day was finding enough food for supper. Much as I wanted to, I never met some of the parents of 8-16 students. Although I phoned every one and sent letters home to the more than half whose children were failing the first marking period, only four 8-16 parents attended Open School night. They were not the ones I most needed to see.

Hoping the kids would learn more if the lessons were more connected to their everyday lives, I tried to make the work in 8-16 less abstract. In early November, for a lesson on "The Better Buy," I tried my first experiment. I brought two large bags of groceries to school —apples, boxes of tea bags, ketchup in different sizes, large and small cans of soup. When I pulled out the apples, the kids were immediately intrigued and the usual din subsided.

I had made two signs—"Marlene's Grocery Shop" and "Carl's Deli," named after two of the more restless students in the hope of piquing their interest in particular. Placing two apples beside one sign and three by the other, I said we were going to learn how to become better shoppers. "Now, at Marlene's, the apples are two for twenty cents," I explained, "while at Carl's, the apples are three for seventy-five cents. Which store gives us the better buy?"

No hands, and I had a sinking feeling that my grocery store was going to fold. "Okay, what is the price of a single apple at Marlene's?" I asked. No hands. "Look. If I can get two apples for twenty cents, how much does one apple cost?" Three students finally raised their hands. "Marlene, we're shopping at your grocery. Maybe you can help."

"How the hell do I know?" Marlene groused, and then pretended to sleep.

"Well, maybe you can figure it out," I persisted, lifting her face by the chin. A few kids laughed, but Marlene didn't. "Marlene, if two apples cost twenty cents, how can I figure out how much one apple costs? What operation could I use?"

"Subtraction," Cora screamed.

"Okay, Cora, now how can we use subtraction?"

"Twenty minus two," she said.

"How would that help us find the answer?"

"I don't know," Cora laughed nervously.

At a loss for what to do, I thought: money—I'll show them with money, and produced two dimes.

"Okay, let's all gather around my desk." They came forward, the money like a magnet. "Now listen," I urged. "If the two apples cost twenty cents, how many dimes is that?" Realization all around, they yelled out "Two!"

"Great! Now, if two apples are two dimes, how many dimes would one apple cost? What do you think, Marlene?" She still did not see the answer.

Ever so slowly I went on. "Now, what operation are we using to find that if we spent twenty cents on two apples, one apple costs ten cents? Are we dividing, multiplying, adding, or subtracting?" I could still not get them to understand that we were using division. I rephrased the question several times and then gave up, wondering how a veteran math teacher would get the idea across.

Finally, I said, "Well, it's division," and I wrote the unit-price formula on the board. *Cost of one item = Cost of a group of items/ Number of items in the group.* I had hoped the kids could come up with the formula without my help. Still, it was some progress. "Now, let's figure out the price of an apple if two apples are thirty cents instead of twenty cents." I reminded them to use division to arrive at the answer, and a few of them figured it out correctly.

We worked through Carl's three-for-seventy-five-cents apples, and, finally—with work on the board showing Marlene's apples at ten cents apiece and Carl's at twenty-five cents—I asked in which store they should buy the apples. A few yelled the right answer, but many called out that they would buy the fruit at Carl's. I wanted to cry. The whole exercise took over thirty minutes. The kids had probably forgotten what it was we wanted to do in the first place. I was having trouble remembering myself.

When the bell rang, Saheedra, one of the sharpest students in the class, whose presence I was always grateful for, approached my desk. "That was good, Mrs. Sachar," she said. "Can we do more of that? I'm going to try it out when I go to the store." A few kids, at least, had caught on. Soon they might be able to move on to a slightly more complicated problem.

But the entire episode discouraged me deeply. The concepts were lost on so many of the kids. How could they ever learn the assigned eighth grade curriculum—exponents and scientific notation, constructing angles and plotting algebraic equations? So many were unable to master the simple math they needed just to survive as adults—math to help them save money at the store or land any sort of entry-level job. It was always the struggles and resistance of the vast majority, not the successes of the top few, that created and controlled my mood.

When I headed down to lunch, I was exhausted and disheartened. The kids clearly had some ability to memorize simple facts and formulas. Yet, too many of them refused to reason or think through the simplest problems. Was it boredom or indolence, disinterest or lack of intelligence? Perhaps it was something else—a teacher who, despite her best efforts, wasn't connecting, who wished to remedy in weeks what had been years in the making.

10

The Knife

Never confront a student in front of his classmates. You will always lose. He will always win.

—Bob Rich, seventh-grade dean, Walt Whitman Intermediate School.

There will be a critical moment when you will have to find a way to resolve disputations and how you assert yourself and the rules that you play by and how students view fairness and how they see your role as chief negotiator. Asserting oneself first as you gain control and seize the moment from the management of your classroom and second, when that critical moment where some form of disputation has occurred. Your strength and your support will be necessary. [sic]

—Late Chancellor Richard Green, in a speech to new teachers, the Felt Forum, August 25, 1988.

"Look, Mrs. Sachar, a knife!"

I was standing at the blackboard in 8-7 when I heard a shout from the middle of the room, then a pop and a click. I spun around and saw a glistening piece of metal in Kevin's hand. My mouth went dry.

I should have known better: I had typed my lesson plan so I

could read it easily, and reviewed it before class. I was well prepared, eager to go, and probably tempting fate.

Kevin stood beside his desk, his feet firmly planted on the scuffed wooden floor, his blade piercing the air. Except for narrowing his eyes against the sunlight that streamed through the musty window, Kevin hadn't moved since he flicked open the blade.

He wasn't tall, or particularly strong or muscled for his fourteen years. His expression was usually gentle, and his eyes often shone with merriment. But not today. I tried not to show the panic I felt as Kevin stood there, motionless, though I was sure the kids could see my hands shaking. My chalk fell out of my hand and shattered on the floor.

"Bring me that knife now," I said in the calmest tone I had.

"No, Mrs. Sachar, I don't think so," Kevin answered. His mouth widened into a smirk. "Look what this knife can do." With a sudden move, he slapped the blade back into the cartridge frame.

The room was quiet. The students stared at Kevin, all eyes wide. Even the two girls in the back, my allies, put down their pencils to stare at this boy whose back was inches from their seats.

The blade snapped again. Pop. Whoosh. The handle was black, the blade that sprang from it more than five inches long. It looked sharp enough to kill.

I had felt many times before that my classes were out of control. But I had never been so close to a weapon, or as frightened. I wanted to stalk to Kevin's seat and wrest the knife away. But his eyes were tight with fury. I was afraid he might slash me or turn the knife on one of the students. I didn't know Kevin's breaking point. I barely knew his name.

I ordered one of the girls at the rear of the room to find a security guard, a dean, or an assistant principal.

"Kevin, do you want the security guard to take the knife away, or do you want to give it to me? Bring it to me now. *Now!*" He did not respond. I glared at him, enraged.

Standing beside my desk, barely six feet away from Kevin, I wanted to will him to surrender, so badly did I yearn to defuse this volatile scene and perhaps earn the kids' respect. But that wasn't how things usually worked—not at this school, not in my classroom. Standoffs did not end easily or quietly, and teachers were often the losers. Today it was my turn.

"I want the knife," I repeated. "And I want it now."

At that moment, it was only me and Kevin, as if the twenty-four other souls in the room ceased to exist. I longed for the bell to ring.

A fire drill. An announcement over the public-address system. A joke from a student. A knock at the door. Anything.

It seemed an eternity since I sent for the security guard, but my watch said it was only three minutes. Should I begin the lesson anew, ignoring Kevin's knife, or continue the staring contest with him?

"Kevin, I'm going to say it one more time." As I spoke the words, I was certain they sounded as ineffectual as I felt. "Bring the knife to me now. I'll give it back to you later." With each word, my voice grew louder. I couldn't believe I was promising to return the weapon. If I got my hands on it, I'd never give it back.

Looking around the room, my eyes pleaded for help from the few students I could trust. Renee, Carlia, Lakeesha, Maxina—they neither moved nor spoke, at best silent allies, willing to help me only if they risked no loss of respect from their classmates. Respect. A big word with a little meaning.

Marlon finally spoke up, disgusted. "Just give it to her. She's not so bad."

Marlon had an uncanny sense of timing, which I had seen him use before to cool situations that went too far. Marlon knew as well as I that Kevin had already won. He had stolen time from the lesson, and frightened me. The class had become his audience, not mine. What more could a disruptive student want?

Confused, Kevin hung his head. Marlon was no ace student—he failed the first two tests I gave—but he was widely admired by the eighth-graders at Whitman. He was a superb athlete with a solid build, a gentle baritone voice, and a tight grip, in every way, on any girl he fancied. He winked at teachers, too. What Marlon said carried weight with these kids, and Marlon had just given the signal to Kevin to knock it off.

Kevin scanned the room, while fidgeting beside his desk, seeking a cue from the audience to go on with his knife act. But their attention and loyalties were divided. Kevin was testing me; Marlon was testing Kevin. I held my breath.

"Give it up, K," said Marlon with quiet confidence. How did he manage it, I marveled. Kevin had still not left his desk, but his head was bowed, his gaze cast sadly downward. "Thank you for bringing me the knife," I coaxed. I wanted to walk to his desk, touch his chin gently so he would look up at me. But I was too frightened to leave my desk. The school's teacher trainer had told me that a teacher always at the front of the room is usually a teacher in trouble, too intimidated to walk comfortably around her own classroom. It was true.

The girl I dispatched for help returned, unable to find any.

"Thank you, Kevin," I tried again. "I'll take the knife now."

Slowly Kevin walked to the front of the room, looking at Marlon as he passed. Marlon, head on his hands, feigned sleep. Kevin was silent as he handed me the blade.

"Thank you," I said. "Now, please sit down and join the lesson." What lesson? So far, there had been none. I put the weapon into my bag and rummaged for a piece of chalk. When I tried to write on the board, I couldn't—my hand was still trembling.

My mind was a cacophony of "what ifs." What if Kevin really wanted to hurt someone? What if he *had* slashed someone or in humiliation turned the knife on himself? What if the next weapon was a loaded gun? Such questions would have been inconceivable in my own tame junior high school in suburban St. Louis eighteen years earlier. But they were completely plausible here, in the heart of New York City at one of its most troubled schools.

With fourteen minutes still left in the period, I was completely at a loss. A teaching pro might give a lecture on school safety, rules, law, and weapons, and pull the class together with a discussion about respect for one's fellow students. I just wanted to keep the kids busy while I attempted to regain my composure.

Trying to sound a note of authority, I said, "Take down your assignment now." The din of murmurs and whispers continued, but it was less upsetting than the taunts and laughs I usually faced in class 8-7. I was in no mood to shout for order, and the kids must have sensed how rattled I was. They bent over their papers, working, or pretending to work.

When the bell finally rang, Kevin approached my desk. "I have nothing to say to you," I told him angrily as I gathered my satchel and eraser to pack away the supplies I carted around. As he came closer, I began to tremble. "Get away from me."

"But it's not a knife, Mrs. Sachar," he declared, his eyes once again lively and mischievous, the way they were when he joked with friends. "It's just a letter opener. Give it back to me," he cajoled. "You said you'd give it back. Please, Mrs. Sachar."

"I don't care what the hell it is. I will not give it back. You had no right to pull that thing out in my class, and you know it. Now get out of here."

"But you promised." Angry and menacing during the standoff, he now looked like the Kevin I observed in the hallways—standing just a bit off balance, his head cocked to one side. He had an engaging smile and, like so many of the boys at Whitman, was eager to flirt, to flaunt a new jacket or high-top sneakers or a gold necklace. Math clearly wasn't his main interest. In class, he usually doodled, copying figures out of comic books, and some of the girls told me he wrote them beautiful romantic poems. Yet this was hardly Kevin's first posturing prank in my class. It was he who had led the desk-rattling percussion section whenever I turned to write on the board.

Though often devoted to making their teacher's life miserable, one on one, the kids seemed like sad angels—innocent, conflicted, and desperate for a place in the world. In my heart, I understood that the rebellious students had a point: evolution, at least in junior high, did not favor adolescent wimps. Often, I felt a surge of hope—the kids might behave, I might achieve an orderly classroom, and they would respond and learn. But listening to Kevin's pleas, I still trembled.

"Kevin, I don't want to say it again. Get out of this room now." I held on to my satchel, so he couldn't wrest it from me to grab his weapon back. I couldn't wait to behold this knife supposedly turned innocent letter opener.

"You heard me," I repeated stiffly. "Get to class."

He finally trudged out with a shambling, beaten shuffle of defeat. It was a three-flight dash to my next class on the fourth floor, and I skipped every other step to make it in time. As I bounded up the stairs, I rummaged in my satchel for Kevin's knife. Alone, in a corner of the fourth-floor hallway, I pressed the button on the switch-blade cartridge. With that same startling pop and click, the blade sprang out, very much like a knife. But when I examined it more closely, gently tracing a finger along both sides of the blade, I realized that Kevin was not lying. It was a letter opener.

A nauseating chill overwhelmed me. I had been challenged, duped, and humiliated. I'd taken Kevin's bait, foolishly overreacted, and he knew it. I wanted to walk straight out, give it all up, and forget my deluded dreams of life as a teacher. But when the bell rang, I saw the students of 8-1, eagerly settling into their seats. "What are we doing today, Mrs. Sachar?" chirped the voice of one of my favorite students as I slogged wearily into the room. It was time for my third class that morning, an introduction to simple interest. It was time once again to teach. At last.

11

Fail-Safe

You can do it, Mrs. S. It don't hurt you none, and it help Pedro. Just this once, you could pass me. Please, Mrs. S. Pleeeeeeease! [sic]

—Pedro, 8-13, Walt Whitman Intermediate School, at the close of the first marking period.

At 7:50 A.M. on Thursday and Friday mornings, I had 8-13 for math, but only five or six kids usually showed up, and rarely was Pedro among them. Before school, the students were not allowed in classrooms or hallways so they waited in the auditorium for their teachers to retrieve them for their first-period classes. If a teacher was absent or the kids a few minutes late, they had to remain in the auditorium the entire first period.

Typically, Pedro was one of the late ones and he generally appeared outside my classroom just as the first-period class was ending and the homeroom bell had rung.

"I no make your class, Mrs. S.," he would declare with a look of utter innocence, as though each time was the first. "What's the homework?" In ninety seconds, I would brief Pedro on what we had done and suggest which students to see for a detailed explanation. He always thanked me. Not only was I annoyed that he made so little effort to get to class, his excuses seemed farfetched: His father and mother, he claimed, often forgot it was a school day and didn't wake him. What about using an alarm clock? "We don't have alarm clock,

Mrs. S." Some days Pedro didn't arrive before 10:30, halfway into
the school day. During the school year, I never saw his parents—they
did not come to the open houses—and when I telephoned them one
evening early in the year, the language barrier defeated me. First-
generation Dominican immigrants, they spoke no English. Their
other sons could have translated, but it would have been an awkward
arrangement for discussing Pedro.

One Thursday morning in October, Pedro made it to my class.
He sat attentively through a lesson on converting fractions to percents, and even tried to answer a few questions. Such behavior was
virtually unprecedented for him. Usually, he slept or stared out the
window or fooled around with one of the Spanish-speaking girls with
whom he had shared a bilingual class the year before.

Pedro was no Kevin or Jimmy—he was never mischievous and
was not an attention-seeker. He was just a genuinely sweet kid. An
ungainly boy, twenty or thirty pounds overweight, he walked with a
slight limp. Nearly six feet tall, he had dark hair, café-au-lait skin,
and dark deep-set eyes. When he did make it to school on time, he
was early, often waiting for me just outside the students' cafeteria.
On those days, he ate the free school breakfast, and he would shout
for me as I locked my car and walked to the entrance. He seemed a
little puppyish in his fascination with every aspect of my life.

"Wash your car, Mrs. S.?" he would ask. "New dress, Mrs. S.?"
Or, "I like your haircut. Maybe Pedro buy you a hair bow."

Keeping to his own peculiar schedule, Pedro made it on time
most Wednesdays and would announce: "We got you today, Mrs. S."
He would tag along after me, his white shirt, always a bit dirty,
hanging loosely over his big belly. Even on cold winter days, that
belly was always showing, and his coat unzipped. "Don't forget, Mrs.
S. Third period." Triumphantly, he would pull out a tattered class
schedule. "Room 309, Mrs. S."

"Thanks, Pedro. I'll be there."

He also brought me little treats. One day, it was a colorful pin
that said "I ♥ Math." He explained: "For you, Mrs. S., not me. I no
like math." Another time, it was a math puzzle he found in a local
newspaper. Sometimes he brought me doughnuts, which I gather he
had sneaked out of the cafeteria.

In those early-morning hours teaching 8-13 was a breeze. The
kids who showed up came because they wanted to, and the class
population never attained the critical mass that so often spelled trouble. If every class held to but a dozen students, teaching would be
pure pleasure. How I loved those first-period classes! No yelling, no

panic, no fights—I never felt overmatched. I could even work one-on-one with kids who needed my help without fearing a revolt from the rest.

But on that particular October morning, Pedro had an agenda that had little to do with math. True, he was paying attention, but he kept smiling at me knowingly. Sure enough, when the bell rang to end the lesson, he approached my desk. Standing awkwardly, he first asked if he might erase the board. I assented and prepared to leave. As I gathered up my things, he stopped abruptly and blurted, "Mrs. S., is Pedro going to pass the first marking period?" He often talked of himself in the third person.

"I don't know, Pedro. I haven't done the grades yet." Actually, most grades were in, but I was undecided about his mark. Pedro's first three test scores were 20, 42, and 25. Then, magically, on the last test, he pulled a 95. I suspected he had cheated, but I certainly wasn't going to penalize him without proof. Yet, even with that dubious grade, his average was only 45. That he neglected to do most of the homework assignments and seldom took notes in class all militated against passing him. On the other hand, were that 95 somehow legitimate, a failing grade after such improvement would be a crushing rebuke to his efforts.

"You can do it, Mrs. S. It don't hurt you none, and it help Pedro," he begged. "Just this once, you could pass me. Please, Mrs. S. Pleeeeeeease! Next time, Pedro do better." This argument—treat me right now and I'll owe you one—was a depressingly familiar litany. These kids borrowed shamelessly on my goodwill.

In four days, the first marking period of the year was to end, appropriately on Halloween. In the week following I was expected to hand in grades for my five classes. Grading Pedro and all the others was so daunting, I began to obsess about it as the deadline neared. To average each child's quiz and test scores for a grade—the way we had been marked throughout my own schooldays—meant nearly all my students, except 8-1, would flunk. Eight out of ten kids were failing. If I worked out some rationale to pass more kids despite their performance, what kind of signal would it send? To me, that was tantamount to declaring I had no standards, that tests meant nothing, and that teaching was a transparent hoax.

I had not set out to be a tough grader, and my exams were well below eighth-grade standards; most of our work so far had been simple and familiar, a review of fifth-, sixth- and seventh-grade material. The most recent test in my three bottom classes had included this question: *If 20 students worked for 2 hours each making curtains for the spring show, how many hours were worked in all?*

The overwhelming majority said 22. When I inquired how they had reasoned through to that answer, many said that "in all" meant that you had to add: 20 plus 2 was 22. When I tried to help them analyze the problem to see that we had to add 2 20 times—which was multiplication—most looked baffled.

Another problem: *If there are 400 seats in the auditorium and 40 seats in each row, how many rows of seats are there?* Only two students of the eighty-eight taking the test used division; the others added or subtracted. One of those who at least did know to use division still came up with 20 rows. One boy in 8-12 explained his logic. "Well, you take your 400 and you take away 40 and then you have 360 seats."

"Yes," I said, "but the problem asks for the number of rows."

"So," he countered, "then you divide by 10."

"Why by 10?"

"I don't know. Because there are 10 seats in a row?"

Pedro was not alone in his jeopardy, and his plea was but the first of many, all buttressing the importance of ironing out every detail of a consistent grading policy early on. If I simply averaged test and quiz marks, 108 of my 150 students would fail. This, I was frankly afraid to do, not because my supervisor, Miss Kowalski, would challenge me, but because the students would. All traded report card information, and when they got wind of my low evaluations, they would revolt, if not also retaliate. Credibility among my colleagues would be lost, too. What kind of teacher failed nearly three-quarters of her students? A failing one.

Seeking clues to how other teachers handled the grading dilemma, I scoured the cumulative record files for the previous years' grades of all my students. For some, the disparity between skills and grades had obviously started years before. It was a rampaging credibility gap. Lester's file was typical. An 8-12 student without a grasp of the basic arithmetic taught in elementary school, he failed every class in seventh grade, whereupon he was duly promoted to eighth; in his first try at eighth, he failed everything but Spanish, and was ordered to repeat the grade. None of that was surprising, but his earlier sixth-grade marks were surely far out of line with both his skills and evident performance. That year, he passed both math and language arts, although his standardized reading and math scores were in the 30th and 12th percentiles, respectively. Had his sixth-grade math teacher taught third-grade work and passed him for mastering it? Or had she ignored test results and rewarded him for effort? Did he show even that?

To convince myself that Lester was not an exception, I checked the earlier marks of another student. Hudson, also in 8-12, struggled with math just as his citywide test results would indicate. His national ranking was among the lowest in the class at the 16th percentile. Yet, Hudson somehow passed seventh-grade math with a 65. Furthermore, although his reading level was also far below the seventh grade, he passed both language arts and Spanish. He even earned a 90 in science and a 75 in social studies—remarkable grades for a student whose reading and math abilities remained well below fourth-grade level. Either he was a monument to doggedness or his teachers had passed off the ultimate hypocrisy.

Clearly, teachers customarily gave grades based on something besides skills, knowledge, or official policy. I wondered what standards they really did use, and stumbled on some answers by accident. One morning, a social studies teacher invited me to watch as my homeroom class performed a series of skits about World War I. She had them write lyrics about the war to be set to the tune of a popular song of the time. Each group was to perform for the others. Some bright girls wrote a song to the tune, "When Johnny Comes Marching Home Again":

When the American boys go marching on, hurrah, hurrah.
   Our boys are going overseas, hurrah, hurrah.
   To fight against Germany, we'll fight for our rights to be free
   When the American boys go marching. Marching to be free.

Many soldiers died in Germany, hurrah, hurrah.
   They were fighting for their country, hurrah, hurrah.
   They died because of bravery. They died defending their country.
   When the American boys go marching, marching in Germany.

When the American troops go marching, on, hurrah, hurrah.
   In Germany, we fought and won, hurrah, hurrah.
   We fought and won victory. We fought hard against Germany.
   When the American boys go marching, marching for freedom.
   Marching for freedom.

The kids loved the assignment, which they had enthusiastically prepared in class, and overjoyed by the results, the social studies teacher said it had one overriding purpose. "I use it to put one decent mark in the book. Otherwise, no one will pass." What did she mean, "a decent mark"? She showed me her marking book, explaining that a student might have marks of 60, 55, and 50, but with a 90 on the singing assignment, he would pass social studies.

She announced the marks for each group's song and performance—100, 95, 90, 95. Every single group had passed with flying colors. "We'll have to do more of these to bring up the grades," she told the kids. I was halfway down the hall when it hit me that the grade of 100 percent went to a song about World War I based on a Civil War melody whose only factual contents—"fighting for our rights to be free," "died in Germany," "defending their country," were simply flatly incorrect. (They did get the "overseas" part right.)

Having such success with World War I, other history-to-music assignments followed. By the end of the second marking period, many students who had failed all her class tests and quizzes were passing social studies. Did her kids actually learn any history? "Who knows?" she laughed. "But you can't fail everyone. You have to give a few assignments where they can get high marks without thinking you're giving up all your standards. It's kind of sneaky, but it's the only way." To her, skills and knowledge were only a small part of the grade. Effort, she seemed to be telling them, meant the most, and even that did not have to come in large quantities.

Another teacher, Ellen Yudow, a language arts instructor, had also loosened her standards, and was troubled by it. Ellen was the kind of teacher who cared deeply about her job and the kids. She was a gracefully articulate woman who often spoke in metaphors and with great passion. An avid reader and gifted writer, she was widely known as a demanding teacher. Many of her students, she conceded, were unable to write a simple declarative sentence, and most could not spell. Since she taught no class lower than 8-7, her students were among the highest achievers in the school. Yet, she often spoke of how much her standards of evaluation had weakened over the years.

She had given the matter great thought, and reached the unsatisfying decision to be relatively lenient. "I'm not sure," she said, "that I can hold up my 1965 standard and wave that in front of a generation twenty-five years later. Some of these kids have been in an intellectual coma for years. When I see a growth, a spark, I want to encourage it. I *have* to encourage it." That meant giving students passing marks for work she would have failed without hesitation years ago. For Ellen, too, skills and knowledge were not the prime determinants of a mark; improvement was paramount.

Another social studies teacher was thrilled when even a handful of students turned in any homework whatsoever. During the closing month of the 1988 Bush-Dukakis presidential campaign, he assigned his students their only project for the second marking period—assemble a scrapbook of newspaper clippings, recording the events leading up to the election. Students could focus on any of the issues —abortion, foreign policy, the economy—but they had to add some personal commentary on how they believed it had shaped the election's final results.

When I walked into the second-floor teachers lounge one morning, the social studies teacher greeted me with a big grin. "Look what I got from one of my kids," he said, proudly waving a red folder. A seventh-grader had carefully pasted newspaper articles to sheets of notebook paper, each with a headline that included the names Dukakis or Bush. All told, there were twenty-two articles and even a few charts breaking down the popular and electoral vote. But not a single word of the student's own writing. I looked at him puzzled. "Is this really the best thing you got?" I asked. "Yeah, pretty good, isn't it?" he beamed, and penciled a big 95 across the front page.

Especially curious were the grading policies of those teachers who defended easy grading as a necessary mechanism for protecting fragile young psyches. A few simply abandoned every academic standard, and likewise attributed all disruptive behavior to students revolting against a system that both called them failures and failed to help them.

Some of these teachers turned the problem back on me. "If half your kids are failing," said one, "then something isn't right with your teaching, because these kids are terrific, capable of anything."

"Even the kids in 8-16?"

She shrugged. "Look, all I know is, if you expect them to fail, they'll fail."

Other teachers were upset at the poor performance of many of the students and held to more traditional ground. "Some of these kids are just plain lazy," Roman Foster, a well-loved social studies teacher, remarked. "You've got to kick them in the pants to get them to work. And they will, if you keep kicking and showing them you care."

Edward Newman, an assistant principal I regarded highly as a disciplinarian and efficient administrator, provided inadvertent insight at one of the eight staff development sessions for new teachers. His discussion of grades was entirely devoted to the mechanics of recording them—what color ink to use on what type of form. No advice was offered on grading philosophy, policy, or practices.

With no computers to compile and record grades, every teacher had to transcribe them from a marking book onto a large document called the Rating Sheet. When each homeroom teacher had a completed Rating Sheet, each student's grades had to be hand-copied onto his report card. This was a cumbersome and tedious process, consuming several weeks. Finally report cards were distributed on Open House nights, to be signed by parents and returned. What they didn't say at the staff development seminar was that many parents never bothered picking up their children's report cards; so homeroom teachers had to hand them directly to the students. Some took them home; most did not. Forging their parents' signatures was a minor industry.

Still wholly in the dark about how to generate a meaningful grade, I approached Newman at the end of the session. Though not a particularly commanding presence physically—of medium height, thin, and balding—his stern demeanor and deep voice always compelled good student behavior. Dutifully, he walked the third floor during morning homeroom, looking for miscreants chewing gum, wearing caps, eating, drinking, or playing radios. He knew the names of nearly all 500 eighth-graders, and they certainly knew him. "Damain, the cap," he would bark down the hall and, before the second syllable was uttered, Damain would yank off his cap and tuck it into his pocket. Students respected Newman like a firm father, yet I rarely heard him raise his voice in anger.

Several weeks into the first term, he had reviewed my Red Roll Book, that critical attendance document, and in a matter of seconds he found five errors, steering me gently through the maze of rules until I saw my mistakes. He had seventeen years of experience, fifteen as a respected Whitman social studies teacher. Surely, he had developed sound ideas about how to grade and what standards to apply. So, after his presentation, I waited until he was alone to express my quandary.

"I need some tips on what criteria I should be using to grade my students. I've got some kids who have failed tests, who don't do the work. But I know they care, and I just don't know what to do about their grades." Newman asked if I had read the 1983 memo on this very topic. It suggested that 10 to 15 percent of the grade be based on homework, 40 to 50 percent on tests and quizzes, and the rest on class participation and performance in class projects.

"Yes," I replied, "but what if a student has done failing work? Should he still pass?" I described Pedro's case: ignorance of long division and the times tables, all his test scores under 45 (plus one strange 95). "He's a sweet kid, and he thinks he's trying," I finished. "Should I pass a kid like that?"

"That's a decision you have to make," Newman responded.

"What would you do?"

"Well, what exactly do you accomplish by failing him?" he asked.

"It's the truth, that's all," I said. "He's doing failing work, so I think I should fail him." Indeed, failing in work that he should have mastered years before, I wanted to add.

"It's up to you," Newman repeated. "But maybe you should pass him to encourage him."

"Isn't there some sort of standard, some definition of what a passing grade is, what sort of work a kid should be doing to pass? Doesn't the school or the Board of Ed have some guidelines we can use?"

"We can't tell you how to set your grades," Newman concluded. "That's up to you. That's part of being a teacher." That is, part of being a teacher was getting no help whatsoever. Passing kids who failed was not a policy—just the absence of any.

He seemed to be talking around the real issue. I was all for latitude and flexibility in setting grades, but what I wanted was some objective standard of what a high mark of 90 meant, and what a mark of 65, the lowest passing mark, meant, as well. To what degree should discretion, kindness, compassion be part of the grading? If they should indeed play a role, I still didn't see how that would ultimately benefit a student like Shereeza. In the last term, she had passed every class, yet all of her eighth-grade teachers knew that she could not read. Even using some subjective notion of "improvement" as the criterion for passing led to blind alleys. Some kids, like Sherwin, came to class and turned in homework every day, yet never had the correct answers, and failed every single test and quiz. In his case, like so many others, not even concentrated effort yielded improvement. How to distinguish between the failures who cared to try and the failures who didn't, especially when I knew a boy like Sherwin would be emotionally devastated by a 50 on his report card?

Good grades were important to the kids, but the work necessary to earn them often wasn't part of the equation. Grades having been exposed as arbitrary, they just wanted their share of the payoff. And

Pedro wasn't even after high marks; he wanted merely to pass, to answer his parents' sole demand: "Did you pass, Pedro?"

A kid like Pedro clearly did not really care about school, not enough to come to class regularly or to do homework or to study at all. Yet he wanted keenly to move on through the system with his friends. School was a sort of obstacle course, with no pride taken in the technique one used to negotiate it as long as one surmounted the hurdles; to be passed was to get past them. I could understand the arguments against harsh judgments that might crush frail egos. But exactly who really was served by the ritualistic fraud of passing kids on, and up, and out—who for eight years of such tender loving care remained as incapacitated as the day they began?

I passed Pedro for the first marking period. I rationalized my decision by telling myself that a failing mark might turn him off just when he might be willing to give math a chance. I was bribing him and kidding myself. And I passed Shereeza—for trying. After painstaking review, I ended up failing only twenty-eight of my students. Although we had been told not to take behavior into account in evaluating academic performance, for me the two were strongly linked. Most of the kids who were flunking were the worst classroom offenders—not so much dumb as mean.

The grades were a sham, devoid of meaning, and I knew it. And I resented the Board of Education for giving me so much freedom to deceive, however well-intentioned my lenient marks may have been. Weeks after the report cards were out—and the kids I had failed almost over their resentment—I was still tormented by many of my decisions. In nine weeks' time, I had become just another cog in the insidious machine of education in New York City, doling out to students with virtually no skills some bogus stamp of competence. Children weren't the only victims—we duped their parents, too. Shereeza's sister told me later, "When you pass Shereeza, you make her think she knows it. She goes around saying she passes in school, when we all know she can't read or do math. That's not fair to a person."

Pedro was so appreciative of his passing grade that I wanted to hide every time I saw him. His thank-yous were a constant reminder of my uncomfortable moral compromise. Then, one day in November, he came to see me, looking forlorn. "Mrs. S., thank you for passing Pedro, but I no deserve it."

He pulled out his sole, excellent test paper, the magical 95, to which I had affixed stickers of congratulations. I was surprised he still had it. Most of the students in my lower class sections threw everything away at the first opportunity.

"I no get this 95," Pedro said, his head cocked to one side. "I get 0. But I still try, Mrs. S."

"Do you mean that you cheated, Pedro?"

"*Sí*, Mrs. S., Pedro cheats." He was near tears, and it was hard to be angry at him for wanting to pass when so few even cared enough to cheat. Nevertheless, his timing could not have been more suspect. First quarter grades could no longer be changed, and I resented such blatant manipulation. Yet, at some level, the admission revealed Pedro's bafflement at what this system really expected of him. Like so many other kids, he was getting a signal from being passed and promoted that he must be doing well enough. Why then, he must have wondered, was every class a struggle? More sensitive than most, Pedro was certainly confused by his frustration and the ambiguous response from his teachers. If he was such a lousy student, why *were* they giving him adequate grades? If it made no sense to me, why should it to him?

"Pedro, you know it's wrong to cheat, don't you?" He nodded glumly.

"But, Mrs. S., Pedro is stupid. Pedro will never learn."

"Pedro, you *will* learn. But don't cheat, for pete's sake. What good does that do?" I wanted to praise him for his candor, however ill-timed, but I was overwhelmed by conflicting feelings. Maybe I was actually encouraging kids to cheat. Maybe they were justified in wanting so badly to pass; we teachers were telling them that if they failed, they would repeat the eighth grade. That surely wasn't an appealing alternative.

And I wasn't sure just how much Pedro *could* learn. He did not seem to be retarded, but he definitely seemed to be intellectually out of his depth in mainstream classes at every level. In some school systems, I was certain, he would not be placed in a regular academic setting.

That November morning, I realized, too, how much I resented the fact that kids like Pedro reached my class without the fundamental skills they were supposed to have. The vast majority of kids at Whitman had reached the eighth grade unable to do even the most basic of basic math; they did not know how to multiply or divide; they did not know what a graph was or how many sides there were on a triangle. Many of them could not explain the difference between a square and a rectangle. Their problems in reading and writing were equally severe.

To be fair, the blame for such widespread incapacity and lack of basic skills lay as much in the special circumstances of Whitman as in the system-wide policies of the Board of Ed. Many of the students were newly arrived from the West Indies and had never attended school regularly or received anything like a comprehensive education in their home countries. Their families moved frequently, and regular school attendance suffered as a result. Age, rather than any particular level of skills, was the criterion for acceptance into the eighth grade at Whitman. The school merely reflected its district, one of the most economically distraught and socially beleaguered in the city: rife with poverty, floundering immigrant families, devastated housing and decimated homes, drugs, crime, malnutrition, and despair.

Other students had been promoted to Whitman from elementary schools based not on merit, but on expedience. The Board of Ed offers only recommendations, not requirements, for promotion to junior high. And elementary schools almost never hold a student back more than once, even if he has failed to pass the reading test, Board officials explained. It was easy to understand how math skills, in particular, could lag so far behind when I learned that no one was held back in elementary school, at any point, *ever*, over math.

Grade reports were thus reduced to a sterile exercise, empty of any objective meaning, yet fraught with the possibility of destroying what little self-esteem and enthusiasm these kids had left. Even though they did not belong in an eighth-grade math course, we all had to live with our daily portion of futility—endless days of blank faces and wrong answers.

I looked back at Pedro, who was staring at the ground. "Pedro keep trying, Mrs. S.," he said. And then the bell rang.

The next day, I found a note in my mailbox. "I no get your class, Mrs. S.," it read. "I try, but I no get. Maybe, you help after school." It was unsigned, but I recognized Pedro's hand. I admired his courage in asking for help instead of simply disappearing after I had shown such displeasure with his admitted cheating. So began my first afterschool tutoring efforts on Wednesday afternoons, right after eighth period. I offered my services for one hour, until 2:30 P.M. Any student in any class was welcome to come to tutoring. Hoping those most in need would come, I resolved to use every effort to bring the kids up to seventh grade math, at least. I announced I would even provide snacks—raisins, apples, and juice.

Few students responded. Pedro showed up mostly because he enjoyed my company. In a typical session, I would try to teach him a rule for dividing numbers by 10—if a number ended with a 0, you could simply knock off the 0. 4,000 ÷ 10 = 400; 400 ÷ 10 = 40, and so on. There was no need to set up a long-division problem, as he always tried to do. Showing this useful trick, I solved several problems on paper. "Now," I prompted, "you try one. What's 3,000 divided by 10?" I looked up to see him in a far fog, his glazed eyes riveted on my chest, his pencil rolling across the desk.

The students' total lack of interest in a meaningless, inappropriate, and abstract curriculum marked the beginning of the end of my illusion of standards. A few weeks after the first marking period, I unilaterally jettisoned the curriculum for my four bottom classes. I resolved to teach very simple math, give even simpler tests and homework they could handle. So, I taught the conversion of decimals to percents, but instead of teaching how to convert .375 into 37½%, as mandated, I taught the conversion of .20 to 20% and stopped. Teaching exponents, we learned that $3^2 = 3 \times 3 = 9$, but I didn't bother to teach, as the Scope and Sequence required, the negative second power, that $3^{-2} = \frac{1}{3^2} = \frac{1}{3} \times \frac{1}{3} = \frac{1}{9}$. I worked very slowly, making each step so simple that any student who paid even minimal attention could pass my tests and keep up with class. The level wasn't eighth grade or even seventh; it was a sixth-grade curriculum with a few daring attempts, here and there, to introduce subject matter on their true grade level.

Grades improved, as I had hoped, and I was delighted at the new enthusiasm I found in many students. Kids who had been getting 40s and 50s on tests began achieving scores of 80 and 90. Only three of thirty students in one class had passed an earlier test; now only three of thirty failed the first test of new material. Handing back those first exams, I told 8-12 to give themselves a hand for making such wonderfully high marks. Beaming at the stickers of success on more than half of the test papers, the students applauded themselves—their success—loudly.

When I put the homework assignment on the board that December Friday, the students copied it with alacrity into their notebooks without the usual hubbub. On the following Monday, more than half the students in 8-12 put homework assignments on my desk. Perhaps, I thought, I had found the answer: If enough of the kids could pass every test, the class might start to pay attention. Then, as their enthusiasm grew, I could gradually build up to the work we were supposed to be doing.

Only one person was not comfortable with this approach: me. Though I stuck to this plan through the rest of the year, it was with a growing sense of deceit and guilt. I had surrendered to the students, and they knew it as well as I. They had shown no inclination to work on the topics I was hired to teach—negative exponents, scientific notation, simple and compound interest—and so I taught instead how to make change, how to read a pay stub, how to determine the better buy when shopping. Even if I could justify these lessons as real-life math more useful than scientific notation, I had, in a sense, broken my contract with the Board of Education. Even more important, the sad truth was that my students, yet again, would leave school at the end of the term years behind, and I would be at least partially responsible.

This new approach in my bottom four classes also spawned a host of unexpected complications. Giving passing marks for elementary work put me in a bind with my top class. It was hardly fair to give 8-1 kids a barely passing grade of 65 when other classes earned perfect marks for material so much easier. Kirkland typified the paradox. On the borderline of failing in 8-1, he challenged me over the inconsistency of my relativistic standards. When I gave him his grade, he said, "I don't see why you can't give me a 75, Mrs. Sachar. If I was in the bottom class, I'd be getting a 100."

"You don't want to go to the bottom class, do you?" It was an unfair reply. Of course, he didn't, and he had a point. Holding to traditional legitimate standards of excellence in 8-1 while abandoning the pretense elsewhere was neither a comfortable nor entirely justifiable position. But I felt I had no choice.

Another inequity became apparent when I learned that the second-term eighth-grade marks were a critical factor in high school acceptances. Nearly 60,000 eighth-graders throughout the city competed for slots in 117 public high schools. Exactly what weight was given to grades, standardized aptitude test levels, teacher recommendations, was never clear to me or the students. But students were cautioned that their second-quarter marks were vital. Big improvements from seventh to eighth grade in major subjects like math and language arts would undoubtedly help a student's chances of getting into his first-choice school. Or so we said.

If so, might applying different standards hurt the kids at the top, skewing the odds against them? Might a kid who sought acceptance at one of the city's top high schools—like Bronx Science or Stuyvesant or Brooklyn Tech, with distinguished reputations for academic excellence—fail to get in? These schools promised to be great gateways—to college, professions, and middle-class security.

Kirkland had his heart set on Brooklyn Tech, and he insisted a low math grade would cripple his chances.

But as the months passed, I slowly became more comfortable with my uneasy compromise for my lowest classes. If those kids in the bottom classes failed over and over, and grew only more disaffected, I might as well stop teaching altogether. The memory of how discouraged they had been the first term was never far from my mind. They had been unwilling even to attempt the work; classroom chaos had been their protest. The hope of passing was fanning at least a spark of interest, which might benefit all of us in the end.

12

Stink Bombs and Other Facts of Life

"Holy motherfucking shit. What's that smell?"

It was seventh period, four days before Christmas, and I was on my own with 8-12, the most difficult of my classes. The lesson had started smoothly enough. Despite the usual din of whispering and flurry of note-passing, I succeeded in getting most of the kids into their seats. At least half of them were copying the Do Now problem into their notebooks: *If a $100 coat is marked down 10%, what is the sale price?*

Into that relative calm came the foul odor and, in its wake, the foul language.

"Oh, gross," one boy moaned.

"Who the fuck did it?" Tawana yelled, pricking the air with her purple umbrella. "I bet it was Sherwin. He's always farting."

"It wasn't me," Sherwin said indignantly, looking around. "It was Jarred."

"No fucking way," Jarred insisted, opening his hands toward the ceiling. "Why the fuck are you saying I did it?"

"Stop it!" I said. "What difference does it make who did it?" Even as I spoke, the odor was wafting up to the front of the room. It was intense. "Part of growing up is knowing when to keep your mouth shut. If someone passes gas, you don't need to make a federal case out of it."

"When it smell like that, you do," Tawana shouted. "Sherwin should control what the fuck he eats. He's always eating them onions."

"It wasn't me," Sherwin pleaded again.

"Was, too," Tawana insisted. "You's always eating them damned onions."

"Oh, no, now I smell it," hollered a boy in the back. He and a friend jumped up frantically, pinching their noses and running to the windows. It was a frigid, windy day, but they threw the windows open high, chanting, "Air it out, air it out."

"Okay, who did it?" Crystal yelled from her post in the row of seats by the windows. "Enough is enough."

Suddenly the other kids were out of their seats, running around the room as if their clothes were on fire.

"If you want to act like lunatics, get out of the room," I called into the hysteria. The aroma was intensifying, so six students bolted out the door and ran down the hall.

A few seconds later, the librarian knocked loudly. *"What is going on in here?"* she boomed. She had two of my students by the collar, trying to herd them back into my classroom. *"Get in there and stay there!"* she commanded, slamming the door behind her as she left.

Rooted to my spot at the front of the room, I was speechless as I surveyed all the overturned chairs and wild kids dashing among them. Finally, I managed, "Okay, if you want to go on with the lesson, come up to the front of the room." Four students came forward; the rest were too caught up in their antics to even look in my direction. Within moments, I was sure, the other four escapees would also be returned by the librarian. The chances were good that I would be disciplined along with the kids. Perhaps the bell would save me.

Another rap at the door—it was a language arts teacher known for her formidable class discipline. Deeply embarrassed, I stood before the wildest classroom disorder even I had yet witnessed at Whitman. She only wanted to retrieve some materials, and left immediately without a word about the racket. I felt a pang: Would she tell the other teachers? Would the eighth-grade supervisors find out?

Again, I tried to move ahead with the lesson. "There is a Do Now problem on the board. Does anyone have an answer to it?"

Just as Sherwin raised his hand to speak, Tawana tore to the front of the room. "He did it again! Sherwin, what's your fucking problem?"

"Tawana," I said firmly, snatching at her umbrella. "Control your mouth, and sit down." She yanked the umbrella back.

"I ain't sitting down, Miss," she parried, "until Sherwin gets out of the room and stops them fucking onion farts." Sherwin was probably not the real source of the problem, and kept rolling his eyes at her in disgust.

"8-12, enough is enough," I declared, trying a tone of righteous indignation. I looked at my watch, thankful that we had only seven minutes to go. "Let's get to work."

I called on Sherwin again. The coat with the 10% discount would cost $90, he told me. "Great, Sherwin. Everyone listen to Sherwin. He has the answer to the Do Now." No one listened; no one cared.

When the bell finally rang, Daniel, an attentive, kindhearted child, approached my desk. "Don't you know what a stink bomb is, Mrs. Sachar?" he asked softly. I had heard of them, but didn't know they smelled like flatulence. Burning rubber or smoke, I would have thought. "It was Jarred's," Daniel said softly.

I wondered how he knew. But that's always how it was—the kids knew what I didn't.

By the middle of the year, my success or failure as a teacher was almost entirely contingent on discipline. I had more or less figured out what to teach and how to teach it and, given half a chance—a mildly attentive class—I could. Yet, just as those veteran teachers had warned me months before, a teacher cannot teach without discipline. Paradoxically, even good discipline was no guarantee that you *would* be able to teach, but there was no question that, without it, teaching was hopeless.

In 8-12, I was almost never able to teach. Other classes also posed periodic problems: if the basketball duo showed up in 8-16—even without their basketball—the period was a washout. If Jimmy, in 8-7, carried on about his need to urinate, teaching was impossible. A class that had started out as a delightful bunch of eager kids, 8-13 was also slowly ruined by the addition of three disruptive boys—one had been arrested twice for car theft, another periodically unzipped his fly and pretended to masturbate, and a third seemed to know every other trick in the book for interrupting the lesson. In 8-12, however, every day was a battle for control—not with the few, but with the many. It was a hideous situation, and always filled me with dread. It was somewhat comforting to hear from school administrators that they, too, had written off 8-12; they understood the teachers' inability to control the class. Still I found it hard to give up. I kept hoping for a miracle.

One 8-12 student, Crystal, showed no interest whatsoever in learning. For her, the school was a stage. I would see her between classes, huddled around the drinking fountain with her clique of mostly overweight, arrogant girlfriends, hatching some new nastiness with which to plague me and her other teachers. While others in the 8-12 class were constantly angling for changes in seat assignments, Crystal sat every day in the first row by the window—the better to stand up and yell at passers-by on the street below. But the yelling was a mild disturbance compared to her hairbrush.

At least twice a week, the hairbrush—a sky-blue handle with a haphazard collection of black bristles—was out on Crystal's desk before her notebook. Then, when her pal, Tawana, arrived, the two would open their beauty salon, right in front of me. Tawana was an odd mix of intelligence and rebellion. Sometimes, she took her designated seat without protest, contributing helpful and correct responses throughout the lesson. Her handwriting was perfect, and, with her instinct for math, she might have kept up with the work. But she had long ago lost interest in academics, and had incurred by now the wrath of every administrator and most teachers at Whitman for her rotten attitude.

On bad days—most days—she sauntered in with an insistent arrogance that was her trademark and settled herself next to her buddy Crystal. Pointing her nose into the air, she would pull out all the bobby pins and rubber bands and other paraphernalia woven into her hair, and surrender her head to Crystal who, with the deftness of a well-trained salon stylist, would set to work.

Tawana detested me from the start, right after I confiscated her umbrella as she was attempting to poke one of the boys in the groin. When I called her mother to discuss Tawana's disruptive behavior, her mother promised to give her a whipping, which was not the discipline I had in mind. At my request, Tawana came to the phone. But as she tried to offer an explanation for her behavior, her mother screamed, "Shut up, Tawana, or I'll shove a fork down your throat." The next day, Tawana appeared in class with a welt on her face. "Thanks for ruining my life, Mrs. Sachar," she grumbled.

Tawana often spent time in Mr. Newman's office, sent there for discipline by other teachers as baffled as I over how to deal with such an insolent fourteen-year-old. One afternoon, she was set to work with a bottle of Fantastik and a wad of paper towels, wiping the words "Fuck me" from the orange walls of the second floor. "Keep it up," Miss Kowalski ordered. "You've still got a long way to go." Matter-of-factly, Tawana explained as I walked by, "I sprayed up the walls and now I be taking it off."

"Tell Mrs. Sachar why you did it," Miss Kowalski prompted.

"'Cause I felt like it," Tawana spat back.

Tawana and Crystal had an on-and-off relationship in which I seemed to be involved. When I was able to interest them in the lesson —only rarely—Tawana couldn't get her hair done. When both were feeling hostile toward me, the salon in the first row was open for business.

One Monday, I went over to Crystal before class. "Sweetheart, could you help me out today and put the beauty supplies away?" A gentle appeal sometimes worked better than sternness, either because the kids felt pity for me or merely liked the individual attention.

"Oh, Mrs. Sachar, please," Crystal whined. "Just for a few minutes. Tawana needs new braids."

This begging was the hardest tactic to confront. If I gave in— whether for hair-braiding privileges or bathroom passes—it always came back to haunt me. But if I held fast, I'd have a fight on my hands. And I might well lose.

"Crystal, please," I said. "Just put the brush and mirror and makeup away, and save them for after school."

"Oh, Mrs. Sachar, we won't talk, I promise." Another dilemma —if they were quiet, I could teach. And if I took the hairbrush away, she would retaliate by talking for the whole period. I was tempted to give in.

"Crystal, put it away." She didn't, and rather than fight, I ignored her, starting the class with a simple exercise. No sooner had one girl begun to recite a solution than the aroma of hair grease wafted up to the blackboard. I turned and saw the brush moving in gentle strokes on Tawana's hair. "Crystal," I said, hoping she would respond to one last gentle reminder.

"What?" she replied sweetly, continuing to brush.

"You know what."

"Well, if she's going to do Tawana's hair, I'm going to do mine," added Jemema. Now two hairbrushes were going. Shortly the girls on the other side of the room would pull out their beauty supplies, and the cosmetologists would rule the room. As if reading my mind, one boy put on his headphones and pumped up the volume. Now, in addition to the giggles of teenaged girls, I had music throbbing.

Brandishing my marking book, I threatened zeros to anyone without a notebook open, as our teacher trainer suggested. She had tried on numerous occasions to help me with 8-12, to little avail. The boy with the Walkman didn't hear me, and the hairbrushers stroked on. A few kids sat up straighter, but they weren't the ones causing the trouble. The noise level steadily increased.

"Who wants a zero? I mean it, enough playing around."

But zeros meant nothing to kids who had often failed entire terms.

I stomped to the door. "Is there an assistant principal out here?" I called into the hallway. My supervisor, Miss Kowalski, came out of her office across the hall.

"Miss Kowalski," I said for the students' ears, "I think we have a problem in here today." As soon as she entered, combs and cosmetics and cassettes were stuffed away in knapsacks and notebooks hurriedly pulled out. In three minutes, the class was in perfect order, and Miss Kowalski had said not a single word. The quiet conditions were temporary, destined to vanish almost as soon as she left the room. I felt defeated at having to call her in, but it was better than another twenty minutes of chaos.

My one consolation was company in misery: discipline was hardly my problem alone. On my eighth-period hallway patrols, I noticed many classrooms out of control, several with students standing atop chairs and desks. In one room, the kids routinely ran around as the teacher's supervisor serenely read the newspaper in his office two flights up. Another teacher did needlework at her desk while the students played cards and radios. Dozens of times over the course of the year, I saw teachers inspecting papers they had assigned for punishment—"I will respect the teacher," or "I will always obey Mr. ———," or even the rather baroquely excessive "I am a poor, disrespectful student" repeated a thousand times across the pages. Obviously, teaching at Whitman was a struggle for many teachers.

In March, one of the music teachers threw a child bodily out of the music room. When the boy, tears streaming down his cheeks, knocked begging to be readmitted, the teacher slammed the door in his face. In April, one boy pulled down another's pants in class; the teacher didn't even bother to report it. One of the basketball duo in 8-16 was caught with a knife. In the middle of another class, two boys erased a teacher's chalkboard and then started dancing on the desks.

Our principal acknowledged at one staff meeting that many classes were out of control and that he himself had seen students jumping on desks while the teacher sat and read a newspaper. Another time, during the standardized math test, students roamed out of their seats and chatted in four classrooms where the test was being given. I notified a supervisor, who sent help to all four rooms, but it was a grim reminder that, in the supposedly secure atmosphere that surrounded citywide testing, chaos already reigned.

Bob Rich, the seventh-grade dean, told of bizarre incidents by the dozens. Occasionally, we would have lunch in his office, and I would watch as up to twenty kids trailed in during the hour. They had spit, cursed, drawn on desks, struck each other, or threatened their teachers.

It was a depressing irony that the most respected teachers had "good control," which generally meant silence. The quietest rooms were the ones in which students were copying notes verbatim off the chalkboard. Silence, of course, did not necessarily imply superior teaching, yet it was the goal to which we were encouraged to aspire. It implied discipline, and discipline implied control.

Two full chalkboards of math vocabulary words to be copied meant fifteen minutes of precious silence from the class. "These kids think if they're filling up a notebook that they're learning," Bob Rich observed. "And their parents like it, too." But such rote work didn't feel much like teaching to me. Even for that highest accolade—her classes are "in control"—it would have been a poor trade-off. Better to have a lively class with a real exchange of knowledge than the dead silence of kids on auto-pilot.

In most schools the "lack of control" might mean little more than a frustrated teacher and a few reckless students. But Whitman was very different. There were real threats to students' and teachers' lives. Citywide, the statistics were ominous—during the 1988–89 year, 1,854 kids were caught in school with weapons, everything from pocket knives to guns. There were 183 robberies, 1,346 assaults, and 105 drug seizures, and those were just the reported incidents. The real numbers were much higher, for many administrators did not report such events to the police or the Board of Ed for fear that the numbers, always played up in the media, would taint the reputation of their schools, and themselves.

The UFT, however, was very interested in the figures:

In junior high schools alone, 54 teachers were assaulted in the first four months of the school year, according to the union's figures. Still, I had convinced myself that our kids didn't carry weapons and I rarely felt my life was in danger. But right after Christmas vacation, I learned otherwise: A loaded gun accidentally discharged in the classroom of a Whitman social studies teacher. She was a kindly woman so worn down by the students' disrespect she seemed hardly to notice it anymore. She often tried to engage the kids in a discussion when they were completely ignoring her, calling out one May day to no one in particular, "Does anyone know what happened today in Warsaw?"

We were not officially informed of the gun incident until the monthly faculty conference on January 23rd. Then we learned that one student had been inches away from death in the accident. Winfield told us that a twelve-year-old boy had brought a loaded gun to school, and that it had accidentally fired in class. The bullet tore a large hole through the coat of a girl standing next to him, then ricocheted off a desk. "If the girl had larger breasts, they would have been eliminated," Winfield said, "and if she'd been turned in another direction, she'd probably be dead." The teacher, Winfield added, did not report the incident because she thought it was a firecracker. The kids all knew the boy had a gun, Winfield reported, but they, too, chose not to mention it.

This was only the first in a series of weapons incidents at Whitman. In February, one dean told me, a sixth-grade girl hit another student over the head with a hammer and was suspended for five days. A few days later, another sixth-grader brought a custom-made .410-gauge shotgun to school, and was arrested. The boy had borrowed the weapon from his fourteen-year-old brother, a drug dealer, to scare another kid at school who was "giving him trouble." A detective from the local precinct said that the boy showed no remorse: "He was quite callous, in fact."

Again and again, we heard that the drug culture—crack, in particular—infiltrated our school. One morning in late October, that reality became more obvious when two of my students broke down weeping: "Mrs. Sachar, one of my friends was killed on Friday night," one cried. The dead boy, also a Whitman student, had supposedly been caught in the crossfire of a drug fight, gunned down on the way to get Chinese food for his family. But another girl told me after class not to believe "that shit," because the boy, she insisted, was a drug dealer himself, often on the hunt for his enemies. Which version was true I never did find out.

A student volunteered one day that he knew where to get drugs if I ever needed them. Drugs did far more than touch our school; they permeated its very fabric, affecting my kids in subtle and powerful ways.

Beyond the occasional serious incident, though, an atmosphere of constant, low-level violence reigned. In the classroom we might control and channel some of the impulsive frenzied energy; in the hallways and stairwells, it ran unchecked.

The changeover between classes, which we called "passing," was wild, with six-foot-tall fifteen-year-olds roaring along corridors designed for four-foot-tall ten-year-olds. None of the normal rules of people moving from place to place—keep to the right, climb staircases on the right, etc.—were observed. The result was human pinball. Kids would career up or down the wrong staircase, screaming and cursing without restraint or any effective regulation.

Then there were the hallway games, which made the haphazard routine rumpus of the corridors seem bland and tame. First, it was Colors. In homage to the Los Angeles youth gang movie, students wearing red bandanas vied with students wearing blue bandanas, each veering around trying to knock over anything or anyone not moving as fast. Twice, that meant me—my pens and books sent flying. One day, a girl with a red bandana flew past, catching her sweater on the metal corner of my file folder, tearing a hole the size of a tennis ball in the weave. Another day, two warring students collided with such force that one suffered a concussion and was out of school five days.

A few weeks after Colors faded, a new game called Posse took over. I never quite figured out the rules of this one. It usually was played in the stairwells. Students would charge upstairs as fast as they could, then suddenly reverse direction and come bolting down. One student, his back pinned to the metal grate of a stairwell, got a broken nose when another plowed into him. When I got caught in the middle of a game-cum-stampede one afternoon, my only alternative was to press my face against the wall of the stairwell and pray as the kids battered my back. At home, I discovered a collection of bright red welts across my shoulders. On still another day I cowered impotent as a dozen eggs were dropped one-by-one from the fourth floor of a stairwell to the third just outside the assistant principal's office. Nor was the dried egg mess cleaned for a week.

Had the school actually functioned by its own Official Behavior Code, Whitman would have looked like a college prep school. There were rules covering every point of behavior and a rigorous follow-up procedure for misbehaving students. Even kids who came to school without pen and paper were to be punished, reprimanded, and ultimately suspended for repeated transgressions. Get to school on time, observe the basic standards of cleanliness and good grooming, carry a notebook, pen, and pencil, turn in homework when assigned—it all sounded great. I especially appreciated the catalog of forbidden objects in class: playing cards, basketballs, handballs, jacks, toys, computerized games, or Walkmans.

Officially, it went, first offense: teacher to discuss incident, give child warning. On the second offense, a parent was to be contacted. On the third, parents got a letter from the school requesting a pre-suspension conference. Four offenses, and a guidance counselor reviewed the case for possible referral to special education. Five strikes and you were out—a principal's suspension from school for up to five days. A number of offenses were considered so serious—vandalism, profanity, fighting, disruption of classes, possession of any weapon or drug, and threats or insulting behavior toward any adult—that they were supposed to lead to immediate suspension.

There was little evidence at Whitman that this vaunted Behavior Code was honored except in the breech. One day in mid-December, a fight erupted between one of my brighter students, Sherry, and Kevin, the boy with the push-button letter opener. Sherry threw a soda can at Kevin, and when he threw it back, she hoisted a chair and heaved it across the room. After I marched Sherry out, I turned her over to the sixth-grade dean. She was neither suspended nor were her parents called. When I phoned her home that evening, I could only reach her uncle, who apologized profusely. He was angry, though, that the administration had not contacted him directly.

When I asked the eighth-grade dean for the forms for a presuspension conference, he only laughed. The forms did not exist. "What did the kid do that would justify a suspension anyway?" he snorted.

Sanctions were threatened but rarely imposed, reserved for the gravest offenses—drugs or weapons. Not only did we fail to reprimand kids who showed up without pen and paper, as the code provided; we were frankly grateful if they put in an appearance at all.

Truly severe offenses were supposedly dealt with by a chain of command. For each grade, there was a dean to whom teachers were to remand serious discipline cases. The eighth-grade dean, however, was more of a legend than a functioning official. He told me that even the threat of suspension was out of the question for minor infractions—insulting back-talk, class outbursts, stink bombs—anything short of conspicuous drug-dealing. When I sent Kevin to him after the desk-rattling episode, he responded, "This is not a discipline problem. Please readmit to class." When I dispatched Marlon of 8-7 for telling Jimmy to "put away yer hairy dick," the dean wrote a character reference: "Marlon is a good kid. You must have heard him incorrectly."

This dean enjoyed a perverse celebrity at Whitman, with a whole catalog of stories, jokes, and rumors flourishing about him. Among other things, he had gotten his job, the one-word answer had it, by "connections." He was said to be friendly with one of the members of the local community school board.

Winfield patiently heard my complaints about the dean, whom he said he had inherited when he took over as principal four years earlier. "This is his last year," he intoned, "so you'll just have to put up with him, as your colleagues have for all these years." All those years, he had never sought to reassign the dean to regular teaching duties. Thus another message to teachers: utter nonperformance, flatfooted dereliction, was acceptable. If Winfield declined to act against this phantom dean, for whom there was widespread contempt, whom *would* he seek to remove?

I was luckier than many of the eighth-grade teachers, with seventh-grade dean Rich's office only two doors away from the room in which I held half my classes. With each passing month, I increasingly called on him for help with my intractable kids. There was nothing magical to his methods, just sure-fire consistency. When a student was referred to him, however minor the complaint of misbehavior, he always phoned a parent. He kept detailed notes on those calls, and he didn't hesitate to demand a parent's appearance if the poor behavior problem didn't promptly improve. And he never copped out by blaming the teachers. "Look, there are probably things you could do differently to get control in your classes," he advised when I was particularly discouraged. "But it's not just you.

Many of these kids have never been taught how to sit still, how to control what they say, how to behave. It's as simple as that. My office is filled with referrals and they're not coming just from one or two teachers; they're coming from a dozen." With that support and his avuncular pat on my shoulder, I could brave my return to the line of duty.

Rich also let me know what to expect in the way of backup from the administration. Little. The Behavior Code had long been abandoned, he explained, because if it were enforced, half the kids in the school would be suspended. Obviously, that was simply not possible. So many parents worked that children who were sent home would lack any supervision at all, which would be a much-sought paradise to the so-disposed. Suspension, in fact, was even less than a disciplinary mechanism of last resort; there was so much public pressure against its use it was virtually extinct.

Yet, more practical, moderate alternatives were nonetheless denied us. A Whitman teacher could not cool a student down by temporary exile, by sending him into the hall; administrators feared that would lead to lone wolves running amok down the corridors causing headaches elsewhere. Nor could we send students to the front office. Both of the eighth-grade supervisors, Miss Kowalski and Mr. Newman, were willing to play sheriff, but they had many administrative responsibilities—cafeteria and auditorium duty, reports, inventories—that took them away to other floors where they were hard to locate. Sometimes my classroom was two floors below their offices, at the opposite end of the building.

Such as they were, the administration's plans to cope with the mounting mayhem in the hallways, although admirable in concept, did not prove realistic in execution. In January, "sweeps" began—several minutes after the late bell, a high-pitched tone sounded three or four times a day, signaling all free teachers to the hallways and stairwells to corral any loiterers, be they students or non-Whitman intruders. Violators would be escorted to the front office to face the principal or security guards. When he announced the random sweep policy to the school, Winfield called it a direct response to the Colors game and the daily melee in the corridors. Some teachers maintained that trespassing outsiders sparked the hysteria in the hallways. Ample evidence implicated our own students, and the problem was not after the bell, but before.

In late May, Winfield imposed what he called a "state of emergency," after a band of intruders barged into a class to "get" a student. In the process of valiantly defending his young charge, an eighth-grade math teacher was attacked and beaten. "Assaulted viciously," in the words of our UFT chapter chairman, who rallied us to "stick together and function as a team," finding the incident as convenient as appalling.

In consequence, the administration instituted a new security regimen—teachers were assigned extra patrols to guard the school's eight first-floor exits and the corridors and stairwells on the upper floors. Fire laws forbade the locking of these exit doors from the inside, and most "intruders"—drop-outs, older kids, drug dealers— were let in by a student accomplice who simply punched the door open from the inside.

Yet, for all the justifiable anxiety about school violence, the most consistent impediment to teaching came not from drugs and weapons but from mundane situations that might seem comparatively trivial—a boy demanding a bathroom pass, a girl unable to resist the latest gossip, the sudden eruption of a he-said-she-said fight. It was the contest for their attention that was so vital. Hoping that if I brought fun into my classes, math might yet captivate my students more than their distracting neighbors, I devised a strategy for 8-12, that most challenging of classes. We would learn by playing Math Baseball.

It was a game I recalled fondly from my junior high days in which students counted off into teams, and took individual turns "at bat," swinging answers at math problems pitched by the teacher. Singles for the easiest, home runs, the most difficult; students could choose the level of difficulty. These kids thrived on competition and their need for fun was an all-consuming appetite.

They were as excited by the idea as I. I had written simple math problems I was certain the kids could do and bought small candy prizes for the winning team. I even found a stopwatch to limit each student's time at bat. With the whole period happily mapped out in my mind, I felt prepared, and in command.

Yet, no sooner had I assigned the kids to teams than things began to unravel. Twenty-two kids assembled on one side of the room and only four on the other.

"What's going on here?" I asked, annoyed. "The Ones on the left, and the Twos on the right. There should be thirteen of you on each team." No one budged.

"I don't want to be on that team," one of the girls whined. "I'm staying here."

Pointing to one of the four boys who sat on the other side, another girl said, "Yeah, I hate him."

"It's a game," I implored. "You don't have to love each other to play."

Numbering the kids off again, they finally fell, more or less, into sullen lines. I urged them to make up names for their teams; they didn't, preferring to mock my unhip display of school spirit.

The Ones came to bat first, the worst student in the class leading off. He asked for a triple.

"Okay, great," I said. "How much is 23 times 14?" I gave him a piece of chalk to work the problem at the board, and clicked the stopwatch on.

"I can't do that," he complained. I bid him to keep trying, but no luck. One out.

The next batter, another out. Then came the third, who got on base with a single. When I pleaded for some cheers for the successful hitter, I got nothing. Two students on the team began arguing, another was drawing pictures. Three boys read Marvel comics. Two others just played cards.

"This is stupid," moped one boy after bombing out in his turn at bat. Three outs, the Ones retired.

We had been playing math baseball only eighteen minutes, with twenty-five more to go. The atmosphere in the room was closer to a circus than a baseball field. I didn't know what I had done wrong.

The other team was due to bat, but they just took up the comic books, playing cards, and radios from their friends. No one was interested in math baseball.

Discouraged and also insulted, I finally boomed, "Forget it. Both sides forfeit!" Wearily I erased the scoreboard and replaced it, angrily, with a long homework assignment. Thankful that there was one ally I could always rely on, I sat sulking at my desk waiting for a ring from my only friend, the bell.

13

Stand, Mrs. Sachar, and Deliver

That teacher in the movies really cared. Because he gave up a good Job Just teach kids that was given him a hard time at frist. But, they come through. He gave up his spare time Just to help them, he gave up his summer without getting payed Just to help them. I can't believe any one or any teacher will ever do that. But he did. I wist I had a teacher like that. [sic]

—Reginald, 8-16, Walt Whitman Intermediate School, on the movie *Stand and Deliver.*

"You got a baby in there, Mrs. Sachar?" Jackelyn blurted out in homeroom one morning late in November. "You're looking kind of fat."

The whole class fell silent. "Well, yes, I do, Jackelyn," I said. "I guess I can't hide it anymore."

"I knew it, Mrs. Sachar," one student yelled from the back of the room. "You look so happy. You want a boy or a girl?"

"Just a healthy baby," I replied.

"When's it coming?"

"In early May."

"Oh, that means you won't finish the year."

"Yes, I will. I'll be back two weeks later, I promise."

"What you gonna name it?"

"I don't know. Maybe you can all help me think of something." Their sudden flood of questions stunned me.

"Is it your first, Mrs. Sachar?" two girls asked at the same time.

"No, my second."

"Gosh, you've been pregnant twice? You're too young."

"Actually, I've been pregnant three times," I told them, "but I had a miscarriage last spring."

"Oh, that's so sad," one said. "Did it hurt?"

"Yes, it did," I said. "It broke my heart. Anyway, I don't look that young," I laughed, trying for a lighter note. "I bet I'm older than some of your mothers."

A few of the girls started whispering. "We'll have to give her a shower." "Yeah, and invite all her classes and all the teachers in the school."

"What's this talk I hear in the middle row?" I teased.

"Oh, nothing," they replied. "Just nothing."

It was the Monday morning after Thanksgiving, and I had little enthusiasm for a return to school after the happy four-day parole. The longer I was away from Whitman, the less I wanted to return. We still had three more five-day weeks to go before the Christmas break. Yet, this fascination with my pregnancy might create a new connection with the kids to carry me through.

Although my condition was becoming more and more obvious, I had never expected the kids to take such keen interest. In just a few minutes, I had become their friend and confidante and mentor, just by having a baby in my belly.

"Can I touch it?" one girl asked while I took attendance.

"There's not much to touch, but sure, go ahead." She put her hand on my abdomen.

"Oh, that's so neat," she squealed. "What does it feel like, Mrs. Sachar?"

"Mostly, it just feels like I'm getting fat. But it is an amazing thing, to be making a life inside your own body." I paused to consider their intense interest, their demands to touch me and hold the baby when it was born. "Amazing, that is, as long as you're old enough, right?"

The bell rang, and most filed out of the room. Three of the girls, though, walked shyly to my desk. "Mrs. Sachar, I just want to give you a big hug," said Stacian, who draped her arms around my neck and kissed my cheek. "I can't wait to see your new baby. Will you let me hold her?"

"What do you mean, *her!*" I asked.

"Oh, I just know it will be a girl," Fabionda declared. "It better be."

"Me, too," said her friend, Trisa. "I love you, Mrs. Sachar."

I was hit with a sudden barrage of questions: Where did I live? How old was I? When did I think they'd be ready to bear children? How long was I married? What was my husband like? What did he do for a living? How old was my daughter? Who were my favorite students? My favorite classes? My favorite teachers? What did I think of abortion? What did I think of Whitman? How young was old enough to have a baby?

The unexpected attention intrigued as much as delighted me. Was it that by knowing something deeply intimate about my life, something they would share with me for the next five months, they had finally accepted me as human? Or in discovering that I, too, had struggled with disappointment and eagerly anticipated the joyful times in my life, that I was more like them than they had imagined? It was hard to know, but finally the kids were willing to open their hearts to me. For the first time, I really understood just how painful our previous failures in math class must have been to them: they wanted to be a family. After seeing teachers as little more than jailors and judges, here was a stunning surprise—an adult who actually wanted a child. And they were its eager godparents.

We soon had far-ranging heart-to-heart conversations, and agreed to make some big changes to ratify our new relationship. In three of my classes—8-7, 8-12, and 8-16—the students confided that the work, despite the curriculum alterations I had already made, was still so difficult that they often felt lost; we talked about how we might structure the class differently. They actually asked for weekly tests to gauge their progress and to lift some of the pressure from the arduous three-times-a-term exams. I assented. Instead of grading random homework assignments, they wanted me to collect and grade every last one. Although the chore would consume all my free time, I agreed. I confessed that their erratic behavior hurt me, and explained that when they refused to give my lessons a chance, it felt like a slap in the face. They solemnly promised to change, and we even wrote contracts, which many students returned to me promptly with a parent's signature. I countersigned each one and had them paste the guarantees in their notebooks.

"We just want you to think we can do it, Mrs. Sachar," one girl in 8-12 told me one day after class. "You think we's all so dumb, and we really ain't. Just 'cause we don't behave don't mean we's stupid."

"I don't think you're stupid at all," I replied. "I just get frustrated because I know you can do better, and I don't know how to get through to you."

"Just stand by me, Mrs. Sachar."

It hadn't really been an overnight change, and it wasn't a revolution. Every step forward could also become two steps back. One week, for instance, soon after a bull session in 8-7 and despite our agreement, only two students turned in homework. I told them how disappointed I was and they agreed to be more diligent. And by fits and starts, they were.

Like so much else at Whitman, our new arrangement worked only partially. We were not making really substantial improvement, but ever so slowly the classes began to come together, with more and more of a chance for me to teach. I tried to take the sometimes brutal antics of the kids and myself less seriously, to laugh with them and endorse their restlessly rebellious spirits with an occasional wink of conspiracy. The improvement—the sense of community—was yet too fragile to endure the test of pushing hard for radical leaps in learning. And my growing confidence was as vulnerable to setbacks as their math progress. Still, there was no question—life at Whitman was improving. I was no longer an obvious enemy, and the kids were far enough away from summer to have stopped resenting the sheer fact of daily incarceration.

For many of the girls, my pregnancy was an almost sacred focus of their interest and, I sometimes felt, the only reason they came to class. They brought me pictures of pregnant women and drawings of babies at various points of gestation. "This is what your baby looks like now," one girl in 8-7 explained every few weeks, leading me through a book on fetal development. One of the girls admitted she couldn't read a science book she'd brought me but, "it has a pregnant lady in it so I thought you would want it." Their excitement astonished me with its unguarded directness. They even took bets on the baby's sex and many pleaded with me to name it after them. "If it's a boy, you've got to call it Germaine," one boy in 8-12 boldly proposed, "for me."

"She can't name it Germaine, you fool," Fianie chided. "Can't you see she's white?"

"Who knows?" I ventured. "Maybe I'll name it Tyrone. And I've always loved the name Sheniqua." The class roared. "Be real, Mrs. Sachar," Fianie said. "The kid will kill you. You have to call it Mary or Bob. You know, white names."

As my relationship with my students began to improve, I took a few minutes of every class for their questions, referring the ones that were too biologically specific or too graphic—"What happens down there, Mrs. Sachar, when the baby comes out?"—to the sex-education teachers.

Some began clinging to me in the hallways for personal chats about babies and bottles and disposable diapers, and sometimes even about math. I talked to them individually in class, as well, finding first-time acceptance by a few of the most disruptive kids, and I approached cliques of misbehaving students now as four or five individuals, with each of whom I finally had some individual rapport.

An old approach—lifting a student's chin with a gentle touch to force him to look me in the eye—was suddenly particularly effective. Ten to 15 minutes of each class were still wasted getting the kids into their seats, but I no longer lost my voice. I still felt like a novice, but as my belly expanded, I was beginning to find my way in the classroom.

Our new rapport was clear to me one day when three 8-7 students raised hands to say they had done the homework together: they wanted to make sure that I didn't consider that cheating. "When you're honest, nothing is cheating," I decreed. As a class, we agreed that some homework assignments could henceforth be done in groups. Finished projects soon began to appear more regularly on my desk.

When the kids' faces were warm with excitement, they also granted respect, and there was no better place. Christmas cards poured in, and although my due date was months away, so did baby presents. Four girls chipped in to buy a porcelain music box; two others, a selection of rattles. Another girl promised to write a lullaby when the baby was born. "To Mrs. Sachar: The Teacher of the Year," wrote Diamond of 8-12 on her Christmas card. "May your baby be as special as you are."

"To the best teacher in IS 246, Mrs. Sachar. From Mississippi. you are the *best!*" She had drawn little hearts all over the card and affixed a picture of a baby.

Monica, a playful girl in 8-1, gave me a card that said: "Well Miss Sachar, you have a baby on the way. I hope you alway's love that baby. 1. If it's a boy I hope he's cute. 2. If it's a girl I hope she's pretty. 3. And if it's twins I hope their loveable and cuddley! Enjoy your Christmas and I hope your little baby inside their enjoy's it too. (Laugh)" The front of the envelope had a sticker that said FOR AWARD

SOLVING MOST THE PLICATED COM PROBLEM, with arrows indicating how to put the syllables in order, like one of my weekly extra-credit logic problems.

There was always the nagging fear that the warm questions and responses were merely ploys to distract me, postponing the math lessons I was supposed to teach. But the misery I had felt in September and October gave way to a tolerable anxiety by late December. I thought if I could take advantage of the students' new goodwill, perhaps I might encourage even better work from them. Test scores in my classes still alternated between heaven and hell. A few students had continued to be disrespectful toward me and provocative toward each other; some persisted in doing no work at all. But the genuine kindness and class effort of some of the most difficult students was impossible to ignore. As the Christmas vacation approached, I decided to give them a treat.

One Friday evening, a sign in a video store in my Brooklyn neighborhood caught my eye. "Now available on videocassette—the critically acclaimed movie *Stand and Deliver*." I had seen it: the story of a novice math teacher, Jaime Escalante, who took near-dropouts in a troubled Los Angeles high school and transformed them into masters of calculus by drilling them all summer and every weekend. He had given the kids faith in themselves, someone to trust, and what he called *gana:* desire. They rewarded his dedication with their own. The film could be more than just entertainment; it could be a true inspiration to my students. True, we were miles from tackling calculus. But if we worked hard enough, we might crack the ice of algebra. I thought there was a good chance I could convince the administration that this was serious classwork, related to mathematics, academic growth, and school pride, especially if I followed the showing of the film with a writing assignment. It had to be better than cartoons.

So that very evening I drafted a memo to the eighth-grade supervisors, Newman and Kowalski, and to Winfield, asking permission to show *Stand and Deliver* to all of my classes before Christmas vacation. I explained the film's academic pertinence and its material relevance. Only a fraction of our students were Hispanic, but otherwise the rough inner-city L.A. neighborhoods of the film's locale and our own dear Flatbush were truly similar: like Escalante's, many of our kids, too, had arrived at recalcitrance from boredom and anger. Turning the screening into an exercise in self-expression and writing, I proposed we hand out questions to guide the students in the writing of an essay, due after Christmas break. I would even supply the monitors to supervise the auditorium. On December 9th, Winfield gave his approval without comment to show the film several days before Christmas break.

That night I went home filled with delight at my accomplishment. If the movie worked, there were other films I could bring to the school—*To Sir with Love* and *Up the Down Staircase*. And a new film, *Lean on Me*, about a nearly all black New Jersey high school whose principal turned his failing school around. The film had been criticized in some quarters for overly glorifying the principal's personality and endorsing his reckless means, but the story of his and the students' accomplishments against great odds seemed inspiring enough.

The film was showing at local theaters; I hoped we could make a field trip out of it.

The typical use of films at Whitman was neither innovative nor particularly educational. Mostly, it was a pacifier. Every day, half of each grade was assigned to the auditorium during second period because there was nowhere else to put them, in a school operating at over 110 percent of capacity. Dividers already split some rooms into two, and, in a few, three teachers taught simultaneously. We were on double session as well, with two separate, staggered school days—one for sixth- and seventh-graders, the other for the eighth grade. Warehousing large blocks of kids in the auditorium during second and third periods—the population crunch times—and distracting them with movies about Michael Jackson was the school's solution. I couldn't wait until Monday, when I could tell the students they would see a real movie at school.

There was much to be done to get ready for the film—scheduling, notifying teachers, requesting audiovisual squads. At Miss Kowalski's insistence, I also checked the film for foul language; in a memo, I noted the five places where the word *fuck* was uttered. "I can promise you," I wrote at the bottom, "that there is no language in this film that the kids haven't heard before." Or read on Whitman's walls.

By the morning of December 22, the film was the talk of the school. Several teachers introduced themselves for the first time and asked if they could bring their classes to see the movie. After an announcement over the PA system that the movie was soon to begin, all gathered at the auditorium entrance. As the students crowded in, I saw that it was full to bursting. Several teachers wanted to separate the students by sex, seating the boys on one side, the girls on the other, in the usual assembly arrangement. But it was my call and I insisted they sit together. Even the veteran teachers deferred.

I distributed a set of questions as a guide to their essays. A few students immediately began folding the sheets into paper airplanes until I threatened to dismiss them. Others started reading through the list of twenty questions. There were these:

- *What type of students was Mr. Escalante teaching?*
  Early in the movie, one student says: "We are not a minority." What does the student mean?
  Mr. Escalante tells his students: "Math is the great equalizer. People will assume you know less than you know because of your name and your complexion." What does he mean?
  Mr. Escalante tells a student, "All you see is the turn. You don't see the road ahead." What does he mean?
  After the students have been accused of cheating, Mr. Escalante talks to his wife. She says, "Regardless of whether they passed the test or not, they learned." Mr. Escalante says: "Maybe so, but they lost confidence in the system they're finally ready to be a part of." What does he mean?
  Mr. Escalante tells the administrators from the testing service, "In this country, people are innocent until proven guilty." What does he mean?
  Mr. Escalante also tells the administrators: "If this were Beverly Hills High School, they wouldn't have sent you to investigate." What does he mean?

The assignment was due January 3, the day we returned after Christmas break. Students were to choose a favorite character from the movie and write an essay of 250 words about their selection.

The showing went beautifully. The audiovisual squad sprang into action; Newman and Kowalski both made appearances to bless the event; the lights dimmed; I felt ecstatic. The only thing missing was popcorn. Though the crisp colors were muted on the big screen and the focus wasn't perfect, most of the kids watched in silence. Those few who didn't, I banished to the front office. Never had I seen the auditorium so quiet.

When the film was over, several students were wiping away tears. Others talked excitedly about what they had seen. As I walked to the front to dismiss them, they offered a round of applause. One group of kids from 8-7 was cheering loudly.

1

2

ABOVE: **Waiting for math class to begin.**

LEFT: **A student displaying a desktop broken that day.**

3

4

5

TOP: *Walt Whitman Intermediate School in Flatbush, Brooklyn.*

ABOVE: *Claude Winfield, Whitman's principal.*

LEFT: *Vikki Kowalski, assistant principal and chairman of the math department.*

ABOVE: In foreground, a desktop from one of many broken desks. Others lie on the floor to the left.

LEFT: Whitman classroom with broken blackboard; requests for repairs had gone unanswered for years.

BELOW: Homeroom at the end of a school day.

RIGHT: A common stairwell scene, trash swept into piles and not removed.

BELOW: Homeroom four days before the start of the 1988–89 school year with teacher's desk missing two legs.

BOTTOM RIGHT: Boys' bathroom.

8

9

10

11

12

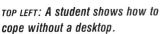

TOP LEFT: A student shows how to cope without a desktop.

TOP RIGHT: Two students before math class; rear, a bag of trash awaits collection.

RIGHT: Students in class in winter jackets; Whitman has no student lockers.

BOTTOM: Whitman's schoolyard just three weeks after repainting in the spring of 1989.

13

14

<u>8.07.01 SCIENTIFIC NOTATION</u>
(2-3 lessons)

PERFORMANCE OBJECTIVES

The student will be able to...

8.07.01.01B   write a standard base ten numeral in
scientific notation;
e.g.,
$$450,000 = 4.5 \times 10^5$$
$$.003 = 3 \times 10^{-3}$$

8.07.01.02B   write a number expressed in scientific
notation as a standard base ten numeral;
e.g.,
$$3.5 \times 10^3 = 3,500$$
$$6.1 \times 10^{-2} = .061$$

8.07.01.03B   multiply two numbers expressed in
scientific notation;
e.g.,
$$(4 \times 10^5) \times (6 \times 10^3) =$$
$$(4 \times 6) \times (10^5 \times 10^3) =$$
$$24 \times 10^{(5+3)} =$$
$$24 \times 10$$
$$2.4 \times 1$$

8.07.01.04B   divide two numb
scientific nota
e.g.,
$$\frac{1.6 \times 10^{12}}{4 \times 10^3} =$$
$$.4 \times 10^9$$

15

A page from the Board of Education's **Scope and Sequence,** *outlining eighth-grade topics.*

SELECTION OF STUDENTS
TO EDUCATIONAL OPTION PROGRAMS

Each cluster has established the selection criteria for cluster programs offered on a boroughwide or citywide basis. Selection criteria are stated on the Directory blue pages. Additional information on school selection of students is contained in the Application Booklet.

Top 2%

Students who score within the top two percent on the reading test are automatically accepted to an educational option program if it is listed as their first choice on the application.

Student Tested Spring 1988 Grade	Student Applies Fall 1988 Grade	for September 1989 Admission Grade	Raw Score Required on DRP —If Student Lists Program as Choice #1 on the High School Application— for Automatic Acceptance.
7	8	9	74, 75, 76, 77
8	9	10	76 or 77 only

Based on citywide standardized reading test score attained in the term preceding application
• 16% of students reading above average
• 68% of students reading within the average range
• 16% of students reading below average are selected.

Half are selected by computer at random
Half are selected by the school

Special Education mainstreamable students in self-contained classes who apply to general education options will be selected for the self-contained parallel option only, on the basis of a review of the student's record according to program criteria. Where there is no identical self-contained parallel option, the applicant will be considered for the school's most similar special education option.

If admitted to the special education option, the student's eligibility to participate in the general education option will be determined between June and the first week in September of the year entering high school by the special education option program teacher, the assistant principal/supervisor of special education, the school based educational evaluator and the assistant principal who supervises the general education option program in consultation with the parent and student at the Phase II IEP conference.

Special Education students in self-contained classes who apply to parallel self-contained educational option programs will be selected by the school based on a review of the student's record according to program criteria.

Resource room students who apply to general education options will be ranked as general education students.

A page from the 1988–89 High School Directory, *for use by eighth- and ninth-grade students in choosing the high schools they want to attend.*

16

17

Remedial reading instructor
Sharon Cohen and her students
crammed into a closet-sized
room with two other remedial
instructors and their students.

18

ABOVE: "Grandma" Gloria Holloway huddling with students
as education associate Louise Gibbons looks on.

BELOW: Social studies teacher Barry Kantrowitz,
one of Whitman's most popular instructors.

19

"I hope you enjoyed the film," I said—yet more applause. "Have a great Christmas break—and don't forget your essays."

Students who had never turned in a homework assignment all year promised they would this time. "I got something to say to you about that film," promised Kevin of 8-7. "You'll see, Mrs. Sachar."

Reginald, my nonreading math whiz from 8-16, also came up to me. "That film make me sad," he said. "I's gonna tell you about it, Mrs. Sachar."

It was a great ending to a rough term.

On January 3, the stacks of essays were piled high on my desk. Looking over the papers, it was clear the movie had deeply touched many of the kids. For all their problems with spelling, organization, and grammar, they wrote about it with real ardor. Several wished for a teacher like Jaime Escalante, so totally devoted to his students. Others said they had been inspired to work harder in school. Happily, I saw that several had written more than I'd required, even answering questions I hadn't posed.

I started with 8-16. Saheedra, the charming and attentive star pupil recently arrived from Guyana, turned in this essay:

> *My favoriet charitar in the movie Stand and diliver was the teacher. The reason why is Because, he shown the kids that he care about there Education. He cared so moch he had them working for two years even over the sommer, instead of having fon. By thinking about a teacher doing that just to teach kids. Math I think that teacher shold get a reward. and I wish I had a teach like that reading so I could be very smart in reading. Out of all the movies I ever seen, I like that movies more than the rest of them. If Walt Whitman J.H.S. was to have alot of techer like that then everone will gradueat very smart. But I don't think so, Because most of the teacher don't care.*

Marlene, a tall, awkward girl with only a minimal understanding of math, tried harder than almost any other student I had, always turning in homework even if she gave up after a few problems. In November, she had confided by a note dropped in my satchel that she didn't know basic arithmetic. "This is form Marlene," the note said. "One day, you teach me long divisorin, okay?" She now wrote:

> *Mr. Escalante was a math teacher who teaching students that wanted to learn but they didn't show it. I hated the women who*

runs the math department. She did [not] want Mr. Escalante to teach calculus because she didn't think the students can do it. Mr. Escalante tells his students, Math is the great equalizer. People will assume you know less than you know because of your name and your complexion, and he's right. The point of the movie is you can be somebody. I feel terrific after the film plus I started bluiding up my confidence.

Delano was a tiny bright boy with an inquisitive mind who was often distracted in class. He wrote:

My Christmas homeworke is about Stand and Deliver. My story is about this man he had a hard time with is class is name his Mr. Escalante He is a nice man and a funny man too. He teach the class how to do fraction percentage he teach them thing over and over. He even use to teach on Saturday But he was a man who have courage two children and a wife.

　　　About 5 chidren in the class had problem in math. Mr. Escalante teach the a new subject was Mr. Escalante goover with them every morning when they come to class He give them a test and see How they do on the test if they do good or not so they study hard for they test When was the big day like after a week the get they redulce and Board of Education did thin they chead But Mr. Escalante when done to the two guy who think the class chead after a Wile he call said they take over the test and every past the test.

I read Reginald's paper last, wanting to savor the special words he had for me. "That teacher in the movies really cared," he wrote.

Because he gave up a good Job Just teach kids that was given him a hard time at frist But, they come through. He gave up his spare time Just to help them, he gave up his summer with out geting payed Just to help them. I can't Belive any one or any teacher will ever do that. But he did. I wist I had a teacher like that, I'm not saying to not get payed Just to teache me. But to help me know my work and know what I am doing. Thats all I have to say But Just By watching that movie makes me want to lean more to pas all my test and to get a good job when I grow up.

In 8-7, only a handful of students turned in papers. I searched especially for Kevin's.

> *In this movie every play a tefferic role. I pick the teacher because of efford to try and help the kids even thought everything was agaist him in doing it and he was detemind ang will to teach them kids and change one renage kid with a mind of his into a brain. I pick the Mexican kid because he was really going through a lot of pressure in the streets and home and through it all he went to school and tryed his best and suceed.*

Carlia, one of my favorite 8-7 students, usually had a sparkle in her eyes and a warm smile. She delivered every assignment and was ranked at the top of the class. She wrote:

> *In the movie Stand and Deliver there was no character that less or more good. The characters in the movie were terrific and it shows when you belive in your self you can make it.*

Finally, in 8-7, there was Trisha's paper. Trisha was responsible and methodical but spoke in an annoying whisper and clung to me in the hallways, offering to carry my books even if she was going the other way. She wrote:

> *The person that I realy liked was Mr. Escalante because. he trys to teach the kids in his class. Who were speaking another language. Who to do math called calculus. To be smarter than other kids and to get better oprtunites for Jobs. When Mr. Escalante got hurt he tried very hard to get better and stronger. So he could be able to prepare his class for the calculus exam.*

The writings from 8-1 especially interested me. I had already promised the kids that if we completed the eighth-grade curriculum, they could begin algebra in the spring. Of all my students, they had the best chance of eventually learning calculus and algebra was the first step. Nonetheless, more than half of them turned in little more than plot summaries. Only a few essays contained reflections of the passionate connection I had hoped for. From Gary, one of the brightest boys in the class and certainly the quietest and best behaved, came this:

> *The movie was an excellent movie. Mr. Escalante was my favorite character because he was a very persuasive person, and*

he always think positively. He was my favorite character be-
cause he never loose hope on the kids, he always knew that they
can do anything they want to, if they really put their mind to
it. although he was teaching a bunch of bad kids, but he still
believe that they could learn whatever they want to learn. When
he first came in the class the kids seems like they didn't have a
future, but later he made the kid see the road that's ahed. The
kids grew to love him very much. I like his character because
he believe in the kids and he believe that they could do whatever
they want to do in life.

And, from a girl I had nicknamed Tinkerbell for her delicate
voice, sprightly demeanor, and magical smile, came this:

My favorite actor was Mr. Escalente because I thought he acted
his part good and also because of how he got the kids interested
in math. Most people on the staff at school didn't think that he
could do it. They thought that the kids were at a minor level.
    During the movie Mr. Escalente made a statement that
"Math is the great equalizer. People will assume you know less
than you know because of your name or complexion." This
meant that people would judge you because your either too
white or too black. But in the movie Mr. Escalente meant be-
cause your Spanish or Black people would think that you don't
know much.
    I think that the point of the movie was that you should try
something before you decide to give up or think that you can't
do it.

Patrick, bright but lazy, wrote his essay when he arrived in class
on the afternoon that the assignment was due. He said:

My favorite person in the the move "Stand and deliver" was
Mr. escalante because he almost died, trying to teach these kids
calculus and trying to give the hispanic kids a better life in the
future.

Another of my favorites, Judith, had this to say:

I thought the movie was very interesting. Mr. Escalente was a
very good teacher who take the challenge to make the student

*think about why and how math is important. The school was
in bad condition and in a bad neighborhood. The student had
experience bad condition at their home. One of the girl mother
an boyfriend that don't treat her right. A second example will
be a father talking his daughter out of school just to help the
family restaurant business.*

*Mr. Escalente set up an excellent example to the student
waht they can achieve just by working hard. By the example
Mr. Escalente show the kids, I think they might have a chance
raching their goals. I thught the movie was very good. I enjoy
it alike. I hope we can see a movie like that again. My favorite
character was the puerto-rican boy that always put his hair in
a pony-tail. I thought he was cute. 160 words composition.*

And Mara, the soft-spoken victim of Tiara's taunts, wrote an
especially heartfelt essay:

*My favorite character in the movie is: Mr. Escalante the
teacher. Why? Because he is an understanding person. When
he first came to the high school, he wasn't very happy with the
kind of students that he saw but, he tried to deal with them the
way they were. The students were very bad, they were like vag-
abond, they came to the class not to learn calculus but to talk
about sex. All they wanted was to talk about boys and girls.
They didn't know anything in math, even $-2 + 2$. They weren't
able to do fractions even the easier ones. But all the teacher did,
was: talk to them and try to make them understand what is the
meaning of math. At the middle of the movie the students
wanted to learn calculus. I don't really know what was the
reason but I think it's because of the way Mr. Escalante taught
them, cause he made the course interesting by making them
laughing and talk to them. Mr. Escalante is a very good person.
He is generous, and patient and he has the kind of humor too.
He is my favorite character because I like people who understand and care for others. Even the students were bad at the
bigining, but he was patient and he wasn't discourage with
them because he knew what he was doing. So this is why I
choose him so.*

*A good teacher can transform bad students into good ones
(he, she) can also prepare good students to become good tech-
nician, doctor, lawyer, engineering etc. . . so that they can contribute to the advancement of the country and ameliorate*

human life. I would like the ingenuity of Mr. Escalante, the teacher, to reflect on all teachers so that we can hope for a better future.

One of the most sophisticated students was Diamond, a well-dressed, outspoken young woman. She wrote:

My favorite character is Mr. Escalante. He was given a class of students, who people said are most likely to fail in life and he gave them the opportunity to succeed. Now they were finally given a choice, before everything they needed to know they were told. And they were always told the same thing . . . you will never rise to your fullest potential.

Mr. Escalante heard this, and he looked past the three strikes against them. One—they were poor. Two—they were Hispanic. And three—the families that did not encourage them. And Mr. Escalante said that these kids are young, bright, and are eagered to learn (if you listen to them closely). All you have to give them is the motivation and the opportunity to learn. That is what Mr. Escalante said to them "You are the true dreamers and dreamers accomplish wonderful things." The students are dreaming about success. About accomplishing their fondest dreams. About as they say, being all they can be.

I also like Mr. Escalante because he put his health and his personal life aside to work with the kids. I shouldn't say kids because he was also helping Hispanic adults to learn English for free. He stop at nothing to insure that they can accomplish bigger and better things. He shouldn't have risked his life. But you can't stop the people whom are staints from doing their heavenly duties. He saw in these stuents what no one saw before . . . a future.

Finally, there was one unsigned paper:

The character in the movie is the teacher. I do not know how to spell the teacher's name, but I like what he tryed to do with the students. The love he showed for the students. He tryed to teach one of the students that wanted to quit because he did not know how to do the math. They were going down a street and the car was going fast, and there was a two roads one was a dead end and the other was a road that just kept on going. But that had to make up his mind fast which road to take and chose the dead end street. I think it meant without an education, you are going nowhere except a dead end.

14

Special Kids, Special Help

If we tested every kid at Whitman for special education, I suspect we'd find that more than half would qualify. I can't tell you how many kids we see who can't read or are emotionally unstable. It's really scary.

—Joann Thompson, PhD, educational psychologist, School-Based Support Team, Committee on Special Education, Walt Whitman Intermediate School.

One December afternoon, over lunch in the teachers' cafeteria, I decided to mention Shereeza, my poorest student, to one of the remedial reading teachers. Sharon Cohen, whose small-group reading program was funded by the federal government, was specially trained to work with kids like Shereeza, and she did so with unending patience. Sharon was in her thirties and had a pleasant, lightly freckled face framed by long auburn hair. She wore her keys on a lanyard around her neck and for months I had assumed that she was a gym teacher. Easy to talk to, gentle and nonjudgmental, she controlled her classes with a deft combination of suasion and iron-clad rules. She did not try, as so many Whitman teachers did, to ingratiate herself with the administrators. True to herself, and honest with me, she had earned my respect and affection for being frank and open.

As we sat down to our fried chicken, I started to fill Sharon in on Shereeza without naming her. "I'm pretty sure," I said, after filling her in on the basics, "that this girl can't read or write at all. She doesn't know that 300 is larger than 30, and it takes her ten minutes to write her own name."

"What class?" Sharon asked.

"8-16," I said. "I have a terrible time teaching that class to begin with—the kids are so loud and disruptive—but I'm sure part of the problem is that some of them should not be in a regular class. Maybe they should be in special ed."

"So what else is new?" she answered, with a touch of resignation. "Half the kids in the school belong in special ed." Her tone was sincere, not sarcastic, and resigned.

"Well, this girl in 8-16 is not a behavior problem, but I just think she misses everything I say."

"Who is it?"

"You probably know her if you teach 8-16. It's Shereeza. Am I crazy to think she's got big problems and needs special help?"

Sharon rolled her eyes. "I'll tell you something about Shereeza," she said. "The other day, I came into the room and I put a word on the board, 'rice.' That's all I wrote. I told the kids to make a tree, with branches coming out from the word. 'Just think of as many words as you can that have something to do with rice,' I told them. Shereeza could not think of a single one."

"Well, what do you have to do to refer someone for special ed?" I asked.

"I think there are a lot of forms to complete," Sharon replied. "I don't know, I've never done it. I work with the kids in such small groups that it's really like special ed already in a way. I have no reason to refer them out of my classes."

I had seen the small-group setting—a room no larger than a walk-in closet, desks so close together that students had to suck in their bellies to squeeze into the seats. During a typical class, three instructors shared the room with three different Aims, Do Now exercises and problem sets crowding the blackboard. The confusion must have been maddening, yet Sharon never complained.

"Do you think I'd be crazy to try to refer Shereeza?" I asked again.

"Well, they always say there's no point in doing it in the eighth grade because the kids will be out of here in June anyway."

"Couldn't it help with a placement for next year? Ninth grade would be better for them at least."

Sharon shrugged. "I don't know how it works."

Shereeza wasn't the only student I had in mind for referral.

Thomas, I had a feeling, was emotionally disturbed. He was constantly out of his seat, shouting meaningless expressions to no one in particular. Carl couldn't sit still long enough to pick up a pencil, much less learn to write or do math; Terrence was so withdrawn I often wondered if he even knew he was sitting in school.

None of the other teachers at the lunchroom table knew much about the special-education referral process. Not a single one had ever completed a referral. They said it was too involved, too time-consuming. That these teachers I regarded so highly had never referred any of their students astonished me. In 8-16 alone, I wanted to send at least four kids for testing, and, in 8-12, there was another handful. I was already working on special help for Jimmy or, at least, getting him transferred out of my 8-7 class. Maybe turning in four referrals at once would label me further as a weak teacher who couldn't control her classes. I decided to wait.

Then, in February, I had an encounter with Shereeza so discouraging I could no longer justify her placement in my class. I had planned to teach the students how to read a thermometer. So many of them spoke of becoming doctors and nurses. However unrealistic those goals, I wanted to encourage them and also introduce them to some of the other opportunities in the medical world—nurses' aides or technicians, for instance. I had to pay for fourteen thermometers and alcohol pads to clean them out of my own pocket but I hoped the lesson would be worth it.

Drawing a large thermometer on the board, I first explained the whole-number marks—96 degrees, 97 degrees, 98 degrees, before moving on to the two-tenth-degree gradient. "Normal body temperature is 98.6," I continued. "What two numbers is 98.6 between?" Shereeza raised her hand.

"Nine and ten," she offered.

"Let's look at the thermometer and find 98.6," I suggested and passed out a drawing with the thermometer's whole degree and two-tenths markings clearly illustrated. I walked over to Shereeza and showed her exactly where 98.6 was on the thermometer. "Now, you can do this, Shereeza. What two numbers is this mark between?" Other students mumbled the right answers.

"Nine and ten," Shereeza repeated. I tried several different ways to get her to see her mistake. But she just looked up at me, uncomprehendingly.

"Can someone else help us?" Saheedra had the answer, and we moved ahead, counting in two-tenth-degree increments.

"Now, let's say when you took the thermometer out of a patient's mouth, the mercury was pointed to this line on the thermometer." I drew a temperature of 99.6 on the board. "How much fever would he have?" Shereeza and some of the other students who seemed consistently lost stared back at me blankly. "Okay, I'll show you how we do this. We start at ninety-nine and count by twos like this: ninety-nine point zero, ninety-nine point two, ninety-nine point four, ninety-nine point six—and there we are."

"Now you try one." I prayed that Shereeza and the others would finally catch on. After all, many of them wanted to be nurses. "Let's try again, Shereeza. How much fever would a person have if they had this temperature?" I marked 100.8 on the board.

"Let's count it out," I said, trying to sound encouraging. "I'll help you start. One hundred point zero, one hundred point two. One hundred point . . ." I paused. "Go on, sweetheart."

"Ninety-three," she said, "ninety-four, ninety-five, ninety-six, ninety-seven." Her finger pointed to the 100.8 mark. She looked up at me hopefully. Determined not to show her my disappointment, I shut my eyes in frustration and bit my lip.

I called again for correct answers. The other students were focused and alert, more responsive than I had seen before. Holding the thermometers gingerly, pens and pencils out, they were keen to tackle the exercise. They also were silent, a sure sign of interest. Ever so slowly, some of them had caught on. But Shereeza was totally lost.

What can I do to make her understand? I wondered, holding my thermometer aloft as if the tangible object might magically solve the problem. I wanted to cheer her and the others on—"Come on, come on. You know the answer. You do!" But she didn't, and her response to the thermometer exercise was only the latest confirmation of the severity of her learning problems.

When the bell rang, I went directly to the guidance office to find Barbara Brown, the only counselor in the school assigned exclusively to the eighth grade.

"Where do I get a special-ed referral form?" I asked. "I have a student who's got to get help."

"What grade do you teach?" she asked.

"Eighth-grade. Math."

"Why would you want to refer a kid now?" she replied. "The eighth-graders will be out of here in June."

"Look, this kid should have been in special ed years ago. She really needs help, and I want to make sure she gets it." I knew I sounded defensive, but what difference did it make what grade Shereeza was in? Were we supposed to ship her off to high school, hoping they would instantly recognize and solve a problem they knew nothing about?

Tall and heavy-set, Barbara looked like a loving grandmother, but despite her good reputation at the school, I had yet to see any evidence of diligence, compassion, or affection for the kids. "We probably won't even get around to testing her," she said.

"Well, I hope you will," I said. "But even if you don't, I want to do the referral. Where can I get the forms?" I had a sinking feeling that the whole exercise was fruitless. Barbara said she had run out of the forms, and, because the copying machines were broken, had not been able to make more. However, she agreed reluctantly to lend me her original set, which I promised to return the next day with copies for other teachers.

I spent the evening filling out the forms for my three neediest students—Shereeza, Kenneth (whom I had nicknamed the Olé boy because he often shouted the word spontaneously in class), and Carl, all from 8-16. Terrence, I had learned, was already getting treatment in a special psychiatric program at one of the city hospitals. Others, like Jordene, needed evaluation, too, but I didn't want to flood the system, losing what little goodwill I had accrued with the administration. Frankly I was afraid that more than a handful of referrals would brand me a hostile, incompetent teacher unable to deal with students' needs.

No instructions or explanations of the referral process came from Guidance or anyone else at Whitman, and I had no idea what to do after turning in the forms. Nor was there any such information on the form themselves. Who did the evaluations? How long did it take? Could a referral hurt my students in any way? Only because I befriended one of the women on the evaluation team did I eventually learn that three specialists would become involved: a social worker would meet the family; an educational evaluator would test the student's mastery of various subjects; and a psychologist would assign an IQ and do a social and emotional study. Then the District 17 office would review the entire workup.

The referral packet turned out to be five pages long and very straightforward. Although I had to look up test-score data and grades from the cumulative records, each child's forms took less than an hour to complete. Some teachers were sure that the forms were twenty pages long and would take days for each child. First, biographical data was requested, then I had to specify my reason for the referral and any previous efforts I had made in school to help the

child. Many questions I could not answer: Is the student taking medication? Is student or family known to outside agencies? How does
the student interact with peers in the lunchroom? I described each
child's behavior, attendance history, and work skills as best I could.
Leaving about a third of the questions blank, I handed them to Barbara the next day.

In February and early March, the guidance office contacted each
of the children's parents. All agreed readily to have their children
tested. One of the evaluation team members said that all the parents
were grateful for the opportunity to talk, not only about their children, but about themselves. It was, a few said, the first meaningful
contact they'd had with Whitman.

Because the guidance office did not routinely inform teachers of
preliminary results after a referral, I myself inquired, in the process
finding an ally in Joann Thompson, the psychologist who did the
largest part of each workup. A friendly blond woman, pregnant with
her first child, she was extremely candid about the shortcomings of
the special-education system and the public school system in New
York City in general. The referral forms, she acknowledged, discouraged many teachers, though her team was willing to act on even
sketchy information. Moreover, she said, parents didn't know that if
they felt their children needed special ed, they could initiate the
process themselves with a simple written request. "We'll take anything. Just a few words from a parent, 'Please test Willy,' is enough.
We'll even help the parent write the note."

After all the bureaucratic roadblocks to getting students into
special ed, I was almost afraid to ask Joann if the programs were
well-run and effective, and if being isolated from the regular-education population would hurt the students. Some experts argued that
even kids with severe learning problems should be "mainstreamed"
—placed in regular classrooms as often as possible. "If regular ed in
New York City wasn't so deficient," she acknowledged, "we probably
wouldn't need special ed to nearly the same extent. We *could* mainstream the kids. But most of the kids we test really benefit from
smaller classes during the whole school day. They need that individual attention, whether their problems are emotional or intellectual.
Virtually the only way to get that kind of small-group help in New
York is through special ed." The sheer variety of special-ed programs
itself usually enabled students who were diagnosed properly to get
the appropriate help. The best programs—the handful that taught
the kids an employable skill—were superb, she said.

"It's got to be better than the alternatives—being pushed through the system year after year in classes with thirty kids to a room," she concluded.

Finally having found someone in whom to confide, I assured Joann that I didn't think every disruptive kid belonged in special ed, but that there surely was a high percentage in my lower classes who did. Was it fair for them to ruin everyone else's education, or right for them to sit frustrated, year after year, in classes with teachers, like me, who did not understand their problems or know how to reach them? With surprising vehemence she said, "I don't know how you do it, you teachers, when I meet some of these kids."

"You mean, most of the kids who are sent for referrals qualify?"

"Are you kidding? Absolutely. Most of them should have been referred years ago. Then they wouldn't come to us in such bad shape."

In New York City, I knew, fully one eighth of the students were enrolled in special-education programs, everything from twice-weekly remedial help in reading or math to full-time placement in a school for physically or emotionally handicapped pupils. But at Whitman, most of the teachers I spoke with knew virtually nothing about the three-woman special-ed referral team or the process itself. This ignorance was particularly unfortunate since Whitman's team proved to be one of the school's greatest strengths. Each of the three women was committed and knowledgeable, putting in long hours on frequent phone calls and site visits to new special-ed programs, and communicating sympathetically with confused parents. The team's social worker, Rosanna Gowell, made four attempts to contact Shereeza's family to explain why she should be tested. Carrie Brooks, the education evaluator, took more than an hour explaining to one parent how she determined the academic level of each of the students.

When the evaluations of my three students were completed, I asked to see them, and was initially turned down; teachers have no right to review special-ed referrals or track their progress. The rule was preposterous, and, after I insisted, the team members relented. With relief I learned that all three of my students had been found eligible for special ed; none, in fact, had an IQ over 70. The background information compiled from the students and their parents explained much that I saw in class. And after ten minutes reading the information on the kids' abilities, skills, and interests, I learned more than in the five months we had lived together in Room 327. I wished I had made these referrals months before, when I had first suspected the extent of the problems. Now I wanted to refer a dozen other students for testing, if only to get the sort of detailed information a referral elicited.

But the relief I felt was joined by anger and resentment. I had been assigned 8-12 and 8-16, two of the most difficult eighth-grade classes in the school. Yet I had never been candidly told what to expect from these classes, nor had anyone ever mentioned the words special education to me. No one had encouraged me to refer students, and some, like the eighth-grade guidance counselor, had actually discouraged it. Information on each student that should have been readily available before I ever walked into a classroom—former teachers' appraisals, for example—was nowhere to be found. Medical information was incomplete; test data were sometimes missing. Family details were nonexistent. If only, in the early days, I had known more about Kenneth, Shereeza, and Carl, months of futility would have been spared us all.

Attached to each evaluation, besides an IQ score and academic and psychological profiles of each student, was a worksheet of social history—by turns illuminating, harrowing, infuriating, heartbreaking. Kenneth was fifteen. His mother had been advised by her doctor to have him tested years before. She felt that he was slow to learn and needed special help, but he liked school and wanted to do well, she said. His history of school problems dated back to Jamaica, from which he had emigrated when he was thirteen. He had been enrolled the previous year in the Gates program, an extensive reading-enrichment program for fourth- and seventh-graders who had failed the citywide reading test and had to repeat the grade. Kenneth lived with his mother, stepfather, and a brother and stepsister. His mother, who was thirty-two, had worked as a home attendant until the birth of her seven-month-old baby. His stepfather, forty-eight, worked as a presser at a dry-cleaning store.

Kenneth had been promoted to the eighth grade only because of his age; he had shown no improvement in reading or math during his seventh-grade year in the Gates program. According to his mother, his gross motor skills, too, had developed late. Now, she wanted him enrolled in a job-training program where, at least—at last—"he might have a chance to make something of himself."

Tests also revealed that Kenneth had seriously delayed writing, speech, and language skills but normal fine and gross motor skills. On the Peabody picture-vocabulary test, in which children are required to identify a series of pictures, Kenneth's score was that of a 5-year-8-month-old child. His ability to sound out words was that of a first-grader. Under "reading comprehension," the evaluator simply wrote, "nonreader." On the Detroit Verbal Opposites test—an important indicator of linguistic reasoning skills—Kenneth scored as a nine-year-old.

"Kenneth has hardly any phonetic or decoding skills and his sight-word vocabulary is extremely low," the evaluator wrote. "He was unable to read any passages. Therefore a reading comprehension score could not be obtained. He did not seem to understand how to solve problems for subtraction, multiplication, or division, even in simplest forms. The written sample was grossly delayed. The content could not be read or understood because of poor spelling and structure."

When he had been interviewed by Joann, the psychologist, for the social-emotional evaluation, Kenneth told her that he wanted to become an engineer.

The evaluator's summary offered this hope: "Kenneth was cooperative, respectful, and tried to perform the tasks requested of him, but was too delayed academically to obtain adequate scores in any area. The examiner feels Kenneth should benefit from a special class placement offering intensive remediation to address his academic needs."

Three other eighth-grade teachers, asked to comment on the referral, had noted similar long-standing problems. Why then hadn't they made the referral? The language arts teacher had not even bothered to return the auxiliary referral form.

I turned next to Carl's review. He had become enraged one day in class when he discovered he was being evaluated, rhythmically stomping his feet and shouting slurs at me. Academically, his report was the most encouraging: his IQ was 68. His parents had told the evaluators they were desperate with worry about him. At home, they said, he was often belligerent and angry, but they had come to accept such behavior as "just Carl's way." Carl had six siblings living with him, ranging in age from seven to twenty-two; his father, forty-four, was a security guard; his mother, forty-two, worked as a factory assembler. Carl had never passed a citywide reading test, even after repeating seventh grade in the Gates program. Although his father had moved to New York six years earlier from Guyana, Carl had arrived with his mother and siblings three years later, a pattern common among West Indian immigrants.

"Carl often does not understand the main details of a passage," the academic evaluator wrote, "and attempts to reread and reread. Carl does not understand computing with decimals, money, or fractions. He also has difficulty with long multiplication problems and with long division. He wants to be an engineer. He is a good-looking boy who was resistant to being tested. Finally, he cooperated and attempted all tasks requested of him. Examiner feels Carl should benefit from a class offering academic remediation for his age category." Carl had turned fifteen in early January.

Developmentally, Carl was fairly normal, with some delays but no gross problems. But I could not stop thinking about the IQs of these children. Whatever the debate about IQ's true scope and relevance, all of the scores indicated definite learning problems. Why hadn't I been told? Didn't anyone at the school know? Children with IQs as low as these, whose problems had been neglected for so long, deserved more help than I could possibly give in a class with thirty students. At the very least, such information would have suggested that I explore new ways to reach the kids and build from fundamentals. And they would have justified an abandonment of the eighth-grade curriculum from the very first days of the year.

Shereeza's referral took the longest to complete because none of the home phone numbers listed on her various school records were in service. Three letters to her home went unanswered. Finally, a social worker made a home visit, seeking her mother's permission for an evaluation. In late March, the team met with Shereeza's mother at the school, and then with Shereeza herself.

Shereeza, her mother said, lived with her and five siblings; her father had died six years before of liver disease. The family had emigrated from Guyana in December 1987. Shereeza had severe medical problems, the mother told the referral team, but her financial situation made expensive treatment impossible. Shereeza had not seen a doctor or dentist in ten years. Her mother didn't know why she walked with a limp and had a lazy eye. Two other children in the family also had unattended medical problems. Shereeza's mother, who was forty-seven, was not even sure whether or not her daughter had repeated the seventh grade in the Gates program, nor did she know if her daughter was now in the eighth or ninth grade. But asked whether Shereeza was doing well in school, her mother said, "The report cards are usually okay."

Of all Whitman's failings, this was one of the hardest things to fathom—students who could not read or do basic math but who, year after year, passed all their subjects. In the previous year, Shereeza had been given 80 in language arts, 70 in mathematics, 65 in science, 65 in social studies, 85 in family living, and 65 in health education—marks that seemed to relate more to her gentle, good-natured personality than to her academic performance. So far, in the eighth grade, I was the only teacher to have given her failing marks.

"Shereeza acknowledges that she has difficulty reading," the evaluator wrote, "but has felt ashamed to discuss it with her mother." In Guyana, her mother said, Shereeza's academic performance had been fair though her reading difficulties were evident even then. But she had never mentioned the problem to her daughter's teachers here.

Language problems were also obvious. As part of a common-sense test, the evaluator asked, "What would you do if a girl much smaller than you tries to fight with you?" Shereeza answered, "Walk away from she." When asked to draw a person, Shereeza drew a five-year-old child. Describing what she had drawn, Shereeza said the girl was alone, had no friends, and didn't like kids or school. Her IQ was calculated at 63.

Joann went out of her way to find a new school for Shereeza. I was ecstatic when she gave me the news. Shereeza would be placed in a job-skills program and could continue there until she was twenty-one, at Board of Education expense. At this special school, a small facility for no more than 300 students, learning a trade would take precedence over academics. The school, which trained kids to be short-order cooks, waitresses, stenographers, and janitors, had a great reputation. Shereeza would have to commute, but that was the only drawback. The alternative was daunting—Erasmus Hall High School, with more than 3,000 students and four more years of large classes. Joann was as elated by the placement as I. "This," she told me, "is how the process is supposed to work."

The next day, when I saw Shereeza, she smiled as I touched her cheek lightly and explained what her ninth-grade year would be like. "You're going to have a new beginning, Shereeza," I promised. "It really is going to be okay. Remember, I told you we'd figure something out. And we did." After so many frustrating months, one of my students was finally on the way to a better life. I had done something right.

15

The Uncivil War

When you're white in a school with this many black teachers, you walk on thin ice. You never know if what you're going to say will be misconstrued.

—A white teacher, Walt Whitman Intermediate School.

Whites don't understand. They'll make you think they do, but they don't. Stick with us if you want an education.

—A black teacher to her students, Walt Whitman Intermediate School.

"I don't know what those Italians in Howard Beach are so upset about," the teacher was saying. "Don't they know they're black? Don't they know they're descended from black people?"

The classroom's wall was thin and several colleagues in the office on the other side heard everything that went on. That day, one of the most militant teachers at Whitman, a woman who had adopted a Muslim name, was speaking to her social studies class about racial violence in Howard Beach, a community of white, largely Italian, families in southeast Queens. Shortly before Christmas 1987, a twenty-year-old black man named Michael Griffith had been fatally injured when he was chased onto a highway by a gang of white youths there. Several of them were later convicted of manslaughter in the attack, which became a symbol of racial polarization in New York City. "The Italians came from Ethiopia," the teacher continued. "And Ethiopia is a black country. . . . So what's all this fuss in Howard Beach?"

"I couldn't believe what I was hearing," a white teacher told me later. "She had her history all messed up. But that kind of thing is typical in this school—it's tolerated, even condoned."

The teachers who gossiped about this Howard Beach lesson were not sure whether the black teacher had reinterpreted history to accommodate her political philosophy or had simply gotten her history wrong, but the results, many felt, were equally offensive, whatever her intent. "She was giving out incorrect information to the kids," one teacher said. "And that's all there is to it."

Not only were episodes like this a frightening commentary on some of the teachers, they also contributed to a deep, silent schism between some black and white teachers. Many white teachers expressed disdain for black colleagues whom they considered intellectually inferior.

"We all wish it weren't so because talking about it makes us sound like patent, undeniable racists, but you would die at some of the things I see and hear teachers teaching," one of my friends, a skilled teacher, told me one day. Some black teachers countered that their white colleagues were insensitive to the needs of black students, who comprised the majority at Whitman. Especially galling to them were some veteran white teachers prone to nostalgia about Whitman's halcyon "white" days in the 1940s and 1950s. Said one black teacher, "I often hear comments like this from the veteran white teachers: 'When the school was white and Jewish, we didn't have these problems. But now that it's a black school, things have really gone to hell.' "

I asked one of my colleagues what she thought of the Ethiopia reference. "Who knows? Maybe black teachers feel that if they can convince the kids that we're all black, even those of us with blue eyes, then they can show we're somehow all alike. Perhaps it's a well-intentioned attempt to dampen racism. But I think it has the opposite effect—it makes the kids feel that the only way we can ever get along is if we all acknowledge we've got black blood in us."

If there was racial animosity between teachers and parents, it was rarely overt. And racial animosity was expressed only rarely between students and teachers. Once in a while, a black student who was being disciplined by a white teacher would make a comment like, "You don't like me because I'm black." One afternoon, I heard a white teacher's reply: "No, I don't like you because of what you do, not because of the color of your skin." Another morning, in March, a fight broke out in the auditorium. One of the more militant black teachers, who habitually wore long skirts and a scarf tied tightly around her head, grabbed the microphone and blasted the students into silence. "You kids are acting like animals," she screamed. "You women, you say you are beautiful black women. I say you are not beautiful black women. What would Sojourner Truth, what would Winnie Mandela, what would they have to say if they saw you here today? They would not say you are beautiful black women. You have no right to call yourselves proud. You are not beautiful black children, as I stand here this day." She had only further angered the black students, at the same time offending several Hispanic and Asian students, several of whom complained to me and one of the assistant principals afterward. "Who does she think she's talking about?" a black student in 8-1 asked. "You know," an Asian girl said, "not all of us are black."

Racial tensions among different groups of students were common—black Haitians at odds with a clique of American-born blacks, for instance. Calling someone a Haitian, in fact, was one of the worst insults the kids could hurl at each other. Occasionally, blacks went after Asians, too. Early in the year, when two Asians in my homeroom were nominated to lead a slate of class officers, a black student stood up to declare, "No way I'm staying here if two slanty-eyed kids is running things." When I replied that being in a democracy, he was free to run also but that he'd have to refrain from racist remarks, he seemed truly shocked. "That was racist?" he asked softly.

And, among teachers the professional atmosphere was outwardly cordial and courteous, without apparent regard to race. At a staff development program in the fall, black and white teachers decided together to economize on the ordering of materials; blacks and whites carpooled together to school. Within my department, one first-floor classroom had become a gathering spot for teachers of both races, spawning a cozy and affectionate atmosphere that led one black teacher to remark, "We're like a family in here. Black, white, we don't care. Just become part of the family." Exchanges in the hallways always seemed friendly to me; at holidays, black and white teachers sent each other greetings and greeting cards.

Yet signs of voluntary segregation were everywhere. In the teachers' cafeteria there was one table at which only blacks sat; the whites, by and large, sat at a separate table. At faculty conferences,

beneath the school motto "Sumus Unum"—"We Are One"—black
teachers gathered in one row and white teachers in another, usually
several rows apart. Social functions and funerals, too, often divided
along racial lines, as did the teachers' lounges, with the one on the
fourth floor becoming the de facto choice for white, male teachers,
while the second-floor lounge was used almost exclusively by black
men and women. White women, oddly, weren't easily included in
either place, and many found their own gathering spots in classrooms or in the few private offices.

Perhaps those separations represented no more than the affini-
ties of people from similar social circles, with shared values and
interests, though those were often the direct consequence of racial
backgrounds. But over the months it became clear that serious and
deep disaffections existed between black and white.

Tense relations with one particular group of black female teachers, and with other individual black teachers, were an undeniable
part of my year at Whitman, despite my efforts to better them. Sometimes it seemed that the more time I spent trying to understand and
ameliorate the problem, the worse it became. Involving such a small
number of teachers, I was even tempted to write off the friction,
telling myself that, in such a large group of people, there were bound
to be a few I just didn't get along with. It was extremely upsetting at
that time, and in the months following the close of school, to think
that I was either the victim, or the perpetrator, of racism.

After I left Whitman, however, I discussed my feelings with other
teachers, black and white. Many told me they had never noticed
racial tensions. Teachers who had their own offices in which to spend
free time were much less likely to have sensed racial friction than
those who spent their free time, as I did, in the lounges. "You're
telling me more than I ever knew," said a highly regarded black
social studies teacher, who admitted that he spent so much time in
his own office that he felt isolated from many of the school's social
interactions. "I really have my head in the sand, I guess." "Shocked
and deeply troubled" by some of the anecdotes I recounted, he admitted that there was "obviously some sort of a problem, but it's
painful to acknowledge it." A second black teacher, like the first very
well-liked by colleagues of both races, said that he "didn't fraternize
with whites" but didn't feel any tension either. "I guess I know my
place," said the teacher, who had been raised in the Deep South.

A black math teacher said she believed she was blind to race at
Whitman, but then recounted stories, thirty and forty years old, that
she said "must influence me still." Traveling in the Deep South just

after the Second World War and being told by a white waitress that she could not be served was an enduringly painful memory. "I'm sure the tension is there," she said, "but I try not to think about it."

When I spoke with fifteen or twenty teachers—about a fifth of the faculty—after I left Whitman, it was the black teachers who most often denied any polarization.

Among the whites, it was startlingly spoken of in terms both harsh and hostile. Black teachers were described as crude, intellectually ignorant, or unprofessional. Discussing "the frequent tardiness" of several black teachers, one teacher said, "You know, C.P.T. —Colored people's time." Another told me that she had seen black teachers striking children countless times, as had I. Once I watched a teacher throw a weeping boy out of a classroom, bashing him in the face with his bookbag in the process. Another black teacher, while I was at Whitman, had told her students that she carried a gun in her pocket. I had once heard her tell misbehaving students, "The devil is in you."

In readily recounting those incidents, the white teachers were aghast and resentful. "It would never cross my mind to call a kid stupid or belittle him, but some of these people think it's their right of heritage. Hitting kids, too, they'll say that's a cultural thing," one teacher said. "But if a white teacher did some of the things the black teachers do, he'd be hauled off in handcuffs or a straitjacket."

Some of the black faculty members apparently believed that black students also shared an antipathy toward white teachers. At the end of the year, several students and two parents complained to me that a few black teachers had denigrated white staff members during class. "You can't believe the things she says about the white teachers. She hates you all—not just you, Mrs. Sachar, but all the white teachers," one of my 8-16 students told me, referring to one of her black teachers.

For many of my white friends—those who said they knew their place and were careful not to step over the line—the problem seemed to stem less from social discomfort than from the fact that they held the educational background and language abilities of some, though by no means all, of their black colleagues in low regard. "You see black teachers who can't speak properly, who can't spell, who consistently show up late for work. No question, it leads to resentment, and that resentment leads to friction," one highly educated white teacher told me.

"A few days ago," a language arts teacher remarked to me one morning, "a kid came in here and he said, 'Miss—— said we don't have to read the whole paragraph anymore to know what it's about. We just have to read the topic sentence, and the topic sentence is always the first sentence in the paragraph.' What do I think? I think I should say, 'Great. At that rate, why bother to read anything at all.' That kind of teaching is indefensible." Another teacher had informed her students that Africa was a state. "You mean a continent?" a student asked. "No, a state," the teacher replied. "You mean South Africa?" the student asked, confused. "No, I mean Africa," the teacher insisted.

The love and respect for language held by many teachers—and the pain that follows its misuse—emerged clearly in many of these accounts. Hearing "Yo chile" and "You be gettin' in my face too much," offended another colleague, who said, "You talk about tension among the faculty. Yes, if you mean lack of respect and anger. When I hear the English language used incorrectly, I bristle. I don't care how desperate we are for teachers. I don't care what cultural deprivation a person has been subjected to. There is no excuse for that in a classroom in this country."

But accusations of incompetence cut both ways. "Just walking around this school, I see plenty of white teachers doing the same things you're describing some blacks as doing," one black teacher said. "It's wrong whoever does it."

I noticed that several black teachers, though by no means all, were frequently late to class and extremely disorganized with their paperwork, yet their jobs never seemed to be on the line. Countless times, the language arts teacher who taught my 8-1 students showed up ten to fifteen minutes late, carrying a cup of coffee. The students joked about her constantly, and several parents of 8-1 students said they had called the school to complain. When administrators passed this teacher in the hall, they noted her lateness merely by a shake of the head.

Winfield, in his fifth year as Whitman's principal, seemed to be part of the problem. A number of white teachers complained that they felt unappreciated by him and said they felt their race had something to do with their failure to win his approval. The principal, they felt, should go out of his way to bridge the gap between the races.

An excellent white teacher, adored by students and faculty alike, had chosen early retirement at the end of the year after several decades at the school. "I cannot continue to work for that man," she explained. "I cannot work for someone who will not say hello to me in the morning, who does not call to inquire when I am sick, who does not ever give me a pat on the back. If you're white and want to earn his respect, you have to be unequivocally, absolutely loyal. Not honest, just loyal. For me, that situation creates racial tension because I perceive the standards to be different."

Another teacher offered the example of the black dean with political ties whose laziness had been tolerated throughout Winfield's tenure even though the principal had openly acknowledged the man's problems. I asked this teacher whether he perceived different standards for blacks and whites. At first, he was reluctant to attribute any motive to Winfield's inaction against the black dean. Then, he ventured, "I guess race does have something to do with it because the blacks in this district are often politically connected, and it does not behoove Winfield to try to get rid of someone who is well-connected. Of course, this sort of thing goes on in white districts, too, and it is just as insidious there." It was often said that the black dean had connections going back for decades to various black political leaders in the Flatbush area.

Oddly, union officials defended Winfield. "Favoritism is how you run a school," one union official said, shrugging.

With so many tensions so near the surface, it was not surprising that occasionally professional self-restraint gave way to public recriminations. One spring afternoon, tending another teacher's unruly class, an exasperated black teacher shouted, "What's this? When whitey walks in the door, you sit down? But not for me?" The white teacher was, in turn, outraged to hear of this incident and accosted her colleague in the hall as kids swirled all around. "I'm not the one who sees color. You are," she screamed at the black teacher as a swarm of students gathered. "I don't care if the kids I teach are purple or covered with green polka dots. You chose the wrong lady to pick on. If I saw color, I wouldn't be in this school." A few of the students came to the defense of their white teacher. "She ain't like that," one girl said. "She don't care if we're pink or blue. She's a great teacher."

Sometimes, whites insulted blacks. Several white teachers used to gossip about one black teacher who had graduated from a prestigious college. "You think she got in on her intelligence?" I heard them say acidly.

Several infamous racial incidents from years before had become part of the school's folklore, told time and again. Twice I heard the story of a white Irish Catholic teacher who had refused at a Black History Month school assembly to stand for the playing of the so-called Black Anthem, "Lift Every Voice and Sing." As the story was told, Winfield confronted her, commanding her to stand. "That is not my anthem and I will not stand up for it," she had replied, "any more than I will stand for the playing of the French anthem or the Canadian anthem. Besides, what is this Black Anthem? What country is it for?"

When I learned that I would be teaching in a school where half the faculty and 90 percent of the students were black, I tried to examine my own racial attitudes and thoughts. Was I prejudiced? Might I say the wrong thing to the wrong people? How would I fit in?

I had grown up in an upper-middle class, white suburb of St. Louis, Missouri—born a century after the Dred Scott case was decided there, four years after *Brown* v. *Board of Education of Topeka* had outlawed segregation in public schools. But through my childhood the only blacks I saw on our quiet, tree-lined street were the maids, the ironing ladies, and the men who cut the grass. I would ride with my mother to pick up our cleaning lady from the crowd of black women gathered on the St. Louis County courthouse steps, where the buses from the inner city dropped them. It was a strange and fascinating event every time to see the women whisked away in so many Ford Country Squires. If our home and our neighbors' were any indication, their only contact with the white women for whom they worked were the day's instructions and the day's pay.

My education was also segregated. My first school was a private girls' school where every student was white. There, the "minority group" in my class meant me and the other Jewish student. We were made to feel uncomfortably different by several students and one teacher for a religious identity I had yet to understand. In fourth grade, I transferred to the local public school, where, again, there were no blacks among the student body or the faculty. Only the janitor was black. The first black student I ever saw was at a peculiar sociological field trip: for six hours, a class of white students from East Ladue Junior High School visited a black junior high on the north side of St. Louis. It was 1974, and the visit was to have been a day of "mutual respect and sharing"; instead, blacks and whites stood on opposite sides of the gymnasium. There was little sharing that day and only the respect of wariness.

At my high school, too, there were but a handful of black students and no black teachers. And even at my college—one of the world's great universities—there were but a handful of black students in my classes.

A quarter century after the order to desegregate American schools, I completed a nearly all-white education. It would be another decade before I learned just how ignorant that had left me.

Before I began teaching at Whitman, I was certain that I had no racial animosities, yet neither did I have any friends who weren't white. I never really gave these matters much thought until at *New York Newsday* my first editor turned out to be a black man. He was incisive, clever, and with a fine ear for language, and it was a pleasure to work with—and for—him.

Teaching in a black school, I thought, would be a chance to have other good relationships with black peers. I was admittedly naive about matters of ethnic collegiality, but I badly wanted to succeed. If I could get along with the city editor at *New York Newsday*, surely I could get along with my black teaching colleagues.

Things started smoothly enough. After my second day on the job, when I was almost ready to quit in despair, one black teacher came to my rescue, suggesting that I rework my seating plan and peppering me with other helpful suggestions. Another shared her treasure trove of logic problems to use as extra-credit assignments for my most advanced students.

Yet, as the months went by, things began to sour. I noticed it most dramatically one day in November when I entered the teachers' lounge and the lively conversation suddenly died. Perhaps the teachers had been talking about me, or perhaps I was now seen as an interloper. No longer were these colleagues inquiring about my classes or even greeting me in the halls.

There was no question I was a misfit. There was also a bit of a generation gap between us. I had nothing to offer except congratulations when they talked about their own children's accomplishments, or their adolescent daughters' emerging sexuality. And there were other social distances: one woman's husband was a police officer and a minister at their church. I knew nothing of those worlds; when she spoke of them my silence may have seemed less like respectful curiosity than alienation. Or she may have felt that the reporter in her midst was a spy, the liberal white lady a self-deluded political enemy.

At times I felt some were directly challenging me, trying to be provocative, as if testing me. One time, in my presence, it was argued that "all whites, all over the world" were "helping to enslave blacks

in South Africa." This posed a double bind—I could not rise to the
bait and retort: "I'm not; and my ancestors were too busy hiding
from Cossaks and pogroms to have enslaved any of yours." But they
seemed not to want my agreement, only to express their anger to me
directly.

When I sat grading papers one day and a few black teachers
nearby started humming "We Shall Overcome," I felt not only was I
not being invited to join in: I was being invited to get out.

It would not have been surprising had this coldness come from
my least professional colleagues, a defensive strategy against the
criticism I might later write. But these were women who knew their
subjects well, who were usually prepared, organized, and diligent.
Perhaps, I thought, race was not the real issue, but me. Maybe I made
them uncomfortable, my occasional questioning seen not that of a
newcomer who wanted to learn, but as the unwanted intrusion of a
snooping reporter.

Still, it was beginning to feel like "the silent treatment," and so
I finally approached the black teacher whose distance was most hurtful; she was someone I admired. One of the most active teachers at
the school, she was coordinating a spring show that was beautifully
choreographed, and was organizing myriad student field trips to
Broadway shows. She taught dance and sex education and had a
commanding presence, a strong voice with equally strong opinions.
As she passed in the hall, I called out, "As long as it's quiet, I want
to ask you something. Could you come in a minute, please?"

"I'm pretty busy," she said, stopping just outside the doorway,
her eyes darting around the room.

I pressed on anyway. "I was wondering, why do I sense that, all
of a sudden, you're annoyed with me? Did I say something that offended you?"

Refusing to meet my eye, she said, "Look, you're a reporter, not
a teacher. How can you really know what we go through?"

"I can't know everything you go through because I'm not a career teacher. But I can tell you, just from the little time I've been
here, I have a whole new take on what it's like. It's damned hard
work, for one. If I write about it, I will say that."

"And what, Mrs. Sachar, are you going to say about the kids?"

"I don't know," I admitted. "I'll write what I see, I suppose."

"Oh, I see." She turned away and said over her shoulder, "I'm
busy now."

Another black teacher leveled with me: "It's not unusual to distrust reporters. That's not racial, it's pragmatic." But it was both,

another suggested: "How would you feel if you were a teacher in an all-white Jewish school and a black reporter came to write about you?"

"Just fine."

"Well, maybe it's not the same: they feel that no one but a black reporter can really write about blacks."

Just before Christmas, the black teacher I had confronted solicited donations for a giveaway of presents to the entire sixth grade. I brought in a stack of twenty-five individually wrapped paperback books. When I gave her my offering, she simply turned her back without a word, but said to some others, in a voice loud and clear, "Don't trust her. She'll burn you."

Soon everything I did began to be scrutinized by this group and criticized for its imagined undertones. When I showed the film *Stand and Deliver*, the most interest any of them exhibited was to call it "a dumb math movie." The day before the screening, I learned that they were encouraging a boycott of the event. "They're saying you're a racist," one of my students said. "That you think we're stupid kids, like the ones in the movie."

"But the movie is about how smart the kids are," I insisted. "How far they've come and how hard they worked."

"But they say you think we have a long way to go and we're really dumb. Do you think that, Mrs. Sachar?"

I felt an impotent rage: it was one thing to belittle me behind my back, but to destroy my credibility with students, by an argument so contrived and petty, was another matter altogether. And it played straight to my deepest fears: that my upbringing had left me insensitive, a liberal who condescended toward blacks and, indeed, was a thoughtless bigot. I did not yet feel secure enough to consider that it might be the other way around.

"I thought at first it was because you were a reporter," a friend suggested. "But it's too mean and ugly. I'm beginning to think it has less to do with your being a reporter than with your being white."

Another ventured, "You're the new kid on the block, but we've all gone through it. If you're doing a good job with the kids, or getting their affection, some people can't stand it. It's threatening to them. You must have heard them telling students, 'Listen to us: white teachers don't understand.' They're terribly threatened by any white teacher's success, however modest."

"You have to understand," a veteran black teacher who was well-liked by students told me, "some of them went to college at the height of the civil rights movement in the sixties. Some of them were greatly influenced by the militancy of the times. And today, they are still very, very sensitive. Some even became paranoid. Don't you think that's only natural?"

In such an atmosphere it was impossible not to make a misstep. Twice over the course of the year I made apparently hurtful misjudgments. In both instances, I wished only to apologize, but I was never given the chance; my every attempt was rebuffed.

The first was a purely professional gaffe. It was my practice to take a private moment with every student several days before report cards were distributed and tell them their grades. I felt I owed them personal explanations, especially since at first there were so many failing marks. It also gave the kids the chance to discuss my grade at home with their parents before the report cards came.

Although I did not teach my homeroom students, we spent so much time together that a sense of family had developed: I saw them first and last each day, and they occasionally came to me with their personal problems. It seemed altogether reasonable to give them their grades in advance, too, in the same private way. The November day I first did so, one of my students had been absent, and the next day asked for his grades. We went to the teachers' lounge where I scanned the record sheet for his marks. "What are you doing with that?" one of his teachers asked me.

"Oh, I'm going to show Roger his grades," I replied.

"You're doing *what?*" she exploded, leaping to her feet. "You're not allowed to do that!" She stalked to the door, announcing, "I'm going to tell Mr. Newman."

"I don't see what the problem—"

"The problem," she snapped, "is that it's a violation of school policy. You have no right—"

At first, I could not believe she considered this such a huge mistake. My reaction, like hers, was anger—for being snarled at rather than civilly corrected. Still, I sputtered an apology. But she clearly knew she had me in a corner and stormed out of the room to prove it. Five minutes later she returned, saying icily, "Mrs. Sachar, Mr. Newman wants to see you."

"He knows where to find me," I replied sarcastically.

"He is your supervisor, Mrs. Sachar, and he wants to see you. Now. In his office."

"He can find me when it suits him." When the bell rang, Newman approached me in the hall outside.

I was prepared for another dressing down, but he simply informed me that my practice was contrary to school policy. He added, "It annoys some teachers."

My accuser emerged from the lounge, smirking. "That'll teach you," she said, heading down the hall with a strut in her step.

Perhaps this episode was nothing more than a professional turf battle. I had acted like a pushy novice and gotten burned. Yet our differing races seemed to have at least something to do with it—she seemed all too thrilled to show me my place, not just as a novice but as a white in her black school.

"How must all this stuff affect the school?" I asked my friends one day over lunch.

"Look around," one teacher said. "This place is a caldron. There are so many problems. We need a heavy dose of human relations—not just for the kids, but for the teachers. We're supposed to be setting an example. Pretty incredible, isn't it?"

In subtle ways, the administration itself, however well-intentioned, encouraged a separation of the races and, at times, was insensitive to the needs of the different constituencies in the school. Every morning, for instance, the principal offered an almanac tidbit. "And now," he would begin, "from our history and culture." Not once during the entire school year did I hear of an action, event, or person of significance to Hispanic, Asian, or white culture. Only black history seemed to matter. "It sometimes seems the Board of Education is more interested in teaching kids to be black than in teaching them to be human or American," one teacher told me. "You can drill Martin Luther King into these kids only so long," another teacher said. "These kids don't have any context in which to place him."

Black History Month, in February, was another production. Packet upon packet of materials were distributed, listing library books and city activities. The students from Spanish, Mexican, Korean, or Chinese cultures were left to their own devices.

The large bulletin board to the right of the front office was a year-long tribute to then-imprisoned South African black civil rights leader Nelson Mandela. The only reference to a leader of any other race was a torn and yellowed photograph of March Fong Eu, a former Asian-American state official from California, posted in the Whitman annex across the street; it had been on display for at least ten years, never replaced when she left office.

Then there were in-school celebrations to which only students and teachers of a particular ethnic group were invited. For the Haitian Day celebration, for instance, no American blacks, whites, Hispanics, or Asians were welcome. Teachers could visit the gathering, a festive assortment of games, songs, and dances, only during their preparation periods. I, for one, had hoped to be able to take my classes, introducing those of other backgrounds to a new culture and giving the Haitian kids the opportunity to show off their roots. The kids had asked to go, but my request was denied. "What does that have to do with math?" one of the administrators asked.

By early spring the frostiness that I felt from my black colleagues in the teachers' lounge was so isolating that I preferred to spend my free time in the library carrels. Quiet, clean, and rarely used by students, they were the perfect place to lay my head down for a catnap or to spread out my work. One day I needed some correction fluid and the librarian had none. So I walked across the hall to the teachers' lounge, which was full and noisy.

A few teachers mumbled greetings when I entered, but most continued their animated conversations. No one responded when I asked if anyone had some of the fluid, so I approached a few teachers individually, none of whom looked at me when they answered. One teacher did have some, but "Not for you," she said, before I could ask. "You have some attitude about you. You think you're better than everyone else; you don't say hello to anyone. No, I don't have any White-Out for you."

I was stunned. I had offered so many unreturned greetings over the months that I thought I was the one being snubbed. This woman had been assigned by Miss Kowalski on the first day of September to be my unofficial buddy teacher but had apparently always been too busy to give me any advice. So all this time she had simply disliked me. She continued to publicly berate me about my "attitude" and "rudeness"; I wanted to disappear. I wanted to shout that she wasn't the only one who constantly felt offended. Yes, I was white, and yes, I had the option of returning to my former profession. Was that my "attitude"? Did that erase my existence as a human being?

Later that day I sought her out to tell her I felt terrible about what she'd said. "If I've ever been rude to you, I'm sorry, really sorry. Please forgive me." I was ready to receive a lesson in racial etiquette, yet I was not, I wanted her to know, her enemy.

Her response was startling. "Another thing, at staff training you had a real attitude about you." She was talking about a staff-training course we'd taken four months earlier. "It was like you were the only one who knew anything and you was so smart or something."

"It was only enthusiasm," I pleaded. "I wasn't trying to be con-

descending. Don't you remember, that other teacher and I at the board were explaining the problem together?"

"All them big words," she said, "you had some attitude on you."

"This is silly. If I thought myself so superior why would I have asked you for help just the other day?"

She repeated, "I just say you have some attitude," and tossed a paper towel in the trash.

I was speechless and trembling, wandering in a miserable fog. When I went to the office to clock out, I wrapped my scarf tightly around my face so no one would see how shaken I was. Other teachers were excitedly sharing Spring Break plans. I went straight to my car and sat a long time before heading home.

"If you are a racist," a friendly teacher reassured me, "the kids will let you know it." That was what I was afraid of. Were my attitudes, in spite of myself, unconscious and uncontrolled?

Three weeks before my baby was due, I got one answer. Two girls from my 8-1 math class appeared at my homeroom door. "Girls," I said gently, "let's get to class." But they were clearly excited about something, happily conspiratorial.

"But Mrs. Sachar, we have something for you. Close your eyes." I felt one of them tugging at my dress below the neck. "There," she said. "Now open them." The girls were beaming. On the front of my jumper they had attached a red plastic pin with white lettering. It read: "Number One Teacher." As I gave them giant hugs, one said, "We made it in plastics class. You have to wear it for the rest of the year. Because it's true."

"Well, I don't know about that—but I'll keep it forever. I can promise you that."

By the end of the year I gave up trying to make sense of every slight or interpret every gesture and decided to keep my focus on the bonds of affection I most cherished—those with my students. Ironically, the surest proof of the strength of those bonds came about in one of the most awkward moments of my year.

I had been asked to chaperone the eighth-grade prom—to serve cake and break up dancing that got "too hot." I was so excited at the prospect of seeing the kids in fancy gowns and tuxedos that when I agreed to help, I forgot I would by then have an infant to be tended.

And so, during peaceful moments at the dance I retreated happily to a quiet corner to feed my child with the assistance of a babysitter I had brought along.

When my antagonists heard of this, they instantly assumed I had brought a "black nanny" in tow, a "Mammy" as one called her, for the purpose of flaunting a black maidservant in their faces.

I felt edgy with guilt and uncertainty. Perhaps it had been a heedless mistake to bring my baby-sitter. But I had no intention of signaling anything about racial superiority. Truth was, I had been too intent on getting to the prom on time to think about the implications to the kids, racial or otherwise, of having a black employee in tow. For me, the event had been a treat—the classroom barriers were suddenly gone amidst the sequined gowns and coed dancing, and the girls eagerly took turns holding my month-old baby.

As the year drew to a close, I asked three of the more hostile black teachers if we could talk. I wanted to explain myself, I said, and to make peace. All said no.

The next September, when the teachers returned for the start of the new school year, I tried again to get to the bottom of my unpleasant relationship among that small group of black teachers. I left messages at the school and at their homes. I asked other teachers to try to set up interviews for me. The woman who had reported me when I wanted to show a student his grades agreed to talk to me, then changed her mind. When I visited the school in October, I confronted two other teachers. They would speak to me about the kids, they said, but not about my year at Whitman and not about their personal feelings toward me. "She's just gonna make the school look bad," I heard one of them say to the other.

Then, late in October, I made an appearance on a local television talk show to discuss my year as a teacher. The moderator asked me whether poor teaching was to blame for the sad state of performance in many of New York City's public schools.

Troubled though I had been by the school's failure to punish the worst teachers, I had never felt that teachers, as a group, were to blame for the system's problems, and I said so as diplomatically as I could. "All I can tell you is if you took the faculty from my school and assigned them to a school on Long Island, the kids would learn," I said. "The problem is not the teachers."

Several days later, Winfield showed a videotape of the show to the faculty. A friend called me that night passing on the teachers' reactions. "You won't believe this, but some of the black teachers are enraged. They said you were putting down the school again."

I thought I was saying that the kids, and especially the teachers, deserved great credit—they were up against long odds and got little help from the system.

"I give up," I said unhappily.

"I know. It's pretty scary. But that's the way it is. If you ever come back, you'll know your place."

I made one final telephone call to the black teacher who had been most hateful to me. She addressed me coldly. "I understand that there has been some compensation for the book you are writing. If you're prepared to share some of that compensation with me, perhaps we can talk. Make me an offer."

"You'll talk to me only if you are paid?"

"That's right," she said. "Make me an offer. I have my son's tuition to pay and lots of other things to spend the money on. If it's the right price, I'll think about it."

I thanked her and told her that I was unwilling to buy information from anyone. I hung up, sadly certain that the hostility toward me was as deep and unsettling as ever.

16

What'cha Think We're Running Here, a School?

LESSON OF THE DAY

We're no longer running schools in this city. We're running the most expensive baby-sitting service in the world.

—A veteran teacher, Walt Whitman Intermediate School.

The boy carefully opened the door to the library and walked over to the front desk, waiting quietly with a pass in his hand. I was there helping a sweet girl who had taken to tagging along behind me after school was dismissed, chattering about boys, girls, her family, school, and also about math. She wasn't in my classes but wanted me to teach her "everything there was to know," she said, because she had recently discovered that she "knew nothing." "You be so nice, Mrs. Sachar," she would say when I tried again to explain that 1,000 is the same as 100 times 10. Except for us, the library was empty.

The boy entered and stood silently at the counter, waiting for help, as the school's teacher trainer, a heavy-set woman, emerged from her office next to the library.

"What do you want?" she asked, a hostile edge to her voice.

"To check out a book," he replied meekly, holding up his library pass.

The woman groaned in exasperation. "I don't believe this," she snapped. "Don't you see the time? Don't you know that the bell rings in five minutes? I can give you five minutes, and five minutes only. Not a second more. I want to get out of here on time, for a change."

The boy, embarrassed, put his pass on the counter and walked slowly to the stacks at the back of the room. The library had new white acoustical tiles recently installed to replace the old, water-stained ceiling, and the librarians worked hard to keep the floor free of trash and the tables spotless. It was one of the few clean places at Whitman. Despite the fact that the school had no study halls, a student could come to the library to read only with a teacher's permission, and it was rarely used by the students. Most often, it was used for periodic state-mandated library lessons or the two yearly book fairs at which paperbacks were sold to students and staff.

The boy stood forlornly amid the stacks for several minutes, then emerged and glanced anxiously at the clock. "Excuse me," he whispered. "Could you tell me where I could find a joke book?" His voice was crisp and clear, even from across the room where I sat. I wished I could help him.

"I don't know," the teacher trainer muttered, an irritated edge to her voice. "Maybe the 900s."

Just then, one of the librarians, a soft-spoken middle-aged man, ambled into the library. At the sight of him, the teacher trainer groaned loudly again. "Where have you been?" she snarled. "There are kids coming in. Are we running a library here, or what?"

"Open reading doesn't start until ninth period," the librarian answered quietly, shifting his weight nervously. The trainer wasn't his boss, but he usually deferred to her.

"You're early," he told the waiting boy. "Next time, get it right." It was 2:14; the boy had come four minutes early. Not until the bell rang did the librarian allow him to check out his joke book.

"Thank you and have a nice weekend," the boy said, looking up at the librarian expectantly, clutching the book close to his chest. The librarian said nothing, and the teacher trainer rolled her eyes heavenward before disappearing back into her office.

In my first months at Walt Whitman, I had been far too busy in the classroom to pay much attention to the mood of the school. Apart from teaching duties, the activities of the teachers and staff were largely a mystery to me. Though I was aware of the after-school committee meetings of teachers working to improve Whitman, the dropout-prevention encounter groups for at-risk kids, and the various responsibilities of secretaries and other school personnel, they had no impact on my job, or so I thought. I spent free periods grading papers or planning lessons or ruminating behind the locked door of a bathroom stall. If the events of the day did not directly involve me, I paid them no mind.

But after the turn of the year, as I began to feel more comfortable in class, I began to take notice of aspects of the school's life that had previously escaped my attention. And much of what I saw was disturbing. Many people working at Walt Whitman, particularly in non-teaching capacities, brought little energy and less enthusiasm to their jobs, and frankly did not seem to care much about the kids.

Equally upsetting, many school employees were condescending to the kids and parents and rude to the teachers. Yet such impoliteness seemed to be condoned—not curbed—by the higher-ups. Whether born of frustration, blind anger, or simple stress, a mean-spirited approach to dealing with others seemed to be the rule rather than the exception.

"It's being inundated with garbage," Miss Kowalski told me. "When you're harassed morning, noon, and night, and you have no dealings with normal human beings over the course of the day, you may lose it. If you spent all day in a factory doing the same menial task over and over, you'd be less stressed out than working in a school. Sometimes, you know you're not being polite, but you have no quiet place to go and regain your composure. So, instead, you jump on people's backs."

Winfield's cold demeanor I at first ascribed to shyness. But whether it was shyness or, in fact, meanness, the result was the same —an atmosphere of callous indifference that permeated the school, from the top down. Winfield rarely said hello to staff members as they arrived each morning; he seldom acknowledged students or staff in the hallways. He did not attend the annual eighth-grade spring show, but stood outside the front office throughout the performance, watching the traffic in the hallways. He may have had his reasons, but these actions were experienced by many as snubs.

Early in the year, I encountered Winfield's curt ways firsthand on, of all days, Teacher Recognition Day. As I was preparing to leave one November afternoon, his secretary invited me in to his office.

"Miss Sachar, did you get your rose?" she asked.

"How nice," I said. "But, no, I didn't. Did someone send me a rose?"

"Sort of. It's for Teacher Recognition Day," she said with a smile. There was no nicer person at Whitman, no secretary more competent. Winfield's door was shut, but she suggested that I wait.

"He's giving out the roses personally," she added, still beaming. "I'm sure he'll have some words for you."

As I walked behind the counter to wait beside the secretary's desk, I wondered what Winfield would say to me. After all, my start at his school had been rocky, to put it mildly.

Then, Winfield opened his door. "Yes, Mrs. Sachar?" he said. "What do you need?"

"Oh, your secretary just said that you had something for me," I blurted, blushing.

"Oh." Without asking me in, he sat down at his desk and pulled a long-stemmed rose from a brown cardboard box, then checked my name off a list. He didn't look up when he said, "Here," and handed me the flower. He looked past me to see if anyone was behind me.

Another teacher—also new to Whitman—was waiting, and Winfield hurriedly scanned the list for her name.

"Thank you," I said. "It's really beautiful." He did not reply.

The teacher behind me received her rose in silence, too, and we left the front office together, signaling our shared astonishment by furtively rolling our eyes.

Several secretaries and administrators also wielded a great deal of power. After the first day of school, the intake secretary, for instance, placed all newly arriving students, and so had the opportunity to alter the chemistry in a class greatly; the payroll secretary could delay or expedite the processing of insurance applications and sick-leave requests. Other secretaries controlled teacher access to the coveted, though usually broken, photocopying machines. Many of them routinely treated parents and staff—teachers, in particular—with disrespect and distrust. Some ruled by mood: the secretary in charge of teacher attendance ran hot and cold. One day she was sweet and good-natured; the next, she would rudely command a teacher returning from an absence to sign the sick-day log. She would let out an exasperated groan simply because a teacher had inquired how many days remained in his sick-day "bank." Her most reliable tone was put-upon annoyance. Her refrain: "How much time do you think I have in a day?" as if teachers requesting her assistance spent their days polishing their fingernails and coiffing their hair.

Another secretary addressed parents, many of whom were newly arrived immigrants, as if they were errant children. "Don't you know you're supposed to bring an immunization record?" she scolded one woman who had only recently arrived from Barbados with her thirteen-year-old son.

Miss Kowalski tried to explain, if not defend, such high handedness: "Imagine having ten parents coming in to see you every hour and half of them can't remember their address or phone number. You're going to get frustrated. It's like the little Dutch boy trying to plug the dike. First there's one hole, and he can stick his finger in. Then there's another hole and another. Before long, the dike explodes and so does the little Dutch boy."

All of the assistant principals I dealt with showed real love and concern for the kids, but their interest was not consistent. A few belittled and berated staff members, even in front of students. Over the months, I felt that we teachers had been given huge responsibilities but were not considered worthy of the most basic trust. I was expected to boost the math score of every student and to keep reams of records in perfect order, yet every day I had to punch a time card as if I might sneak off at any moment. Although the punching-in procedure was finally eliminated, we still had to move our time cards back and forth to show we were in the building. One afternoon, a dean with a near-perfect attendance record over more than twenty years of service was required to bring a note from a funeral parlor after he attended the funeral of a close relative. His word was not sufficient for Winfield.

The manner in which supervisors sometimes addressed us was often unfeeling and caustic. One assistant principal, Edward Newman, whom I greatly respected, called me to his office one spring day. "Have a hard day, Mrs. Sachar?" he began, leaning back in his chair, a stern look on his face. It seemed a reprimand was coming.

"Actually, no, it was great." It *had* been a good day. I had taught probability using dice and gaming wheels. The kids had loved the hands-on lesson. For once, I felt strong and capable.

"Well, your room wasn't great," he retorted. "Paper everywhere. Desks out of line. It was a real mess."

As I thought back, Room 327 probably had been a mess. The students had worked in groups, and I had not put the desks back in rows. We'd done problems together, right up to the bell, though the last five or ten minutes of class time were supposed to be for straightening up. There was so much excitement in the room I hadn't once checked the time. Besides, the unwritten rule at the school was to leave the rooms a mess. Nine times out of ten, I walked into a classroom as disordered as the one for which I was now being reprimanded. The condition of the rooms *was* an appalling state of affairs, but I wasn't going to change the situation singlehandedly. And the problems—even the problem of messy rooms—went so much deeper than whether desks were in straight lines.

Instead of two well-meaning, harried adults attempting to work together to do a good job, we were more like a warden and his defensive, ignorant clerk. Yet Newman was not a petty or punitive man. He had helped me to arrange my *Stand and Deliver* project by doing the vital paperwork and scheduling. Though stern, he was wonderful with the kids, quick to give the benefit of the doubt to students I was nearly ready to give up on. "Lots of them are pussycats," he told me once. "They just want to scare you." But working at Whitman seemed at times to turn even the most compassionate people into patronizing vindictive bureaucrats.

A woman whom I grew to respect greatly as an administrator, a teacher, and, especially, as a warm-hearted human being, Vikki Kowalski, too, "lost it" on occasion. She was extremely conscientious, arriving at school hours before required. By the middle of the year, she was offering me workbooks, teaching materials, and brilliant ideas without my even asking. In her vast fund of teaching experience, she had lots of tricks for tackling math. For instance, to teach the addition of positive and negative integers, she suggested: "Use warriors. Let's say that five negative warriors and eight positive warriors have a battle one-for-one. Now, who wins?" She drew a quick picture. "Of course. The three positive warriors."

Like Newman, Kowalski seemed nonetheless to have become an unwitting victim of an overburdened, insensitive bureaucracy that tolerated cruelty and indulged condescension. Once, having earlier urged me several times to "play a more active role in the dismissal of kids from the auditorium," she berated me in front of the kids, this time for sitting down during a movie in the auditorium. Another time, the stairwells were jammed with classes converging simultaneously on the auditorium for Picture Day. Miss Kowalski was at the door to usher all of us in, and though I had lined up my charges in a semblance of order in the hall, by the time we descended two flights of stairs and traversed another corridor, my class had turned into a disorganized mass of teens. When she saw my group, so bunched up in the narrow stairwell, her face hardened into a frown.

"Mrs. Sachar," she boomed, "can't you get your students into lines?" Her eyes pierced me with anger. "You know better than to bring a bunch of screaming lunatics down to the auditorium." Embarrassed by this outburst in front of my kids, I hastily ordered the kids into two rows.

"That's better," she said without a smile.

Later that day, I told her privately that she had humiliated me by the public dressing down. "When I screw up, tell me in private,"

I said. "I feel very awkward being disciplined in front of the kids. I'm trying as hard as I can."

"I don't mean it personally, Mrs. Sachar," she replied. "There's just a job to be done."

Miss Kowalski was, in fact, a warm, giving person whose long tenure as a math teacher had generated numerous accolades. She had taken her students to amusement parks and picnics, and, though the kids nicknamed her Killer, they appeared universally to respect her. The system and the school had simply hardened her so much, she said, that she no longer realized how harsh she sometimes sounded. During auditorium assemblies, she was quick to yell at the kids for talking. "Okay, if you want to be treated like babies, I'll go out and buy you some diapers," she shouted once. Another day, she threatened to cancel the school's graduation ceremonies. "Babies don't graduate," she told them. "I guess that means you won't graduate either."

She said the sternness and cutting sarcasm with kids and teachers alike was "merely a show, a way for me to make sure I don't swerve off my course." That she might on occasion have hurt my feelings or those of other teachers and students upset and embarrassed her. "Look," she admitted, "I'm part of the problem. I guess sometimes we're so busy just trying to keep our heads above water that we say things we don't mean."

Months later I asked her, "Why does the system do that to people?" She sighed. "This year I've got the responsibility for the entire eighth grade in addition to my duties as math department supervisor. That means checking senior dues, paperwork for sixteen classes, dealing with the problems of 600 eighth-grade kids. You end up having to harass people to get what you need. There's always too much to do. Too little time to do it in. We start to act like machines."

One teacher I admired greatly put it simply. "If these administrators were doctors, we'd simply say they have no bedside manner."

Far from being limited to condescension and the occasional insult, the administration's attitude also extended to matters crucial to the kids' education. Often, it seemed that their needs were ignored whenever it was expedient. The eighth-grade assembly gatherings, for instance, had begun with the worthy notion of guest speakers discussing everything from career opportunities to study tips—and had devolved to showing the cartoon version of *Phantom of the Opera*, and films like *Princess Bride*, Michael Jackson's *Thriller*, and *Super-*

man I and *II.* We also watched a movie about a youth who crashes his car while trying to get his drivers' license, and another with kissing scenes that made the kids squeal, and a thirty-year-old black-and-white film about black widow spiders.

Little annoyances, like the constant announcement "Testing, Testing," that was broadcast three or four times a day over the public address system in September and October, also made it impossible for the kids to concentrate. So did the announcements slapped into every room in the school once the PA went into full operation in November: "Excuse the interruption, will Miss So-and-so please come to the front office?" These we heard an average of five times a day. One morning, the first period was interrupted thirteen times by the principal announcing there would be an "extended homeroom." One of my students stood up and screamed to the loudspeaker for all of us: "Shut up already. We done heard you the first time." Winfield's constant interruptions were the joke of the school. "He likes to hear himself breathe," one teacher used to say.

Sometimes the administration's insensitivities were neither audible nor visible, but the kids felt their effects just as strongly. The day of the eighth-grade social studies test in May, the woman in charge of testing arrived thirty-five minutes late, forcing students and teachers alike to wait an hour before beginning. Arriving at my homeroom, supposedly stocked with the test materials, I was short two booklets and one answer sheet. Many students were unnerved by all the waiting, and I could hardly blame them. Later that day, the tardy testing administrator hunted me down over the PA system; apparently answer sheets from three of my twenty-nine homeroom students were missing. After searching desperately through her office, we found that she had mixed up her papers, something that happened twice more with other teachers, and that all the work from my class had, indeed, been handed in. She did not bother to apologize for stealing precious time from our lunch or for interrupting our classes.

A staff training program required for new teachers twice started late because the instructors didn't come on time; on the third day, the instructor, an assistant principal, failed to show up at all. This lackadaisical attitude contributed to an atmosphere in which meaningful standards—other than for paperwork—were few and rules were made to be broken.

The administration might have helped new teachers improve simply by explaining to each of us which of the various supplemental and special programs our kids were in and who taught them. Only

in November did I discover that three of my classes—8-12, 8-13, and
8-16—took an additional Corrective Math program several times a
week. Had Corrective and Regular Math teachers coordinated lessons to avoid duplication and offer reinforcement, we might have
helped the kids considerably.

Nor was I informed of the difference between the Corrective
Math lessons and the Resource Room lessons in which some of my
students participated. In some classes, students were pulled out
whenever the "Resource" teacher appeared at the door. Much later
in the year, the school psychologist explained that the Resource
Room was a special-education pull-out program in which students
who have mild learning disabilities got small-group instruction several times a week in several subjects, including math. And no one
explained the logic of taking a kid out of my math class, thereby
forcing him to make up the work later, so that he could get an extra
twenty or twenty-five minutes of language arts.

Neither did I know how to get a kid onto the math team, or even
that there *was* a math team, until several months had passed. When
I asked the team coach, whose identity I discovered only by accident,
she encouraged me to give her names of interested students. But after
I did, those students said they were never contacted, and it wasn't
until April that I found out that the math team met informally for
coaching and testing; it was up to me to coach my kids, in my free
time.

There were whole departments at the school, like the guidance
office, whose functions were never explained and whose services I
did not know how to tap for my students.

It would have helped tremendously if there had been some built-
in system—regular math-department faculty meetings, for instance
—to inform and encourage us to work together. Instead, the math-
department faculty meetings were held during school hours when
the twenty-member department could never gather all at once. Had
I been better informed, I might have been a better teacher. However,
the quality of my teaching seemed to matter considerably less to the
administration than my paperwork and discipline. The color of the
ink in my Red Roll Book seemed far more important than referrals
for special education or after-school tutoring. I received four memos
on Red Roll Book procedures, but nothing at all about accurately
diagnosing learning difficulties.

Finding any kind of basic math-related supplies—be it dice or
protractors—for teaching such topics as probability and angle construction was always hit or miss. The resources and materials were

there—like the erasable maps used in social studies that I might have used to teach ratio, proportion, and scales—but their existence was a well-kept secret.

Arranging field trips was an equally chancy proposition with shifting procedures and permission granted according to Winfield's whim. No administrator ever explained how to arrange such an event in the first place. The films *To Sir with Love* and *Up the Down Staircase* were rejected without explanation. Then, in February, I heard that two classes were going to see the Broadway revue *Black and Blue*, though front office secretaries had bluntly informed me that the district office did not allow "noneducational" entertainment like movies and Broadway shows. In March, Mr. Winfield had given me a similar retort when I asked if I might take the kids to see the film *Lean on Me*. "The district office does not allow the showing of movies to the kids," he said. "And besides, I don't agree with what that principal did." What about the Michael Jackson videos in the auditorium? I wanted to ask.

The atmosphere at Whitman mirrored the disinterest of the district office. I saw the district superintendent, Thelma Harper, appear only once at our school, after a gun was fired in a classroom. The district's math coordinator disappeared after the first week of orientation, despite her promises to give numerous training sessions during the year. Supplies promised to teachers who attended a district staff-development program never materialized. Nor did the pay we were promised—until late March, four months after the last session, and only when many of the participants threatened to file a union grievance. (Like almost every function arranged by the district office, these training sessions started late—roughly thirty minutes into the ninety-minute scheduled session.)

There were many good programs in place to help kids, and capable people running them. But the programs themselves often seemed out of touch with the students' needs. The Dropout Prevention Program targeted truants and students with poor attendance records for special help—a small, weekly group encounter session run by a guidance staff member. The woman who ran the Wednesday-morning sessions allowed me to sit in on several occasions and watch. The sessions often started ten or fifteen minutes late, and the activities, although amusing, seemed to have no relevance to the kids' attendance problems. One day, the leader brought in a shoe box wrapped in Christmas paper and passed it around, asking each student to tell what he wished was inside. Another day, the counselor posed a sinking-boat dilemma: with limited space in a lifeboat, which of the passengers did the students think should survive—doctor, lawyer, accountant, teacher, homeless man, or pregnant woman? "The idea is just to get the kids talking," she told me after one of the sessions. Had the program done anything to improve school attendance? "I don't think it makes much of a difference," she answered. It was, however, a costly program—in our school alone, two people worked exclusively on dropout prevention. The whole premise—that truants would appreciate school more if they were rewarded with prizes for attendance—seemed to me less a worthy idea than simple bribery.

One morning in January, a small boy quickly took a seat in the back of my 8-13 classroom. "Excuse me," I said. "I don't know you. Are you new in this class?"

He was only four-feet-six, weighing perhaps eighty pounds, with unkempt clothes and, for all his small size, a strangely sinister look in his eye. He did not smile, and his head seemed permanently cocked to the right. He offered no answers when I asked where he had come from, who had assigned him to my class, or even his name.

While other students poured in, I said, "I'll have to see your transfer form." Every new student carried this slip of paper from teacher to teacher on his first day in new classes.

The boy pulled a paper from his back pocket and tossed it at me. It fluttered to the floor, and I bent to retrieve it. His name was Steve, it revealed, and he had just arrived from the West Indies.

Five new students had already been added to 8-13 in the past month. I had thought carefully before making their seat assignments —some were buddied up to help classmates; some needed to be in front to see; others had to be separated from friends. It was a delicate balance. Although his height suggested a front- or second-row seat, I placed Steve in the back, not wanting to disrupt the class any more than I had to.

He was apparently hyperactive, hopping out of his seat seven times that first day. When I called on him to answer a few simple questions—my way of showing I knew his name and wanted him to feel comfortable—he was unable to answer. A week later a test showed me the true level of his skill. Steve's eyes had roved all over the room that day, obviously hoping for answers from a classmate's work, and he was the last to turn in his paper. He had answered only two questions. He couldn't write his own name.

At my next free period, I rushed downstairs to see the secretary who made these class assignments. For weeks I had been annoyed because her selection of new students for 8-13 was steadily destroying the chemistry in the class. Newman had handpicked the 8-13 students the previous spring, and, as he had promised, the class had been less troublesome than my other low-ranked classes. We had started smaller—only twenty-three students—and better behaved. At least five of the kids in 8-13 were adept enough at the computational part of math to have been in 8-1; only language problems—few of them spoke English well—had frustrated their progress. The inclusion of five sharp kids had been an undeniable help to the other students in 8-13 and to me. These more able kids were willing to help their classmates and strong bonds developed between some buddy teams.

But as new arrivals began to dribble into the school in December and January, 8-13, so small and vulnerable, was given an extra share of the new admissions. The class was smaller and had "room" for more kids, regardless of their temperament or abilities. Yet it was obvious that no attention whatever had been paid to Steve's placement: if he couldn't read, he didn't belong in a regular class.

In addition to Steve, two other troubled newcomers brought problems. Larry had been arrested at least twice, charged with stealing cars. Only two days after being assigned to my class, he was ordered to appear in court to answer one of those indictments. Barron, the other boy, seemed unusually bright, but could not sit still. Other students said he was in a rough gang of crack distributors and frequently flaunted his gold—gold chains, gold teeth, gold rings. Although he occasionally failed to show up for class, when he was there, he stole the show. Tall and crafty, he often tried to fondle girls in the hallways.

To this rough-hewn group, we now added the less vocal but no less troubled Steve, seemingly illiterate and given to venting his frustration by hyperactivity.

When I snagged the intake secretary, I implored her, "I need help with Steve, a new kid in 8-13. He's totally lost. He can't even write his name."

"Yeah, so?"

"Well, I was just hoping we could put him somewhere else. 8-13 is falling apart with all these new kids, and this one should probably be in special ed anyway."

"What do you expect me to do?" she answered without looking up. "We've got to put him somewhere." I didn't move.

"Okay, okay," she finally said, irritated. "Don't worry about it.

We know about him. We'll try to do something." I had a good relationship with this secretary. She was overworked, trying to do it all,
with the inevitable side effect of cranky moods.

She told me to ask the school's administrative assistant what
had already been done for Steve. "I think she's doing a testing referral."

"Do you remember why he got put into 8-13?" I asked. "I
thought that was being reserved for kids coming out of English-as-a-
Second-Language and bilingual classes."

"Not anymore. We've got to put the kids somewhere when we
get 'em. You've got to take your share, just like everyone else."

The administrative assistant's office had never impressed me as
competent. The administrative assistant was in charge of security—
but we already had seen ample evidence, besides gunfire and the
constant intrusion of non-Whitman students, of how lax security
was. She was also in charge of testing, yet she had a habit, too coin-
cidental to escape notice, of showing up late, even on test days,
though to my mind, she had one of the easier jobs in the place—no
teaching duties.

It took all of lunch to track her down and it wasn't worth the
effort. She did not know anything about Steve, although she was
supposed to be doing his special-ed referral. The cumulative record
file on Steve was missing. "Could someone else from your office be
working on it?" I asked. She just shrugged.

No one seemed interested in helping Steve. I filled out another
special-ed referral form in March, but the only biographical information I could find was his date of birth and address. His cumulative
record folder seemed to have evaporated altogether. To specify the
reason for my referral, I wrote: "Although I have known Steve only a
month or so, his skills seem extremely weak. He appears to be illiterate, or close to it, and has extremely poor motor skills." Steve could
not hold a pencil tightly enough to write. "I don't know whether
these problems are a result of his background or a mental deficiency.
But I believe he should be tested."

Much later, I learned that Steve had never been evaluated. On
three separate dates, his parents failed to show up for appointments
with the school social worker to sign the consent form for testing.
The case, by law, had to be closed.

If Steve had been an exception, his assignment to my class would
not have been so troubling. But of fourteen students added to my
classes, five needed intensive remedial help that I could not provide.
If a reading test had been used to screen these kids—theoretically

the official policy—they would surely have failed, leading to prompt testing for special help programs early on. But the test was used only when the intake or administrative secretaries had time to administer it. More often, I heard the intake secretary simply asking of a new student or his parents, "How do you read?" The answer dictated the class placement.

Some of the students added to my classes were either attending school for the first time and had no skills on which to build or were seriously learning-disabled and needed special help. Most told me that reading tests had not been administered; they had spent less than ten minutes, they said, in the placement office.

Sometimes, the heedless class assignments did not involve disruptive students, merely slow ones. Two students assigned in the spring to 8-1, the top class, had virtually no understanding of basic math. When I asked the secretary why she placed them there, she replied, "They were nice boys. I knew they wouldn't bother anybody." She was right. They were nice. But they were also lost. When the year was out, one of them told me, "Thanks for putting up with me, Mrs. Sachar. I know I'm way behind. I don't know how I got into this class."

As the school year advanced, my colleagues and I watched helpless as our classes grew larger and larger. First, every roster was brought to twenty-nine students, then to thirty. When more students arrived in April and May, some registers were increased above their legal limit. 8-1 ended up with thirty-one students. By year's end, all but one of my classes had thirty or more students. In each, as well, the cohesion of the group and the students' enthusiasm had been strained.

Part of the tragedy at Whitman was that most students did not comprehend how weak their skills were, and those few who did had little idea where to get help. As little information as the administration gave its teachers, it gave even less to the kids.

Perhaps the most important academic concern in a student's eighth-grade year is gaining admission to the best possible high school. For many, it can mean the difference between a chance at participating in the skilled work force of the middle class, or falling into a world of poverty. New York City has 117 high schools, including one "zoned" school in each neighborhood to which area students are guaranteed acceptance. In the Whitman neighborhood, that high school was Erasmus Hall. Erasmus had a long and distinguished history of academic excellence. However, despite the attempts of a conscientious staff and principal, it had deteriorated sharply over the years and now had a reputation as one of the roughest schools in the city. Nearly every student I taught desperately wanted to go elsewhere. But the actual application process was so complicated that few students at Whitman understood it—nor did many teachers. The 1988–89 high school directory, which listed the programs offered at each of the high schools, was the size of a small phone book, more than 400 pages; extremely thorough, it was also incredibly confusing—utterly useless for students with the serious learning deficiencies of so many at Whitman.

Assuming that a student was interested in business programs and could find the page in the directory that explained the criteria each school used to select students, he would come upon this passage:

> *The programs in CLUSTER 13 are educational option programs. Based on Citywide Reading Test administered in the term preceding application, students accepted must include 16% above the average, 68% who score within the average range, 16% who score below average.*

It was critical that every student understand at least enough to put those schools he most wanted to attend at the top of the list on his application. That vital information was buried as a Special Note at the bottom of page 45. It said:

> *Half of the applicants to EDUCATIONAL OPTION programs are selected by the computer based on student interest (the higher the student lists the program—i.e., 1, 2 . . . etc.—on the high school application, the better the chance of random selection).*

How many of my students even understood what "random selection" meant? How many, I asked, had read page 45?

"Are you kidding?" one boy in 8-1 told me. "I just threw that book away and put down the schools I wanted to go to."

"And how did you know the schools you wanted to go to?" I asked.

"My cousin picked them for me."

In 8-16, the class of Shereeza, Reginald, and Carl, the kids anxiously hunted through the book, trying to find schools that had nursing and medical-career programs. Most of them were lost, unable to use an index or a table of contents.

After two years as an education reporter, even I did not understand the manual, the forms, or the process. Our school did have an eighth-grade guidance counselor, part of whose job was to coach the roughly 500 eighth-grade students through the three-tier high school application process. She had a part-time assistant to help answer questions. But the assistant talked to the kids in condescending tones, making little effort to explain the entries in the high school directory or help the kids make a good choice. "Just get down your eight choices," she said during one of her typically brief information sessions. "And make sure your name is spelled right on the form."

The guidance staff had no time to offer individual counseling to the kids on this critical decision. Students who might well have had a shot at one of the city's more prestigious schools got no special attention. The one exception was an after-school course that began in October for those students who wanted to take the exam for one of the city's specialized science schools—Bronx Science, Stuyvesant, or Brooklyn Tech. I learned of this class only by word of mouth, and then I was told that it was full. The five students I had who appeared to have an excellent chance at making it could not get into the tutoring sessions, so I ran my own after school, allowing in even 8-12 and 8-16 kids who had no realistic shot at acceptance. Despite repeated requests, I could not acquire a copy of any previous year's exam to use as a guide.

When high school assignments were finally made, several 8-1 students whom I had expected to be attending the more coveted schools were assigned to Erasmus. One particularly bright girl had merely not understood the application process well enough to apply to the better schools and had given up. She, too, was slated for Erasmus.

Particularly sad was the situation for some of the kids in 8-16. Though they had little chance of acceptance at one of the better schools, it seemed they had been written off by the guidance assistant before they had a chance to try. I was teaching 8-16 when the assistant detailed the application process in a presentation superficial and far too brief. "Here are the books," she said, passing out the massive high school directories, "and here is the application. You must hand this back on the date I'm going to give you." Then she walked out. The students looked completely stumped, and I spent the rest of that period trying to help, though I was almost as ignorant of the confounding process as they.

Several days after Newman criticized me for leaving Room 327 a mess, I visited him to set things right between us. I stood awkwardly in the doorway for a few seconds, looking for a graceful segue into what was bothering me. He saved me the trouble. "Got a minute, Mrs. Sachar? Sit down. Are you okay?"

"No, I guess I'm not," I admitted. "This place is really starting to get to me. I've never worked in a place so rife with humiliation and hate. I don't know, hate's probably not the right word, but I just feel lousy working here, and it shouldn't be that way. I've never felt like that in a job before." He said nothing. "I mean, take the Red Roll Book. That damned roll book is more important than anything I teach. If my roll book is out of order, I could get fired. But if I'm a lousy teacher, who gives a damn? Does anyone care how I feel? Does anyone care how the kids feel? Or do we just care that there's no White-out on the Red Roll Book?"

"Look," Newman said, in a near whisper. "If there's anything two decades in this system has taught me, it's that you need three things to survive in this school system. Not just here, but at any school."

"What are they? I'd like someone to finally tell me."

"Clean bulletin boards. Impeccable paperwork. And a tidy classroom," he said. "Oh, and one more thing. Discipline. If you've got that, you've got it all down."

"You mean, when you get right down to it, you don't really have to teach all that well?"

He shrugged. "You'll never get me to admit it, but . . ." Newman had been a great teacher; every teacher in the school and a few students whose brothers and sisters had been his students had assured me of that. He cared about the kids. I had seen it myself. But he knew the pragmatic, sad reality. Claude Winfield had told the new teachers our first week of school that it wasn't necessary to love kids, even to like kids, in order to teach. Now, Ed Newman added the corollary; it wasn't necessary even to teach kids to survive in a school in this school system.

We talked about why the school so often treated people—students, parents, teachers—without respect. The day before, Winfield had told a faculty conference that the physical condition at the school—the graffiti all over the classrooms, the grime, the filth, the chaos—was largely the fault of the teachers.

"I guess," Newman said "we treat the teachers the way the teachers treat the students."

"But which comes first? Who sets the example around here?"

"I guess we think that by having a certain amount of control, we're doing something, the system's working. Like the roll book. If I can go over those roll books and see that every *i* is dotted and every *t* crossed, then I can feel like something is going according to plan."

"Yes, but think about the way you spoke to me the other day. I really resented that. It hurt me. You talked to me as if I were an incompetent who needed to be lectured like a four-year-old. Was it a power play? Why can't we just talk to each other like human beings, like peers?"

He shrugged. "Look, why do we go into teaching? Because we need to be in control. I mean, sure, we care about the kids and all that, but it's really because we want to exert control—over the kids, over our environment."

"So we give accolades to teachers whose rooms are the epitome of order and control, regardless of whether they know anything or are teaching anything. You know, it starts at the top in this school," I went on. "Were you there at the faculty conference when Winfield told us, in that harsh, threatening voice of his, that he would be making visits to classrooms after the spring break? Why does he have to talk to us like that, as though we have something to hide, like we'd better be on the alert because he's about to pounce?" Newman only shrugged. "Why not just say: 'I'll be coming around during April to back you up, to give you some help in the classrooms. I know it's tough working in this place, and I want you to know I'm here to help.' Is the idea that I'm going to teach better if I'm a nervous wreck? There's got to be a better way." I sighed.

For more than an hour we talked—about why I had taken a leave from my newspaper job, about why he had become an assistant principal, what he thought of Whitman, how he felt working in the school.

"You know," he said, "you really won't know what it's like to teach unless you do it for one more year. You should come back next year."

It was my turn to shrug. Whether a second year would be magically different from the first I couldn't know. But I knew I would not return. The frustrations were too many for the slim chance of success.

"You make me think about things, Mrs. Sachar," he said as I rose to leave.

"Call me Emily, for pete's sake. You know me better than anyone in this place. Okay?"

He smiled. "Okay."

We shook hands and both left the school, but we did not walk out together. Administrators and teachers rarely did.

17

The Veterans

Those who can, teach. Those who can't, go into some less significant line of work.

—Quotation on a button given to me while I was a teacher at Walt Whitman Intermediate School.

I was frightened as soon as I heard his voice.

"I can't talk, dear," he said quickly. "I'm not well."

"What do you mean, you're not well?" I asked. Thoughts of cancer raced through my mind. It was two days before the start of the new school year, and I had been out of touch with some of the friends I had made at Whitman the year before. I had phoned this teacher on a Sunday to chat about the coming year and to gossip a bit about the school administration.

"I'm in the midst of a diarrhea spell," he said.

"What's wrong? Did you eat something bad?"

"You know what's wrong," my friend said. "I've got to go back there in two days."

"Back where? You mean to Whitman? I thought you liked it."

"Like it? It's awful. I feel like a piece of dirt in that place. The diarrhea's just the start of it. I get headaches and uncontrollable vomiting, and I've been crying, too."

This was a veteran teacher with a good reputation at Whitman, a man whose company I had cherished during the year. He had spoken of retiring, how every day of teaching brought him one day closer to it, but I had always assumed the complaining was part of the professional banter. After so many years as a teacher, so many Septembers, wasn't he used to it by now? Teachers like him, who had taught for so long, were immune to burnout, I thought.

"But your classes are so good, you handle the kids so well," I said.

"What's control when you've got no respect?" my friend replied. "The kids don't respect me. The administration doesn't respect me. Times have changed, dear," he said sadly. "When you walk into a place and you can't believe what you see—graffiti and litter, mice and roaches—after a while, you become part of it. It's a simple question of survival now."

"Why don't you get out? Do something else?"

"Like what? This is what I do. I'm a teacher."

What could he do, this nice family man who had spent almost his entire professional life as a junior high teacher at Whitman? "You could go to another school," I suggested.

"What's the use? It might be even worse someplace else."

I didn't know what to say. For me, such a choice would be easy. I wasn't a career teacher who had worked up to a $50,000-a-year salary with summers off, counting on a pension in five years. I didn't have a large family to feed and clothe and educate. If I wanted to change careers, my husband would help support the transition, just as he had during my year of teaching. If I was beaten down by the school system, I had another career to return to.

"Why does this happen?" I asked my friend. But I knew the answer. A teacher's dignity could easily be washed away after too many harrowing years in the wrong school. He was one of the kindest people I'd ever met, and a darned good teacher, too. "You should be rewarded and thanked."

"Nice of you to say so, but I really don't feel I'm good for much of anything."

Some weeks later, after the school year had started, I called him again, hoping his spirits had improved.

"I'm stuck here. I have to make a living." He told me that there had just been a stabbing in front of the school. "Who knows what it was about?" he said. "The neighborhood is terrible. It's not just the disrespect you face. It's the violence, the fear. I feel helpless. You have a principal who says the school is great when the school stinks. He tells you about all these great programs that exist. He tries. But Winfield buries himself. He doesn't really know what's happening." His voice trailed off.

I asked my friend why he had never tried to become an administrator as had other Whitman teachers. "The administrators basically came up the ranks by hurting other people. It's disgusting, and I decided long ago I wanted no part of it. These people don't deserve to shovel coal, much less become administrators."

"Well, maybe you could be different, better?"

"It's not worth trying," my friend responded. "I'm white. They want blacks and Hispanics running the system now."

He was upset, and much of what he said was illogical: Of the five assistant principals, four were white, including the most recently appointed. Maybe my friend didn't know how to put out a yearbook, but surely he could help run the attendance office or the school treasury, posts that would take him out of the classroom for at least part of the day. But he wasn't speaking of logical matters—this was how he felt.

"Aren't there any rewards for you at all?" I finally asked.

"When a kid comes back to thank you. It happens, but for the most part, it's very hard to teach these kids anything. Their parents don't care; the kids don't care. They don't see the value of an education. I have one of the top eighth-grade classes now. You'd think they'd be good, but they stink. Year after year, they're pushed ahead, these kids. And then, ready or not, they graduate. It's a farce."

"Did you always feel like this?"

"I started out feeling great. I had good lesson plans, loads of energy, a real belief in what I was doing. But once the school changed, in the late 1960s, it all changed very quickly for me, too. I burnt out. It used to be a darned good school, when it was mostly white middle class and largely Jewish. Now, it's all poor, and it seems the only way to teach these kids is with threats, even though they know I can't actually follow through on them. Winfield tells us to pass everybody, to get them out. But he knows most of them aren't good for much of anything when they leave here."

This man was one of the forty-five Whitman teachers referred to as "the core"—about a third of the staff, those who come back to the school year after year. Whitman had a hard time keeping its finest teachers. The lure of high schools or easier junior highs pulled many away, even in the middle of the year. Only half-jokingly a student sang to me, "Will you still teach me tomorrow?" after another of his teachers left abruptly. An excellent social studies teacher jumped ship the week before Christmas, explaining, "The board called me down and offered me high school." Overnight she was gone, her locker emptied, her dazed classes handed over to a substitute. An administrator could only sigh, "Here today, gone tomorrow."

At the school year's end in 1989, twenty-six teachers left or were not hired back, among them a dozen highly regarded veterans. Three teachers retired. One, a stellar math teacher, transferred to a school closer to his home. The math team coach departed for a high school job. Another math teacher, threatened physically one time too many in class, abandoned teaching altogether. Our only pottery teacher, a real gem, found a job closer to her Staten Island home; without a replacement, the pottery program was abandoned. Every department had its casualties.

Even the promising rookies didn't stay long. One, a French teacher, quit after eleven weeks. "These kids don't know English," she said on her last day, in early December. "How can I teach them French?"

About one-fifth of the faculty was new to Whitman when the fall 1988 term opened. Two days before the start of the next year, Vikki Kowalski was once again still filling vacancies in the math department, just as she had been one year earlier when she hired me. The school's scheduling chairman and head of our teachers union chapter described the effect of so many vacancies.

"Chaos," he said. "Pure and simple chaos."

If the constant exodus of fine teachers told a story, so did the perseverance of those who stayed. How did the best of them, the talented veterans, do it year after year, motivating themselves for a job others found so disheartening. Why did they stay? Why and how did they continue to care? What did they really think of the frequently maligned New York City school system?

While I was teaching, I was too busy, too tired, too afraid to ask most of these questions. But when the year was out and the pressure off, many of these teachers were more than willing to talk. They spent hours with me over long, congenial meals, talking about their most memorable students and classes. They were grateful to be asked for their opinion. In their years of teaching, few had been asked their opinions on anything, they said—even which textbooks to purchase for their classes.

But too many sounded like my friend with the nervous stomach. They no longer savored teaching; they remembered the Whitman of decades earlier, when they taught kids who wore suits and ties and who revered teachers as much as parents. They stayed now for pensions and summer vacations and because of personal and professional insecurities. Many spoke painfully of chronic depression and believed that contemporary society held them in low esteem. Marriages and family life had suffered, too, during their years in the school system. "Teaching is one of the loneliest jobs in the world," one said, "not just because you're alone in the classroom, but because it is so difficult to explain your plight to anyone else—how degrading it can be to stand in front of a class of kids who have absolutely no interest in what you have to teach."

Teachers who were once enthusiastic and still highly skilled lived in a world of constant irritation, a system unable or unwilling to distinguish between the best and the worst teachers. In New York City, at the teachers' union's insistence, any teacher, regardless of ability, knowledge, or competence, receives the same salary as any other with equivalent experience and educational credentials. Removing bad teachers is nearly impossible. In the elementary and junior high schools, any principal who wants to proceed with disciplinary action is bound by stringent time limits.

Ironically, the most tangible and meaningful reward a school administration can give its best teachers is to relieve them of classroom duties, and many Whitman teachers aspired to that status. Countless tasks that could have been assigned to secretaries or administrators were instead used as rewards for teachers, though, at Whitman, these posts were as likely as not to go to undeserving teachers. One woman who assisted in the guidance office spent her time gossiping and joking; to the students she was curt and condescending.

The hope of assignments outside the classroom seemed to be the only thing sustaining many teachers. Such jobs might reduce a teaching load by one-third or one-half. The head of the scheduling office had to teach but one period per day. Even those whose teaching assignments were cut only modestly could relinquish other onerous duties like hall patrols and homeroom paperwork. The teacher who helped out in the attendance office had only sixteen classes a week, no homeroom duties and no hall, cafeteria, or auditorium patrols. By contrast, I had a homeroom, twenty-three teaching periods, one auditorium patrol, and four hall patrols, allowing for only eight free periods per week. The audiovisual room chief, who delivered the televisions, overhead projectors, and movie equipment requested by teachers, taught seventeen periods a week and had no homeroom or patrols. The school treasurer taught sixteen periods. He also cut another good deal. He was given no class lower than 6-10, and was promised a six-year lock on his job.

The school's teacher trainer during the 1988–89 year worked out an especially attractive arrangement, teaching only twelve periods a week. Although she was supposed to work with struggling teachers the rest of the time, she was, to all intents, unsupervised. "Claude lets me do whatever I want," she told me. "He trusts me."

The most enthusiastic and skilled teachers worked with small groups of children or had moderate classroom duties. Many also had private offices in which to spend their preparation periods. "A place to call your own makes life as a teacher so much better," Miss Kowalski told me. Teachers supposedly had to prove their worth before they earned these attractive benefits, and, indeed, the teachers I most admired had well earned the special benefits they received.

Sharon Cohen, the remedial reading teacher, was one of the most inspiring teachers I met. She was unusually candid: in frightening detail she described the problems she confronted in her reading room.

"The students are so lazy," Sharon told me one afternoon. "They want everything spoon-fed to them. If I try to elicit the Aim of the lesson from them they go absolutely nuts. 'What do you mean, no Aim?' they say if they don't see it on the board. And then they'll suck their teeth or roll their eyes or pretend to go to sleep.

"Their problems run the gamut. Some can't pronounce the words in their books. Others can read every word aloud, but have absolutely no idea what the words mean. And, they don't pay attention. You ask them, 'What just happened in that paragraph?' and you get a blank stare."

How do students get to the eighth grade unable to recite or understand simple words like *cat* and *dog?* "The specific problem can be any number of things. Some of these kids have never mastered phonics. They don't know that the letter *B* makes the sound 'buh.' How they got to the eighth grade unable to do phonics, I don't know. Some are immigrants who never learned to read in their native countries. The kids who've gone through our school system probably just got pushed along by teachers who didn't care enough or who figured they couldn't keep a twelve-year-old in third grade indefinitely."

"What about the kids who can read the words but who don't understand what they've read?"

"That's a different question. For some, it's a language problem, but not for most. For almost all of these kids, the problem is not stupidity, it's lack of interest. They see absolutely no use for reading in their lives. They'll say to me, 'I know how to read. No problem. I can read.' It's really sad—they have no understanding of what it means to read. They don't read books, they don't read newspapers, they don't even read road signs.''

In spite of Sharon's rigid classroom rules—no gum-chewing, no eating, no bathroom passes—some classes deteriorated during the course of the year. "I have a class this year that comes in late, chewing gum, eating potato chips, as if they're doing me a big favor to show up. One kid comes up to me with her progress card and asks me to sign it, a kid who makes no effort and who pokes fun at kids who try to learn. I was very straight with her. I said, 'Don't come in here anymore if you don't want to learn. If you're going to disrupt this class for everyone else, forget it.' She was delighted. 'Really?' she said. 'I don't have to come anymore?' That's their attitude. They don't want to be here. They see no purpose in it. What are we supposed to do with kids like that?''

Every month, each child in her class had to write a book report. She used especially easy material, a simple fairy tale at first. Later in the year, she would add biographies, sports books, mysteries. Of her 118 students, only twenty-five actually did the book reports. Of those, none was a true book report. "I have kids who copy one chapter of a book word for word and then hand it in. 'Sure, I wrote it,' they'll tell me, 'that's my handwriting.' To them, writing a book report just means putting words down on paper, any words. I'll ask if they read the book. 'Oh,' they say, 'you're supposed to read the whole book?' 'Yes,' I say, 'from the first page to the last.' ''

"What do these kids think reading is for?''

"For school,'' Sharon replied. "Neither they nor their parents have any concept of how reading can be a part of a daily life. When you have home lives like these kids—parents who aren't around when they get home from school or during the evening or over the weekend—it's no wonder that these kids can't read. Their parents have never read to them. They never see their parents reading. And no one is communicating to these kids why school matters. Teachers can't do it alone, not in six hours and twenty minutes a day.''

Still, Sharon said she wouldn't dream of leaving teaching. "A lot of these kids have heard only negative things in school—what they can't do, what they don't know. When they sit down with me and get something positive, they're amazed. And that can be thrilling, for them and for me.''

One day, Sharon gave the students in 8-16—some of whom read on a third-grade level or lower—a story about troopers parachuting out of an airplane. "I just put the word *parachute* on the board and asked: 'What do you know about this word?' In five minutes, the board was filled, and the kids were absolutely astonished. When you see a kid who can say, 'Hey, I may be in the lowest class in the school, but I know plenty,' it's great."

By working with smaller groups, Sharon was able to build a particularly trusting atmosphere. "When you're working with kids whose problems are so exposed, to me and to the other kids in the class, you have to get them to trust you and trust each other, to feel that we're all working on this problem together. Once there's trust in the room, I can really do things with them. And that can be beautiful to watch. You'll see a kid like Shereeza, who has such severe problems, and you'll see how hard she tries. That makes me feel wonderful."

Roman Foster, a skilled social studies teacher, used another approach. While Cohen set rigid limits with her students, keeping a comfortable distance, he befriended the kids. Nicknamed Bambi by his students for his gentle manner and boyish face, Foster had been at Whitman five years and ran the audiovisual room. He was so easygoing one wondered how he controlled his classes. Yet, he did, with a combination of resourceful teaching and charm.

"I can get the kids charged up," he explained. Once he had talked with his students about the fatal shooting in 1989 of Yusef Hawkins, a fourteen-year-old black youth in Bensonhurst, a largely white, Italian enclave in the heart of Brooklyn. Convicted of murder in the attack was a white teenager named Joseph Fama, allegedly angered that a black had invaded his white community. "We all agreed that there was racism in that situation, but I took it a step further. I said, 'What is the difference between you and Fama? I hear some of you calling kids a Haitian, like it's a put-down. Isn't that just as racist?' We batted it around for a long time. I told them they have to look in a mirror sometimes. I want to be provocative. It's not always possible to show them this kind of connection, but I try."

Foster gave his home phone number to some kids and let them eat breakfast with him in the audiovisual room before school. He had an especially close relationship with Marlon, one of my 8-7 students who was repeating eighth grade and who, in spite of a pleasant personality, was totally turned off by academics. It had taken me months to break through to Marlon, to discover that geometry could engage his interest. Foster had connected with him the first week of school. "I want them to think of me as a big brother," Foster said. "Kids feel comfortable with me. If you make yourself available to them, they appreciate it."

Foster's painstaking attention to the details of movie-making fascinated the kids and drew them in, although he, too, was sometimes discouraged working with junior high kids. "Kids this age are very confused. Sometimes it's hard to teach them. Certain classes, you'll have kids who are lazy, in a way. They don't believe in working hard. They may be sloppy. Sometimes, every five minutes you have to tell them to shut up. But I say, 'Hey, this is reality. Either I can succumb or I can try to overcome the obstacles.' "

Like many of the best teachers at Whitman, Foster never relied on the deans to rescue him from trouble in the classroom. "When I have a problem, I solve it myself," Foster told me. "That's part of how I build relationships with the kids."

That such an easy-going man was able to instill discipline puzzled me. "I don't like to pressure kids," Foster said. "I used to have teachers who were all over you if you made one wrong move. I tell kids they have responsibilities. You come in, open your notebook. I just say it like it is. 'If you do such-and-such, you are violating the rules of this classroom.' I don't have to raise my voice. Sure, sometimes they forget. They're kids. But, I usually win them over. I pat them on the head, and they see I care. And I assume they're competent, whether it's writing an essay or handling a piece of equipment in the AV room."

Could Foster's optimism survive for long at Whitman? "This building was built to be an elementary school," he lamented. "Physically, it's depressing for an adult to be in here all day. This city expects us to work miracles, but a few days ago, in Room 205, paint fell on the kids' faces. Why should that happen? I try to stay hopeful, but it doesn't always work.

"Sometimes I feel I'm being told it's a bunch of dumb little black kids who don't care, and I'm supposed to turn it all around. Sometimes I wake up and think, 'How can I tell these kids there's hope with people thinking these things about them?' But it's not the kids' fault. I want them to spend the little time they have with me relaxed, learning as much as they can."

Teachers like Foster parlayed goodwill into respect; the kids listened to them. There were others like him.

"It's a delicate line to walk. On the one hand, you have to be relaxed and open to the kids so they'll trust you," said Vivian Nobile, who gave up a job as a hospital administrator to work at Whitman. She was credited with straightening out the girls' gym, which had been a chaotic mess until she arrived. "On the other hand, you can never let your guard down or they'll walk all over you. You can't say that you don't know what to do or are confused or don't have the answer. If you're confused, they'll be confused."

Nobile, thirty-six, was in her sixth year of teaching. Of medium build and weight, she was alive with energy. One of the few at Whitman who offered to help me early in the year, she introduced me to one of the more inane tasks required of us—preparing the biographical portion of the answer sheets for homeroom students every time a standardized test was given: four times a year, we had to blacken in hundreds of little circles (we called it "bubbling") for the students' names, identification numbers, school codes, and ages. "It drives you crazy, but we've got to do it," Vivian moaned after she had filled in more than a thousand little circles. "After a day of these forms, sometimes I want to leave. These kinds of things are so degrading."

She dealt with more alarming pests than many other teachers at Whitman. The gym was renowned for the variety and abundance of its vermin. One day, while she was taking attendance, a plump gray rat with a foot-long tail ran up the wall. She screamed to the kids to follow her and bolted for the door. "A bunch of the kids stood up and ran, too," she recalled with a shudder. "The rest of the brave little souls just sat there. 'Come up—let's go,' I'm yelling. 'It might bite you.' 'Don't worry, Miss Nobile,' they said. 'It's only a rat.' "

Her day, like that of so many Whitman teachers, didn't end when the last bell rang. She took graduate classes after school to earn the degrees necessary to work her way up the salary scale. In New York City, new teachers must get a master's degree within five years just to retain their jobs; they need a second master's degree to reach the top of the salary scale. In 1989, a teacher with twenty years' teaching experience and two master's degrees could earn $50,000. Nobile was making $30,700.

She had had some rough moments at Whitman, she confessed, the worst several years before when she was on cafeteria duty, a dreaded patrol most teachers can expect to receive every six years. "There was a girl in the cafeteria who wasn't supposed to be there," Nobile recalled, "so I asked her to leave. 'Fuck you!' was the response. I asked her again, and before you know it, it became a shouting match. I kept calling for help. Finally, another teacher appeared and this kid told her, 'I'm not leaving until I fuck up the white bitch.' I couldn't believe my ears. I was the only white person there. She meant *me*. The next thing I know, she's on top of me, punching me hard. It took three people to pull her off." Nobile was out of work for three weeks, recovering from bruised bones and a battered ego.

"It was really an awful experience, but I wanted to come back as soon as I could. I knew if I didn't, I'd never teach again. And when I did come back, the kids were great. The worst kids in the school would come up and say, 'I would never have wanted that to happen to you, Miss Nobile. The kids in this school really love you.' When you hear that, it makes all the bad stuff worth it."

In contrast, her experience with Project Egg was one of her teaching highs. Among her goals each year is to teach responsibility in her sex education and health classes. During my year at Whitman, she had given each kid in her class a raw egg and she told them to care for it as if it were a baby. The students were divided into groups: intact married couples and single parents, separated, divorced, or widowed. Suddenly, eggs that might earlier have been thrown into classrooms or down stairwells became prized possessions to be treasured and nurtured; some students decorated and dressed theirs. Project Egg became the talk of Whitman, and Sharon Cohen, the reading teacher, even opened a day care center for the "babies" during the school day.

One girl, Joniel James, wrote an article about the experience for the student newspaper.

> *Most mothers kept the fathers away from the babies if they were not living together. Married couples shared the responsibility of taking care of the egg. Single parents, however, took full responsibility. I was a separated, single parent who devoted my time before and after work to my baby. This experiment should be given in all health classes. It gave me a sense of responsibility, and also informed me about pregnancy, childbirth, diseases, and the happiness of the mother and child.*

"I had no idea how the kids would do with it," Nobile recalled, "but one kid came up to me and told me it had changed her views on getting pregnant. She said she'd never realized how much was involved. On days like that, you love your job, and you love the kids. Sure, some days I want to quit, just like anyone in this business. You spend five periods in the gym, tend to all the stupid paperwork, and then do a patrol and find kids throwing rocks in the stairwells. That part is no fun, but I stick with it because I know I matter to the kids. They need me. There's no other occupation I can imagine where I would feel so needed, where I could give so much."

· · ·

Even the more stern teachers could communicate their passion for teaching and their affection for the kids. In Miss Kowalski's case, it was far easier to see a tough side than a tender one. Some days, she didn't even nod when I passed her in the hall, and, when I sought her out with questions, she might answer without lifting her face from her work. She was tough with the kids, as well, believing that "rules were made to be enforced," and enforcing them. Students caught drawing graffiti on the walls spent hours scrubbing them off with rubber gloves, rags, and a bottle of Fantastik. When I observed that Fantastik seemed a pretty mild product for removing indelible ink, Miss Kowalski replied, "It's better that it not work so well. Then the kids can see what a delightful mess they have made."

Yet Miss Kowalski confided that her tough demeanor was merely a show. "I'm mean, but I'm fair," she insisted. "The toughness isn't really me. I want to teach the kids self-discipline. I want to be the rock, not someone who's erratic." Within her firmly held standards, her behavior was compassionate; one day she was gently helping a student understand square roots, the next remonstrating with another for failing to turn in homework. Often alone, she did not lunch in the teachers' cafeteria and rarely showed up for faculty social functions. She was not the sort to reveal her feelings easily, although once in a while, she let her guard down, and it was obvious then how much respect she had for her occupation and how much pride she had in her own work. One day when I was especially discouraged, I asked her if things would ever get better for me in class. Indeed, they would, she promised, and related a comforting, sympathetic tale to cheer me up. A few years earlier a student had stuck her hand through a pane of glass in school and had to be sent to the hospital. The girl insisted that Miss Kowalski be at her side in the ambulance. "Why do you go into teaching?" Kowalski reminisced. "For days like that."

At the end of one school day, as we stood in a dark stairwell between floors, she surprised me completely. A few days before, I had asked her what else she might have done with her life if she hadn't entered teaching. She had quickly changed the subject. Finally, in the dim light, she told me. Many years before, she said softly, she had entered a convent, planning to become a nun. Her boyfriend had been killed in Viet Nam and she sought desperately to find some spiritual meaning. "Almost as soon as I got there, I knew I was running from something, maybe from myself. It didn't feel right." Clutching her keyring for the climb to her office, she sighed and once again donned the familiar impenetrable mask.

Although she never discussed it, it was widely known in school that Miss Kowalski was helping to raise a coterie of nieces and nephews. Once, when I asked if I could leave school early to attend my daughter's performance in a school show, she warmly acquiesced. Some months before, she had flatly denied my request to miss a faculty conference for personal reasons. "A mother's work is never done," she said with a smile the day of my daughter's show. "Let your daughter make you proud."

My last glimpse of her tender side came on the final day of school. Sitting in a chair at a student's desk, she was distributing our payroll checks. I bent over to hug her. "Thanks for a great year," I said. "You taught me more than you'll ever know." She neither looked up nor returned my embrace, but, as she prepared to check the next teacher's name off the list, she turned in my direction. "I will miss you, Mrs. Sachar," she said.

In one of my last conversations with her, Vikki Kowalski was almost apologetic. "I'm not even aware sometimes of how I am coming across. I never meant to hurt you or anyone else. But just as the school can be a pressure cooker for you, it is for me, too. There are always the 154 forms due yesterday and the constant demands of so many kids who need so much help. Sometimes you do want to run away into your office. And sometimes you jump on people because it's your only way out." She paused. "We don't have time to be nice."

Gloria Holloway was another forceful presence at Whitman. A math teacher known to all the kids as "Grandma," she was sixty-four and "still had a good eleven or twelve years left." She had been teaching for seven years and even the toughest boys tipped their hats when they saw the gray-haired Mrs. Holloway in the hall. At forty-eight, she had begun working her way through college so that she could become a teacher; she had first worked at Whitman as a teacher's assistant. Killer and Grandma, outwardly so different, were fast friends. Holloway taught a remedial math program to very small groups, sometimes as few as ten students, in a makeshift room on the first floor. She refused to teach a topic unless she was certain the students could use it in their everyday lives. "I teach things the kids are actually going to need," she told me, "how to balance a checkbook, how to read a map. I'll even do dot-to-dots with the kids if that will give them a tool for understanding number concepts."

A big advantage she made no bones about was her strong connection to Winfield. "If I don't agree with him, I tell him, but I have known him for years, and I believe in him and what he's trying to do here." His unwavering support made her love her job even more. Others felt such encouragement from Winfield less frequently. "I know some people say he's insensitive," Holloway said, "but they just don't know him well enough."

She was not afraid to tell parents to work harder with their kids, she said, "When I listen to parents saying they can't do X, Y, and Z, I tell them, 'Look at me.' I did it all. My kids behaved and they did well in school. I had three kids, and I was active in every PTA in every school they went to."

Why was she able to command so much respect from the kids at Whitman? "I can relate to these children; I know their glands are changing and they don't really know what's going on. I make friends with them and try to give them a little TLC. It's what a lot of kids are looking for." Was that, perhaps, where her nickname had come from? She smiled and nodded. "One day, a girl told me that her grandmother had died, and she asked me if she could start calling me Grandma. I said, 'Sure, sugar.' I think some of the kids really think I am their grandmother."

Ellen Yudow, a teacher in the language arts department, had a view similar to Gloria Holloway's about the importance of teaching kids about life. Yudow, tall and statuesque, had a commanding presence in the classroom which she used to great advantage, refusing to begin her lesson until the kids were silent and looking directly at her. She was marvelously well-read, and she quoted widely from the classics. But her most choice phrases were all her own: "Teaching is the most important job in the world, but society has made it the hardest one," she said once. Another time: "Teaching isn't just about producing diplomas, it's about producing lives."

Like the other superior teachers at Whitman, Yudow grew indignant at the disrespect sometimes shown by students. "I sometimes say to parents, 'If you ask me to do two tasks at once—discipline your kid and teach your kid—I'll do both badly. I am here to teach. You are there to impart discipline. Don't make me do your job, too.' But the reality of these times is that we must do it all. We are social workers and baby-sitters and mothers and aunts and, if there's time left over, we are teachers. I've stopped believing that I can undo what's been done for thirteen years to some of these kids. But maybe I can put a dent in it."

She had become particularly close to a Whitman student who was selected, from all the students in the city, to read her own poetic tribute at the memorial service for Richard Green, the schools chancellor who died in the spring of 1989. Yudow had bound the girl's poetry into a pretty booklet. "I know that girl is going to do something amazing, and, years from now, I'll look at that book I put together for her and feel so proud that I helped. There are a lot of success stories, a lot of special kids. This year, I got a batch of compositions and one of the kids wrote, 'I don't know why God let me be born.' That breaks my heart, but if I can make a difference to that kid, then that's enough reason for being a teacher."

It was not surprising that, in a school with such vast and varied problems, a wide assortment of teaching styles evolved in the search for something that would work. Yet, the best teachers showed a few vital traits. They were consistent, they sought their own self-improvement as well as the kids' and, most of all, they liked the kids. Barry Kantrowitz, who ran marathons and paced classroom floors, spoke intensely: "For a kid to succeed, he has to know what he is succeeding at. A teacher has to say what he means and mean what he says. It's like a relationship between lovers: If you send out mixed signals, you'll get mixed messages. You bond very early with these kids. If the kids don't understand, they have to have the opportunity to ask, to explain, to clarify. I tell the kids, 'If I have to answer the same question thirty times, it means I explained it wrong thirty times.' And I'll try again.

"Second, kids have got to feel good in your classroom. You can't beat learning and success into them. They've got to want to come into your class. I'm lucky to be teaching social studies. It's a wonderful subject: there are good guys and bad guys, heroes and villains, things we're ashamed of and things we're proud of. For instance, we were talking about the importance of Jamestown. If, by talking about black slaves and tobacco farms, I can get them to begin to understand Jamestown, then I can get them to understand the racial violence in Bensonhurst four hundred years later. What you teach has to matter to you or it won't matter to the kids.

"When your lesson is dying and they look at you—they're bored or, worse, they're hostile—that's a rotten, rotten feeling. It's a horror. I've been there. But now, I go into my classes with the sense that this period these kids are going to come out smarter than when they walked in. They're going to feel better about themselves and me and the whole world forty minutes later.

"When I see every head turn and follow me and I know that every eye and ear is taking in my telling of the tale of greedy Cortez playing on Aztec superstition and religion, and that they're loving it, I'm just thrilled. I feel so lucky to be able to do this for a living." In his ardor he sounded all fresh and new. In fact, he had taught at Whitman for sixteen years.

Did he feel like one of Whitman's heroes? "I'm not the miracle worker who's going to save Whitman. But I've defined myself and my work, and I'm happy. This year, my boundaries are the 150 kids I teach. Then there are the teachers who come to me for books, supplies, advice. I run the social studies bookroom. And I'm happy in there, with the books and the maps and the charts. Those are my definitions. A poet once said that the most contented people are those who take delight in the ordinary, and that's true. I think that's me."

As a great teacher, how did he feel about his many mediocre colleagues? He answered thoughtfully, "I had a friend, Allen, who was the finest teacher I ever knew. He left teaching after seven years to sell ladies' clothing because it troubled him so much that the system didn't distinguish between minimum competency and real talent and energy. He was a man of great pride; he's since become very successful. We argued about it many times over the years. My feeling is you have to accept what is possible and also what isn't. You do what you can. I have my ethics and my personal decisions. I work very hard. But there are people who work even harder and they fail. Not everybody is trained to handle this profession."

Kantrowitz said one reason he loves teaching so much is that he feels there is always the challenge to do better, to perfect his craft. "One of the things that rankles me most is the idea that teaching can be mastered in one year. It takes five years before you can even consider yourself a teacher, and only then do you realize how much you still have to learn. It takes fifteen to twenty years to become a great teacher. The sad thing now is that there's tremendous time pressure to make it quickly or you won't survive emotionally in this system and these tough classrooms. But it takes years of introspection to know: What kind of teacher am I going to be? Am I going to be dazzlingly creative or very structured? Am I going to be a teacher whose kids never forget him? This is not a physical science where if you add this and that, you get the answer.

"Anyone who assumes we're in this because it's easy and because we can't do anything else couldn't be more wrong. This job is really tough. It's physically demanding, too. And we take enormous pride in trying to overcome all the difficulties."

. . .

In August, two months after the school year ended, a little slice of audiotape on my telephone answering machine defined for me one of the truest rewards of teaching. "If this is where Mrs. Sachar lives," I heard a student's voice say, "Mrs. Sachar, this is for you. If this isn't where Mrs. Sachar lives, I'm sorry for bothering you. I just want to say thank you for being my math teacher."

I played that brief message over and over. More than anything tangible, that voice was the souvenir that would preserve the most precious rewards of my year as a teacher.

18

A Real Board of Education

In the philosophy of instruction that we practice in the city, and in the nation, we feel it's desirable not to deprive children of exposure to the mathematics that's being taught at their grade level simply because they're lacking the computational skills.

—Susan Zakalak, director of mathematics, New York City Board of Education, during an interview, October 1989.

Pedro had me on the spot. "Mrs. Sachar," he shouted from his seat one rainy morning, "I don't get this shit." Usually when Pedro was discouraged, he closed his notebook quietly and put his head on his hands to sleep. Today, he was angry. "Why can't we do something fun? This stuff is stupid."

Pedro didn't usually make it to our Thursday class at 7:55 A.M.; if his father forgot to wake him, he usually missed the first few hours of school altogether. But there he was, sleepy-eyed and willing to try, and I was ruining his day with a lesson on scientific notation.

"Sometimes, math can be frustrating," I acknowledged, sympathizing. "But keep trying." I patted his back. Then for the fourth time, I tried to explain why 0.4×10^6 is the same as 4×10^5. Even the brightest students looked bored and uncomprehending.

Few of the kids I taught at Whitman were so blunt in acknowledging their frustrations. But the combination of an untried teacher, an unrealistic math curriculum, and few appropriate teaching tools added up for many of my eighth-grade students to a wasted year in math. Over and over, I asked whether the Board of Ed or the district had materials explaining how to implement this curriculum, which was so beyond the students' abilities. Nothing. There were a few puzzle books and tips from Miss Kowalski, but no overall plan for rendering this arcane math sensible for my students.

"How do you teach scientific notation to students who don't know basic addition and multiplication?" I asked her one afternoon. She offered a few tips—review place value (explain that, in the number 98,765, the 7 holds the hundreds place and the 9 the ten-thousands place); review exponents ($10^3 = 10 \times 10 \times 10 = 1,000$); review the need for scientific notation (by asking students to describe the size of, say, a sperm cell or the distance from earth to the sun and discovering for themselves how helpful a shorthand for writing 62,000,000,000 or .0000003 would be). Oh, sure, I thought.

Suggestions like those helped little, given the fact that the kids didn't know multiplication. They couldn't understand place value because the meaning of numbers was a mystery. The virtues of scientific notation were equally moot because they saw no practical uses even for more basic math. To teach this topic, must I first teach multiplication to eighth-graders, drilling the kids with flash cards? Or give them calculators? Did Whitman have calculators, anyway?

There were few avenues of help. Miss Kowalski was adept at finding new strategies for teaching old subjects, but she was overwhelmed with her own paperwork and her duties as a novice assistant principal—students who had just graffitied a hallway for the fifth time that year; teachers who, halfway into the school year, still could not get their students to sit in their seats. The teacher trainer was, in fact, a language arts specialist who offered help with discipline but was little help in teaching basic math. The mentor I had been promised in September didn't materialize until the mentoring program was finally funded, in the third week of December. Mine was a superb teacher who suggested that I "use hands-on materials," but was too busy to give specific help in creating the dozens of lessons I needed. I tried a few ideas of my own; some worked, some didn't. Surely, there were teachers who had already been through all this and had strategies and suggestions that could help me. But where were they? How could I find them?

· · ·

In the back of a closet in my homeroom was a stack of eight games I had ordered with my supplies money the first week of the school year. When the games finally arrived—in January—I had been disappointed but shelved them to examine again later. Each game, called Budget, came in a sealed plastic bag. There were typographical mistakes in the directions, and just to begin to play, the kids had to master "purchase options" and "budget bonuses," savings certificates, and stock options. After spending more than an hour wrestling with the instructions, I decided that the financial rhetoric was too complicated—for me, let alone my students. It would take days to explain, if the kids ever sat still. And, how could I rationalize using such a game in classes where students did not know how to add, when the April citywide math test was less than three months away? Even with my watered-down approach, I had not yet gotten through even one-quarter of the curriculum. Shouldn't I be drilling and drilling and drilling? What would my supervisor think if she walked into my classroom and found us playing games?

In March, though, I decided the citywide math test be damned, it was time for drastic action. I had nothing to lose. By that point, I had given up on the old saws about a quiet class being an attentive class or one that was learning. My ability to keep the kids quiet was far from the ultimate indication of success. Except in my top class, lecturing was futile, as was assigning problems in class and going one-on-one around the room while students attempted to work them. There were just too many kids screaming for my attention. Perhaps playing Budget would reinvigorate us all.

The day I arrived in class 8-12 carrying eight copies of Budget, the kids looked as wild as ever. Tawana flaunted herself in a pair of skintight jeans and a revealing sky-blue polyester blouse; she carried the four-foot-long umbrella that she often pointed at the groin of any boy she disliked. Crystal, though quiet in the first row, was armed with her blue hairbrush. Sherwin, as usual, had his notebook out, but he was the only one in the room who was ready to work. Junior was arguing with Patrick, the boy who had told me the first week that he would make more money dealing drugs than I ever would as a teacher.

Deciding to break completely with tradition to get the kids' attention, I put no Aim on the board and no Do Now exercise. For the first time all year, I sat in a chair behind the teacher's desk at the front of the room and waited for the chaos in the room to subside. I smiled to myself at some of the whispered comments as the kids settled down.

"She's in labor."

"She had the baby."

"She's having the baby *right now!*"

"She's mad. Maybe we all failed the last test."

"I bet she's gonna tell us she ain't coming back after the baby comes."

"What's all them plastic boards on her desk?"

"I think we should get the school nurse. She's breathing funny."

"We better sit down. She ain't in no mood to play."

When the room was finally silent and the students at their desks, I stood up. "On my desk is a new activity," I said. "It's a game called Budget, and we are going to play it once a week until the end of the year."

A few kids clapped, and others cheered. "Allriiiiiiight," one boy said, "a gaaaaaaaame." For a change, no one looked bored. I explained an abbreviated version of the rules to give them just enough information to start—and divided the class into groups of four. The first good omen: no one complained that best friends had been split up. They quickly moved the desks into clusters, laying out the boards and putting the money in piles and sorting out all the other game cards—the savings and stock certificates and the mortgage statements.

Some of the most disorganized students in the class carefully sorted the money into piles of different denominations. Finally, everything was neatly lined up at the banker's desk for each cluster.

"How much money we get to start?" one student yelled.

"Who be going first?" asked a boy who had not participated in class all year.

"Okay, let's go over a few basics again," I said. "To decide who goes first, every player gets to spin the spinner. The person with the highest number goes first and then you go around the group, in a circle." The game suggested starting with $3,000, and together we worked out how many five hundreds, how many twenties, and so on, each student should have. I told the students to watch the chalkboard for other pertinent details.

In fifteen minutes, the room was abuzz. Almost immediately, kids had questions about all the financial jargon on the board, and we spent the first day trying to answer them all. How to decide whether to buy insurance? What if a down payment had been made on a house, and you then landed on the Apartment Rent spot? I told the kids to use common sense. "Why would a person who had a house need to rent an apartment also?"

"What happens if you don't buy medical insurance and you land on the spot, Surgery $500?" Crystal asked, her hairbrush forgotten. "Let's talk about what insurance is," I suggested, and we did. Crystal realized that any player without medical insurance would have to lay out the money. One student even asked about deductibles, and I gave a five-minute outline of deductibles and co-payments. Finally, here was a real-life example of percents that the kids seemed to understand. "If you have a $200 doctor's bill and a 50 percent copayment policy, how much money must you lay out and how much will the insurance company pay?" Students began to understand that each side—insurer and insured—had a $100 liability.

Especially fascinating to some kids were the stock-purchasing aspects of the game, leading to a discussion of what a stock dividend is and how it gets paid. They wanted to know whether they had enough money at home to buy stock, how to buy it, and if the value of their stock in the game would go up. This led us to stock appreciation and stock splits. They were so intrigued that we decided to set up a mock stock market game in our classroom in May and June.

Their comprehension and interest stimulated imaginative explorations. The banker of one group in 8-13 introduced some new rules of his own. He would allow cash-poor players to take out loans from his bank for a modest fee—for every $100 he lent them, they had to pay $5 each time they passed Go. The rules said nothing of such a role for the banker—his sole task was to make change—yet here was a student who had realized one of the benefits of capitalism. One player in his group had borrowed to buy a savings certificate, another to buy a house. Both found themselves better off. So had the banker, who waited impatiently to reap his next $5 bounty.

Students who had seemed catatonic were suddenly filled with energy. Those who had once refused to do simple calculations now wanted to be Budget banker. Some who could not calculate the change from a $10 bill for a chalkboard problem were learning how to make change with play money. They wanted to know how insurance works and why people buy life insurance and whether their parents should know about it. Where do banks get the money to pay interest, how do checking and savings accounts differ, payroll taxes, income taxes—their questions were wide-ranging and eager.

Beyond teaching the kids how to budget money, here was finally a way to teach about real things each one of them would have to deal with some day; in the process, they learned more math the one day each week we played Budget than they did the other three days combined. Kids who had struggled with addition and subtraction began to memorize simple facts—facts all my earlier efforts to teach, in traditional ways, never got across. In spite of its many rules, tedious terminology, and abstract concepts, Budget worked. Hands-on play had turned on the most turned-off kids.

Flush with the success from Budget, I searched for another game. In Grandma Gloria Holloway's big, well-stocked supply closet, I unearthed a game of bingo, which I soon adapted to simple math problems. Instead of calling a letter and a number, I called a letter and a math problem, whose answer was the number part of the puzzle—B/the square root of 25. The kids loved Math Bingo, especially when I provided small prizes, like a Hershey's kiss or a piece of butterscotch.

Yahtzee, a dice version of poker, required players to take chances on rolling certain desirable combinations—three-of-a-kind, a full house—in order to score points. It proved a valuable tool for helping the kids see permutations and combinations at work. Although the game does not require a mathematical knowledge of probability, a gross sense of the odds can certainly help you win. In each turn, a player has three rolls and should reroll only those dice most likely to help him win one of the required combinations. One very reserved girl, who had so far failed every test, was playing one day and rolled a 1-2-2-6-6. "Is it better to try for three sixes, or should I go for a full house?" she asked, immediately coming up with the right question. We looked at the options together and she let me stand right next to her, a hand on her shoulder. If she threw back the 1-2-2, she would have three chances to roll a 6, we decided. But if she gave back only the 1, she would have only one chance of rolling a 2 or a 6. We did not get into the other complications and probabilities, but her curiosity alone was a miraculous sign of hope.

Every game I tried was an instant hit with every class. I worried that perhaps this learning that seemed so real to me might be just an illusion. So, I decided to give a test to find out objectively whether the new approach was really working. Rather than questions about scientific notation or permutations and combinations, or converting fractions to percents and percents to decimals, I asked real-life questions like these:

■ *If you put $40 into a stock and it doubles in value, how much money will you have?*
If you want to buy a $50 stock and you have to pay a 10%

commission, how much will you spend for the stock and the commission altogether?

If you have rolled four 3s and you have one more chance to roll one last die, discuss the odds that you will get a Yahtzee (five 3s).

If you have a $10,000 loan on a house and you have to spend 10% per year on interest payments, how much money will you be paying out each year in interest?

If I call "B/the square root of 81" during a bingo game, what spot on the board do I want you to cover?

In my four lower sections, including 8-16, the average score was just over 80, by far the highest we had had all year. Reginald, the math whiz who still struggled to read, earned a perfect mark, although I had to read him the problems. Some students who had consistently failed my tests also earned 100s. It seemed almost impossible, but my students were suddenly hungry to learn.

I was no less exhausted after a game period than after lecturing or doing problems. But my dignity was intact, and the students had never looked happier. Why, I couldn't help wondering, hadn't the Board of Ed armed me with a games strategy from the start?

In early May, I assigned an essay asking all my students to describe what they had learned playing Budget. Sadly, some who had learned most were still unable to communicate their newfound knowledge because their writing skills remained so poor. As a group, though, the essays told me what I most wanted to hear—that they felt they had learned about both life and math in the playing. It was the first real evidence I had that I could reach—and teach—not just individual students or classes, but all my kids.

Marieann, a strong student from 8-13, the class with the innovative banker, wrote:

From the game budget I learn when you borrow money from the bank you have to pay more than you borrow.

The game had inspired great visions in Hieu, one of the brightest students I taught and the boy who had come up with the new banking rules and roles.

One of the things I learn about this game is how to manage a bank.

Tasheema, her essay gaily decorated with colorful thank-you stickers, wrote:

> *The game budget is a very interesting game it really does help children our ages to learn about the real world. And what good things are being given to us. I think that budget will help me when I grow up. And thanks for teaching me the values of money.*

Some kids, like Prairie, were simply thrilled to succeed at something in math class. She wrote:

> *This is what I learned from the game budget. Frist of all I did't know a game could thaugh you so much of about life. I leaned how to buy stuff that I needed. It also gave me alot of ideas in how to invest in my money. Best thing I liked about the game was when I got Rich.*

We had talked about how to lose at a game like Budget, and how to win. The students shook hands with one another when the game was over each day, and soon discovered that gloating was out since this week's winner could be next week's loser. Two boys even brought ties and wore them when they were the bankers. Steve wrote: "What I learned in budget. 1. I learned how to handle 2. how to be smart in the real world 3. how to trade when to buy 4. I saw how Wall Street work 5. how to be a good sport."

By any measure, Budget had been a success. The kids had learned some math and some social studies and were genuinely excited about coming to school. That excitement turned into painless, measurable learning. I wondered why more teachers didn't use games and similar materials, why the Board of Ed had not introduced a curriculum more sensible—and sensory—than the gobbledygook of the Scope and Sequence.

When the year was over, I discovered that the board had indeed created dozens of useful manuals for teaching math—including some that offered detailed lesson plans for every topic to be covered in several of the grades. Why weren't these valuable resources available at Whitman? The frustrating answer: the board charged local school districts a fee to use them. In the other two middle-school grades—six and seven—the board had created a curriculum called CIMS

(Comprehensive Instruction Management System). Every topic in it was accompanied by lesson plans, which included ideas for games, hands-on activities, worksheets, and tests. There was also a workbook, which, to use the program effectively, every student needed. But the workbooks cost $2.50 each, and districts that didn't want to foot the bill didn't get them. The same was true of the manual that guided teachers in implementing CIMS; each manual was priced at $18.

"Everyone working here in curriculum development feels we should be able to give out these materials free," Jerry Haber, acting assistant director of mathematics for the city, explained. "Unfortunately, right now we're not capable of doing that. We just don't have the money."

"But I was using expensive textbooks that were outdated and useless," I protested. "And you're telling me that for the price of replacing fifteen of them, I could have had a workbook for every kid and an instructional manual for myself and I could have used the seventh-grade CIMS program?"

"Ah, but you were teaching eighth grade, and we don't have an eighth-grade version of CIMS," Haber retorted.

"But the seventh-grade version would have made more sense to four of my five classes than the crazy stuff I was supposed to teach them."

Haber nodded. "Yes," he acknowledged, "things are screwed up."

The board's math curriculum division had virtually no contact with teachers. When I visited the division four months after my year at Whitman had ended, I found a manual on the use of games in math classes, which I had never seen before. Although "Exploring Mathematics Through Games" discussed only six games—most played with toothpicks—it might have encouraged me, had I read it, to try something new much earlier than I did. Why hadn't they told us about any of a dozen other materials available from the Board of Education, all of which might have helped those like me be better teachers—curriculum guides, sample lesson plans, lists of useful hands-on materials, complete with discussions for classroom use?

And why had I never seen the seventh-grade Scope and Sequence? Because I was an eighth-grade teacher who could make no use of seventh-grade materials? Because my students had supposedly mastered the seventh-grade material? Why wasn't there a version of CIMS for the eighth grade? Or a more detailed version of the Scope and Sequence, with lesson-plan ideas?

"We're hoping to do one this year for the eighth grade," Susan Zakaluk, director of mathematics for the New York City public schools, told me. "As for why you never saw one for the other grades, did you ever ask?"

"For something I didn't know existed?"

"You could have gone to one of the teacher centers," she said.

"The what?"

In several boroughs, including Brooklyn, she elaborated, the board and the teachers union jointly operate centers at which teachers may borrow materials, review textbooks and curricula, watch videotapes, and "network." The people who work at these centers, "very often act as consultants," Zakaluk said, "making visits to schools to do model lessons."

"Why on earth don't you tell teachers about these places?" I asked. "How would a new teacher like me know?" She had no answer. "Why didn't one of the people from these centers visit my school?" I asked. Again, she didn't respond.

The teachers union, too, apparently offered helpful programs— workshops throughout the year on how to teach math, how to control chaotic classrooms, how to write innovative lesson plans. But I was unaware of these programs, too, until the year was nearly over and a friend who works in the public relations office of the union mentioned them. What did "regular" teachers do? Perhaps I had overlooked these resources in all the papers, memos, and bureaucratic directives that both Whitman and the Board of Education had deluged me with. So I reexamined every piece of paper I had received since I began teaching. There was no mention of teacher centers or union-sponsored workshops, only memos from the Whitman administration detailing procedures for recording grades and making timely entries on attendance records.

"The curriculum you were given is premised upon the student entering junior high with some mastery of elementary school mathematics. It also assumes that students will continue the study of math in high school," reasoned Bruce Vogeli, professor of mathematics at Columbia University's Teachers College, which, for more than one hundred years, has been one of the great innovative forces in American education. "Probably neither of these assumptions was reasonable for your classes."

The author of 150 math textbooks used by 10 million students nationwide, Vogeli said he endorsed my decision to "toss the curriculum out the window." But, he added, "in a minimum competency environment where kids are tested at various intervals, you might have been in trouble." My students probably would not have passed such tests, he said. Vogeli was right. They had not done well on the annual standardized test, although statistically they had done no worse than the Whitman average.

How might I have taught the curriculum more effectively? I asked him. With geometry topics, he suggested, exercises in carpentry and drafting are useful. "If you start a mathematics classroom by drawing a transversal cutting parallel lines, you'll blow the non-mathematically-oriented student completely off the road." I had done exactly that. The casualties—the bored faces of confused students—were all over my classrooms. "If you give them some cardboard and scissors and pose a problem in which the construction of something interesting is required, you'll have a better shot. Then you quietly mention which angles are alternate interior angles and which are supplementary angles, and you don't worry whether the students master the vocabulary—you worry about mastering the math problem at hand.

"You can teach almost any topic from the junior high curriculum to any group," Vogeli believes, "if you do it in a way that is extremely graphic and concrete and experiential rather than expository. But teachers are not always good at that, and it takes a tremendous amount of time to prepare and execute the lessons. And, if you teach that way, the curriculum moves very slowly; you won't get through more than half of it. You're caught between a rock and a hard place. If you teach it right, you're never going to cover everything. You have to speed it up, which usually means you have to teach it wrong."

Vogeli was uncertain, in any case, whether the curriculum I was given should be taught to bottom students, even with such hands-on techniques. "If kids don't have basic skills, which comes first: understanding what an alternate interior angle is, or mastering commercially relevant survival skills that will allow a kid to earn a living?"

All the months that I had spent trying to teach kids decimals and percents by having them convert numbers back and forth were wasted, according to Vogeli. "It means nothing to a kid to change a percent to a decimal and multiply. Instead, you have to buy a few packs of Monopoly money and have the kids play the roles of storekeeper, salesperson, and customer. Give them practical problems, say 'This $100 dress is 30% off.' See if they can figure out how much to give the shopkeeper. You build an informal understanding that rather than handing over $100, they'll hand over $70 instead. Then they can go on to a formal understanding." I had been miffed months before when my academic background, work experience, and sheer enthusiasm had been insufficient for the Board of Ed. Now, I could see they had a point. Teacher training *is* critical.

In the absence of formal education training, it would have been enormously helpful for me to have talked to Vogeli or someone like him before I entered Whitman. And Vogeli, I reflected, could teach the bureaucrats at the Board of Education a thing or two as well, though he said he had never been approached by them. Perhaps an entire curriculum framed around such ideas could really have helped my kids, rather than the random attempts I'd made to use practical examples.

A colleague of Vogeli's, Frances Bolin, directed a program in elementary education at Teachers College when I spoke with her in November 1989. She agreed that the curriculum sounded irrelevant and the training I received too cursory to be effective. "The moral thing to do when teaching is to begin where the children are, and not a step above. But we get pressured by circumstances, and we have to make compromises that are often devastating for students. We decide to cram it all in to make up for the deficient earlier years, and we leave them even more confused.

"Here are kids who don't understand the concept of a number, and we're going to make them learn how to multiply? It doesn't make sense. How can a kid who doesn't understand what it means to multiply understand something as complex as scientific notation?"

According to Bolin, the whole focus of the city schools should change. "We have this notion that teaching is standing up in front of a group of young people and delivering the material, and either they get it or they don't. That just won't work anymore. The kids aren't getting it. We know that, and we have to make changes."

When I returned to the Board of Ed to hear Susan Zakaluk's responses to these professionals, I found that she stood solidly behind her curriculum. To make it work, she said, I should have required the students to write in "learning journals." Zakaluk used a good deal of educational jargon when she spoke. "Articulation is a very important part of the processing of information," she said. "Journals can be extremely beneficial in increasing the students' retention of the material they study."

"What if the kids can't write?" I asked.

"This is not easy and requires a lot of development and persistence. You don't assume that they know how to write. You have to do a lot of modeling and a lot of discussion of how and why it will help them. It isn't a simple solution."

What should the kids write about? "It should be in response to the prompt, 'Today I learned how to . . .' Then, when they are able to do this, you get them to respond to another prompt, 'One question I have about what I learned today is . . .' " On and on she went, detailing all of the prompts to which my students could respond.

"I don't mean to be critical," I replied, "but that approach seems totally out of touch with the level of the kids I was working with. It seems so forced."

Precisely because the children had trouble with it, she said, I should have been doing it. And journal-writing, she added, is effective in all disciplines.

A fourteen-year veteran of four high schools, in teaching and administrative posts, Zakaluk had never taught junior high school. In her three years as a math curriculum director for the Board of Ed, she had visited only twenty or so junior high classrooms.

"Do you think there's any chance that you're out of touch with what's going on in most of the city's schools—like the one where I was teaching?"

She answered with an emphatic "no" and began firing more ideas at me for better teaching. "You might have tried collaborative groups," she said. "Pose a problem and team four or five students together. Give them a clear and structured timetable to solve the problem—say, how do we convert the fraction ½ into a decimal and a percent? Maybe one student can articulate how it's done and another can convert that articulation into a journal entry in response to a prompt."

I wasn't trying to be contentious, I told her, but in most of my classrooms, teaming kids yielded arguments and card-playing, not excitement about fraction conversions. My only success with group learning, I told her, had been the playing of Budget and some other games. She acted surprised. "Really? Collaborative learning groups usually work well across all topics of a curriculum."

What about scientific notation for kids in the eighth grade who couldn't multiply and didn't understand how to give change?

"Scientific notation is there because they need it for science, to prepare them for more advanced work in high school with exponents. But, with a class like the one you had, one of the most important benefits you can get is to reinforce place value."

"Why should I be reinforcing place value?" I asked.

"For the kids to build up to an understanding of scientific notation and its use in the world."

Zakaluk had moved fairly quickly from teaching to administration; I asked her why. "Because I felt I had so much to contribute. Training teacher trainers, working with districts in implementation of curricula, things like that."

I left her office armed with a spate of paper. There were books with titles like, *Essential Learning Outcomes—Mathematics* and *Compilation of Resource Materials for Staff Development—Mathematics Instruction in the Middle Schools, Grade 7.*

I hoped Susan Zakaluk might one day have the opportunity to follow her own advice and ask a class of eighth-graders reading on a third-grade level to write an entry in a learning journal after her lecture on converting 0.4×10^6 to 4×10^5. Just how would she help Pedro and Reginald and Shereeza and Jimmy?

19

Second Chances

I ask a principal, "Would you want this teacher teaching YOUR children?" If not, then don't put him in a classroom with somebody else's.

—James Stein, director, Office of Appeals and Reviews, New York City Board of Education, on why principals should bring disciplinary charges against incompetent, morally deficient, or vengeful teachers.

In my more miserable moods at Whitman, I was tempted to blame failure—mine to teach, the kids' to learn—on the kids and their parents. Too many times, students had disrupted my classes, spoken back to me, and spurned my desperate attempts to entertain and teach them. The parents of many were too busy, too tired, or perhaps too inexperienced in the demands of raising children to discipline and inspire them. However, as the year unfolded, I saw that others were sometimes as much to blame for the kids' failures in school as the kids and the parents themselves. Unhappily, some of my own colleagues. Equally dismaying, I noticed that the Whitman administration seemed unwilling to dismiss, or even attempt to improve, the worst teachers—those too burned out to be effective, too irresponsible to show up on time, unable to teach competently or treat the kids fairly. Poor teaching was condoned rather than punished.

When I had covered the Board of Ed as a reporter, I visited several principals who took seriously the cumbersome and uncomfortable task of weeding out the worst teachers. But such administrators were apparently rare. It was true that the system urgently needed warm bodies to staff classrooms, yet that seemed an inadequate excuse for allowing rank incompetence in the schools; my hiring was itself somewhat awkward proof of that.

During my year at Whitman, I came across far too many teachers I would not want teaching my kids. Some, unable to control their tempers, would fling students out of the classroom in fits of rage. Students were wounded, emotionally and physically, by such acts of uncontrolled aggression. Some teachers' attitudes toward the children were plainly hostile: one at Whitman used to say, "Aren't they disgusting, the little twirps?" or so-and-so is "worthless," "a stupid piece of slime," or "an ignorant bastard." Other teachers simply lacked sufficient knowledge of their subject areas, could not spell, or were disorganized or lazy.

Yet even those who performed most appallingly the year I taught at Whitman earned a Satisfactory performance rating; every one was still working there the next year.

What kind of school system would tolerate such dismal performances? Surely, there had to be ways to weed out the very worst.

When my teaching year was over, I spoke for several hours with James Stein, whose office at the Board of Ed is responsible for helping principals get rid of bad teachers and helping local school boards discard ill-performing principals. As director of the Office of Appeals and Reviews for the board, Stein's job was to provide technical assistance to administrators in documenting cases against teachers for incompetence, moral turpitude, or use of corporal punishment (illegal in New York State). I also spoke to several union leaders, including Randy Weingarten, counsel to United Federation of Teachers president Sandra Feldman. And I discussed the subject of accountability in the city school system with Winfield. Stein had no difficulty digging up dozens of cases that showed the incompetence, cruelty, or irresponsibility of teachers. The shock was how infrequently a dismissal was attempted and how unlikely it was to succeed.

A first-grade teacher—enraged by her students—removed her high-heeled shoe and used it to strike a boy repeatedly on the head. A ten-year veteran when the May 1987 case was filed, she then stalked twenty feet across the room and hit another seven-year-old boy on the head with her shoe. Both boys were so badly bruised and bloodied they required hospital treatment and multiple stitches to close the wounds.

The Board of Education sought to have her fired, but a three-man panel convened to hear the charges found that penalty needlessly harsh. The panel reported:

> *First, Respondent did not intend to inflict harm. . . . She wanted the students to refrain from disrupting the educational problem* [sic]. *She did not seek to injure. . . . Second, while Respondent struck two students sitting at opposite ends of the room, her actions were part of a single event. . . . Third, we found Respondent to be genuinely contrite as to the inappropriateness of what she had done. It would be unduly harsh to discharge a ten-year teacher with an otherwise unblemished record for having "lost her cool" for a few moments on a single day.*

She was suspended instead without pay for fifteen months and was to return to teaching in the city school system in January 1990.

The statistics were eye-opening. During the 1988–89 school year, out of roughly 62,000 teachers, only 606—fewer than 1 percent—were rated Unsatisfactory by their principals. The remaining teachers received Satisfactory ratings, including the vast majority of those who had not yet been granted tenure, which is awarded after three years of probation.

"In a school system where 99 percent of the teachers are satisfactory," Stein said, "there is no accountability and no need for a rating system. Nowhere in the world, in no work force of which I am aware, does the percentage of satisfactory ratings come close to the percentage we have at the Board of Education. Therefore, we must conclude that the current system is meaningless."

Weingarten agreed. "The Board of Education does not train people how to observe and evaluate or how to manage."

In the eleven-year period between 1979 and 1990, the Board of Ed tried to fire only 104 tenured teachers for incompetence; in only 19 cases was the effort successful. Although more than half the teachers brought up on charges resigned or took early retirement during the proceedings, 37 were found guilty, yet were not dismissed. They received fines or suspensions, and all were allowed to return to teaching.

The year I taught—1988–89—the Board of Education succeeded in firing only three tenured teachers. At any one time, the board was likely to be dealing with only a handful of cases of incompetent teaching, perhaps the most insidious problem because it is so hard to prove and, therefore, to punish. In March 1990, the board was handling only 29 cases of incompetence.

More alarming were statistics on physical assaults on children. During the 1988–89 school year, Stein's office took reports of 778 incidents of corporal punishment (the catch-all title for any physical striking of a child). Yet the board was no more likely to succeed in dismissing teachers accused of this than those charged with lesser offenses. During the eleven-year period in which Stein had maintained records, the board had attempted to have 65 tenured teachers fired for striking children. Of those, 11 were dismissed, 31 received penalties such as fines or suspensions, and 23 resigned or retired.

Principals were even less likely to receive unfavorable reviews. During the year I taught, only one principal out of nearly 1,000 citywide was rated Unsatisfactory. In the previous 10 years, only 18 had received U ratings. And in the same decade, only 5 principals were denied tenure.

"Is that because everyone's doing such a great job?" I asked Stein.

"No," he said. "It's because supervision and accountability are nonexistent in New York City schools."

There are three ways, increasingly harsh, to discipline unfit teachers. A principal may give an Unsatisfactory rating at the end of the school year. Or, a principal may let a teacher go during his three-year probation or recommend that tenure be denied when the probation period has expired. Third, a principal may initiate proceedings to have a tenured teacher fired. But Stein's statistics (and my own experience at Whitman) suggest that these sanctions are not used nearly as often as they might be. Students are not getting the quality education to which they are entitled, and inadequate teachers are degrading the professional honor of the vast majority of their colleagues who are dedicated and competent. "We will not solve these problems," Stein said, "until we resolve whether we are a keeper of the public trust or merely an employment agency."

A floundering teacher should certainly receive warning that he or she is in trouble. Yet, a principal's most effective tool—and often the first or only—is the yearly rating. Supervisors are supposed to observe teachers in the classroom throughout the year, and find buddies or mentors for those who need help. They are also supposed to complete reports and arrange conferences with teachers to discuss their performance. Uncorrected difficulties are to be noted in each teacher's file to substantiate the yearly rating.

Each teacher who works twenty days or more each year is evaluated by his or her principal. Except for the rarely used rating of D (for Doubtful), there are only two categories: Satisfactory and Unsatisfactory. Teachers are supposed to be judged on Personal and Professional Qualities, Pupil Guidance and Instruction, Classroom or Shop Management, and Participation in School and Community Activities. At the bottom of the evaluation form, one composite rating is called for—S or U.

A U rating, I assumed before speaking to Stein, would lead to dismissal. In practice, a U has little effect on a teacher's long-term prospects in the system. In the short term, the teacher's salary may be frozen, but only if he has not reached the maximum salary. At the maximum level, a U-rated teacher continues to receive those increases mandated by collective bargaining agreements, but may be required by the principal to take a three-credit education course. Such a teacher will not, however, lose his benefits, his license, or his job. Some teachers receive U ratings year after year and continue to teach; one teacher received nine in a row, Stein told me.

The greatest impediment to giving U ratings is the fact that the principal who gives one may not transfer a U-rated teacher out of his school for three years. Said Stein: "There are principals who say to teachers, 'You should be getting a U but I'll give you an S if you'll agree to get out of here.' It's like a game of Old Maid."

A tenured teacher receiving a U has the automatic right to appeal to the Chancellor for a final decision. The union provides these teachers with legal representation.

Since teachers with tenure are so difficult to dismiss, a principal's most potent weapon is usually the tenure review, which follows the mandated three-year probation. Any teacher granted tenure is allowed to stay in his "home" school for life, unless a principal subsequently brings disciplinary charges against him. "Once you've got tenure," observed Stein, "you've got a suit of armor around you."

Faced with the prospect of having an ineffective teacher around forever, principals might well be stringent in their tenure reviews. Yet, tenure is rarely denied. In the 1988–89 school year, only 10 teachers of the 7,000 reviewed were refused tenure. Another 32 were dismissed during their probationary period. An elementary or junior high teacher who is, in the parlance, "discontinued," is free to seek work in any other district, though a high school teacher so branded may no longer teach in any of the city's high schools. As with the U ratings, teachers denied tenure are entitled to an automatic review by the schools chancellor.

Termination can result from the intricate process by which local school districts, with the help of Stein's office at the Board of Ed, try to remove teachers. The process is fairly simple for nontenured teachers. Charges drawn up by a Board of Education lawyer, with Stein's help, are presented to a single hearing officer who makes a recommendation to the chancellor. During the 1988–89 school year, 20 nontenured teachers were brought up on charges. As of March 1990 three had been fired; the other cases were still pending.

With tenured teachers, however, the process is cumbersome and strewn with obstacles for administrators. The paperwork requirements alone make building a case extremely difficult. As in any legal proceeding, a school's administration must keep copious notes of wrongdoing as evidence and must enter timely letters in a teacher's personnel file noting the problems and the administration's efforts to rectify them. Every time such a letter is drafted, the teacher, with union representation, may fight its inclusion in his file. Teachers whose schools have effective union leadership are often able to quash these letters completely, leaving an administration without the necessary written evidence.

Even with the letters, building a case is difficult because of severe timing constraints. In junior high and elementary schools, evidence more than six months old may not be presented at the time the local school board votes to bring charges. Thus, if a teacher with a history of losing his temper whacks a kid, say, every seven months, only the most recent incident may be considered. In the high schools, the time limitation is three years.

In a school overwhelmed with problems, where administrators are saddled with an unending stream of nonacademic chores, there often is not enough time to document a case sufficiently to warrant disciplinary proceedings, my supervisor, Vikki Kowalski, said. "Even if a teacher smacks a kid, there are letters, conferences, a whole dragout routine. It's like bringing a criminal to trial. The whole year goes by in just a few simple proceedings. What principal would think it's worth it? Not one already up to his ears in problems like school intruders who have to be dealt with right away."

Even when charges are brought, the chances that a teacher will be fired are slim, mostly because of the way the cases are adjudicated. One member of the review panel is actually designated by the teacher, and is usually another teacher. A second is a designee of the Board of Education, usually an administrator. The third member is an arbitrator agreed to by the other two representatives. In almost every case, a teacher is found guilty of at least some of the charges, frequently of them all. However, the arbitrators virtually never vote to fire the teachers. "We get convictions," Stein remarked wryly, "but rarely terminations."

For good reason, the UFT's Weingarten adds. "We're simply better at defending teachers than the board is at prosecuting them. Is that the union's fault? That's the least we owe our members."

Stein offered a different view. "Arbitrators are afraid to fire teachers. They think it's like leveling the death penalty. That's because they're not educators themselves. The whole problem with this type of adjudication is that we have lawyers, not educators, ruling on the competence of teachers. It would be like having engineers judge doctors or lawyers." A panel's ruling is binding, but either side may appeal to the state Commissioner of Education or the courts.

Prior to 1979, it was much easier to fire a teacher in New York City. Once a panel reviewed the file, its findings were forwarded as recommendations to the Board of Education, which ultimately decided the case. The new system, which became law in 1979, is both time-consuming and costly. The Board of Education spends $33,000 a day in salaries (as of March 1990) to suspended teachers awaiting decisions. Once the Board of Ed or a local district brings charges, a teacher is removed from all classroom duties, but continues to collect his salary. Through 1989, the typical case took thirteen to fifteen months to prosecute, because the Board of Education had only five lawyers to handle the cases and poorly paid arbitrators often refused to schedule timely hearings. An expedited hearing system was implemented in early 1990 and was expected within several years to shorten the process.

The sad reality at Whitman was that even when administrators knew of real teaching incompetence and even when particularly disturbing episodes were actually documented, there was virtually no follow-up. One spring afternoon, one student stripped another from the waist down, yet their teacher neither reported the incident promptly nor sought help in controlling the children. Even with a strong and explicit letter of reprimand from an administrator in his file, the teacher got a Satisfactory rating and returned to Whitman for the new school year. Had the administration sought dismissal any time after November 1989, the statute of limitations would have prevented use of the "stripping" incident as evidence.

Justifications are many for an administration's reluctance to give U ratings, deny tenure, or bring tenured teachers up on disciplinary charges, I learned from Stein, the union representatives, Winfield, and my own supervisor, Kowalski.

What surprised me most, however, was Winfield's candid assessment of his own staff: many, he told me, did not meet his expectations. Twenty percent "are giving what I ask for," he admitted, and another 10 percent "are making an effort, they are trying."

"Why don't you at least get rid of the very worst?" I asked.

He paused for a long time before answering. "Is it right to take away someone's livelihood? Don't we have the responsibility to try to turn that person into a decent teacher? And is it fair to the teacher if the administration doesn't have time to help him improve?" He also offered a pragmatic view, one that was particularly understandable given the high staff turnover rate at Whitman. "I know what I've got, but I don't know what I'd be getting."

"But is it fair to the students to let an incompetent teacher stand at the head of the class?" I countered. "You and I both know that the parents of these kids aren't going to fight for decent teachers. The administration must assume that role."

"Is it so obvious just when and where to draw the line? Should I have dismissed you because you were struggling as a new teacher?" Winfield asked. "Today, it's okay for you to be struggling to teach because you're new, but tomorrow, you'd better know what you're doing?"

I had to admit that in the early months when some of my classes were often out of control, I probably would not have met a demanding administrator's standards of competence. By the end of the year, however, I had improved greatly and was on the road, I thought, to becoming a decent teacher. To be fired just as I was making great strides would indeed have been a real blow. Yet, surely there is a difference between a struggling rookie and a tenured veteran who fails to maintain a certain level of competence with experience.

Stein understood Winfield's predicament, but suggested another, more political, reason for some principals' hesitancy. "Many are afraid of the teachers union and they're reluctant to spend time on documentation. They see no point in giving U ratings because they know it does not automatically remove a teacher. As for the principals, the superintendents who evaluate them are often at the mercy of the school boards who hire them. If the principal got his job because he was a friend of someone on the school board, you might well infer that the superintendent is going to be reluctant to risk his position to have that principal fired." In school district 27 in southeastern Queens, criminal charges were brought in the fall of 1989 against two school board members who, it was alleged, were using the district as a patronage mill.

Union officials with whom I spoke insisted that they did not want incompetent teachers working in the schools. "But our members are entitled to legal counsel and to due process," said UFT communications director Bert Shanas. He and Weingarten described a new peer intervention program, begun in 1988, intended to weed out the very worst teachers. In its first year, the program counseled fifty-seven teachers who voluntarily sought help. About half had already received U ratings; a dozen others had been warned that they would if they didn't improve. Twenty-one of those U-rated teachers improved sufficiently under stricter scrutiny to earn an S rating the following year.

"We agree that incompetent teachers demoralize everyone," Weingarten said. "The bottom line is teachers need more help all along the way. More mentors, more buddies, more training to reach their potential."

In Stein's office, I examined the public records of teachers convicted of serious charges. Many reports dated from the mid-eighties; the most recent detailed episodes from 1986 and 1987 that had, by 1989, still not been decided. Records of pending cases, or those in which teachers were found to be innocent, were sealed by law, but what was available for scrutiny offered a picture of the kinds of cases that came to trial and their outcomes.

There were teachers who, like me, had been extremely frustrated, but who had lost control and physically lashed out at their students. Others offered only disorganized lessons that rambled with inaccurate, often confusing, information.

For every case I read, there were clearly many others that had never been pursued. The suspiciously small number of incompetence cases ratified Stein's words about the lack of supervisory accountability. "The tragedies in this system are not the isolated guy who flashes his private parts or tries to seduce a young student, but the professional sleaze—the man or woman who simply can't teach, who has no spirit," Stein said. "That's what's killing us."

Though Stein's office is overwhelmed with pending cases, the Board of Ed had not allocated funds for more personnel to prepare them. Instead, he said, "The system is clogged with cases of corporal punishment, moral turpitude and other headline-grabbing crimes. Because we're so short of staff, those cases reduce our means to deal with the incompetents."

Sometimes, even the kids expressed indignation at how little they were learning. In one remarkable instance, they took matters in hand, organizing a letter-writing campaign to then-Mayor Ed Koch. Their high school history teacher had a habit of presenting arcane material and disorganized lessons that, to his supervisors, seemed less a rendering of the curriculum than of personal political attitudes.

"Dear Mr. Mayer," one letter began, continuing:

> I would Like for my social studies class to make some changes first of all when I be coming to school the door be locked up I can't get in the class after a long hour of ride in the train I have to stand outside in the hall way doing nothing. Mr.——— is usually late when all of the classes be working we don't be doing anything. He just writes things on the board and make us copy it. he be blowing his nose in the garbage can. When he ask us a question he excpect an answer write away. before he finish saying waht he have to say. He let this girl in the class take attendance and marked me absent twice when I was here. Thank you.

"I will like to tell you about my Social Studies teacher Mr. ———," another student wrote.

> I never learn anything in his class I get a good grade for doing a little bit of work He always comes late and when he do come he spit and blow his nose in the garbage. I will like to tell you more but I want to tell you face to face. Thank you.

Another complaint read:

> Dear Mr. Mayor Everytime we come to school Mr.——— is never in. He do not teach us enough for us to get an education.

*He don't even let us ask him questions? Now me and my class
mate's will like to have something done about it so that we can
learn something. P.S. Please change my class.*

The Board of Education, in 1987, sought to fire this high school
social studies teacher, who had been recently tenured. The charges
ranged from insubordination to incompetence to chronic lateness
and absence. In September 1988, the three-person panel ruled that,
although he was guilty of most of the charges, he would not be fired.
Instead, he would be suspended without pay for eighteen months
and allowed to return to teaching in the spring of 1990.

The panel was convinced that the teacher had serious difficulties
in the classroom. The chairman wrote:

*Mr.——— needs work on organizing his thought processes. His
analysis is foggy, and this leads him to teach in a disjointed
and disorganized manner. His lesson plans bear evidence of
this fact, as well. His refusal to accept this is indeed disturbing.
. . . For instance, Respondent's use of a McDonald's franchise
to illustrate colonialism was incorrect.*

The panel pointed out numerous erroneous statements made by
the teacher to his students, though none, in their judgment, was
egregious enough to justify discharging him.

The main argument the panel offered in his defense was the
administration's failure to help him sufficiently in the classroom. "I
cannot hold that ——— is beyond remediation, given my conclusion
that no meaningful efforts to help him have yet been made," the
panel chairman wrote. The administrator's frequent observations of
the teacher were "sudden and relentless," the panel wrote. They
"could well have caused him to lose both his confidence and his
vitality."

The teacher returned to the classroom in February 1990, and,
following a common practice at the Board of Ed, he was allowed a
fresh start at a new school.

In another case, the hearing panel did not fault the school's administration, yet still refused to fire the teacher. The case involved a
tenured high school math teacher against whom charges were
brought in June 1988. The litany of charges filled hundreds of pages
in the hearing file. The teacher had failed to prepare his students
adequately for Regents exams, let them play with yo-yos and cards
during class, had given incorrect explanations for math problems,

and given homework assignments of more than 100 problems several times in a week.

One day, he spent half an hour reviewing the single algebraic equation $2x = 12$, although the problem was well below the level of the class he was teaching. On other days, he spent the entire class time on the Do Now problem, which is supposed to be introduced and reviewed in the first five minutes. He required no notetaking, spent most of each class introducing and defining formulas, and followed no meaningful progression through the course syllabus. Jumping from topic to topic, he confused his students and often, the board alleged, himself as well. He also was chronically absent—forty-two times between September 1985 and June 1987.

Class observers found students sleeping in his classes. Attendance was poor, often with no more than half the students present. Many parents had asked that their children be transferred out of his classes. Despite all this, the panel majority found he had "potential" and in December 1989 ordered but a six-month suspension without pay after which he would be reassigned to a new school.

While he has displayed incompetent service on numerous occasions, the panel is convinced Respondent can be an effective teacher. . . . 1. When Respondent wants to, he can teach effectively. 2. He has subject-matter knowledge to be a good teacher. 3. Although stubborn, he now knows he must follow rules.

There was a strenuous dissent by the Board of Ed's member on the panel.

His teaching is like his lesson plans—confused, unrelated to what came before or what comes after, messy, abstracted. . . . He is incapable of changing. His attitude toward authority and his apparent personality needs diminish his capacity to learn as shown by his failure to listen to suggestions, to interact with the suggestors, or to modify his behavior except in a most insulting manner.

Stein was particularly disturbed by this case, commenting, "We've accepted mediocrity as the standard. To have people like this man in our schools is a sin."

Even physical abuse wasn't enough to get a teacher expelled from the school system. In several cases in which the panels found teachers guilty, they ruled that termination was "not warranted."

One case involved a junior high teacher whose special-ed classes had no more than five kids. One day in January 1988, he grabbed a boy around the neck, then struck, choked, and scratched him. The panel said the student was "an aggressive young man. He previously had been suspended from school for fighting and was institutionalized because, in his own words, he 'cannot control his impulses.' His Individual Education Plan reports an 'antisocial' veneer and a psychological evaluation describes him as 'oppositional and aggressive.' "

"I am going to kill you," he had threatened the teacher earlier that January. On other occasions, too, he had exploded at the teacher, shouting, "I'm not going to stay in this fucking shop, you motherfucker." He had also kicked another student in the face, been arrested for assault, and suspended from school more than five times.

The teacher had been warned repeatedly not to use physical force in the classroom. The panel ruled:

> The use of excessive force in this case was misconduct of a most serious nature. He had been warned just two weeks earlier to keep his hands off students. . . . It was precisely because his students had attitude and behavior problems that he was never given more than five per class. That day, there were just three. It was one of his obligations to try to avoid a physical encounter, and if one occurred, to try to contain it. . . . He did neither.

In February 1990, the panel ordered a two-month suspension without pay and added a warning: "Any wrongful touching of a student henceforth may reasonably be expected to result in his dismissal from service."

By any definition, the case against a tenured Brooklyn science teacher was bizarre. When he stopped taking his lithium medication, he exhibited what was termed as "obscene, abusive, insubordinate and unprofessional behavior." Over a period of several days, having decided on his own to stop taking his medication, he told teachers that a carved stone he possessed could smash a face in. He then banged the stone on a table and a windowsill. Over the next few days, he called another teacher a "fat, ugly piece of shit" and accused someone else of wanting a "fucking Fascist school." A third teacher was a "racist," a fourth a "twitch-faced, wimp fuck." When the principal and assistant principal came to investigate, he called them "the two shitheads" who "stand with their hands in their pockets, wear fucking ties and don't do anything." The principal, a "shithead," an "asshole," and a "prick," was unfit to "administer a shithouse."

The name-calling continued in his classroom. He told one student who had brought his sister to class to "Get that piece of shit out of here." He called several of his homeroom students "assholes" and "shitheads." He read to the class a letter written by the school's principal. "They can kiss my ass," he said to the kids of the school's administrators. He told another student that his mother had had no right to come to the United States; he told his students that many people had "shit in their blood," and that he, a biology teacher, could prove it.

The Board of Ed sought to have him fired. He would not promise to take his lithium regularly, the board maintained, and he had used poor judgment in deciding, on his own, to discontinue it without his doctor's knowledge. When he was off the drug, they argued, he was in a manic state. He had himself acknowledged that he could not control his actions unless he was taking the drug. And unlike many lithium users who function reliably and responsibly, he had a long history of acting improperly in school.

The panel was unanimous in finding him responsible for forty-two separate violent attacks, verbal and physical, on others. But, the panel chairman wrote:

> *We conclude that Respondent's behavior, even if unusual and bizarre, should not prevent his return to teaching duties. It is clear that these were isolated incidents.*

After the panel decided on a $2,000 fine rather than termination, the Board of Education's delegate filed a strenuous dissent.

> *Public schools require the attendance of students and staff and our service to children in these schools is a serious public trust. We have no right to expose them to a known risk just to allow this teacher's continued employment.*

He is now teaching at a high school in Queens.

By any measure, a special-education teacher whom the board sought to fire took a rather unusual approach to teaching at another Queens high school during the 1986–87 school year. In November, he allegedly told a female student with a sore throat that it was the direct result of a sexual act. The student snapped back, "Fuck you," to which he reportedly replied, "Not here."

When, after a flu illness, the girl returned to school, he taunted her in class for two weeks, the board argued. Referring to her sore throat, he said, "That's what happens when you swallow it." He allegedly told the class that the girl had been absent "because she did what she wasn't supposed to do."

With other girls, too, he apparently had acted provocatively, telling one she had "a nice shaped butt" and pleading with two others repeatedly to "model" for him after school. When one of the girls said that she intended to inform her mother, he responded, "Your mother doesn't have to know."

His defense was that the girl with the sore throat had misunderstood him—he was not, in fact, making sexual references. As for the after-school modeling plans, it was entirely appropriate for him to help the girls assemble portfolios since he was their teacher and they aspired to be models.

In April 1987, he was charged with "conduct unbecoming a teacher" and suspended with full pay. Eleven months later began a series of three hearings. In February 1989, the panel found him guilty of sexual harassment of female students. The punishment? After an expenditure of $92,125 in salary for the two years during which charges were pending, he received a ninety-day suspension and a transfer to another high school.

Stein maintains that the guillotine does not fall fast or often enough; Sandra Feldman, UFT chief, says, "The main problem is that it's not easy to fire people. No one likes to do it."

20

Finishing Touches

This is Alice in Wonderland *and* The Emperor's New Clothes, *all wrapped up in one.*

—A social studies teacher, Harry Van Arsdale High School, Brooklyn, New York.

We're not going to have a situation where, because of the way it might look in a report, we have to have a certain quota of children who pass. No, we are going to have high standards for our kids—high standards academically in terms of thinking and behavior-wise as well, because kids need positive reinforcement when they're right and they need to know when they've done something wrong. Challenge the administration if they seek to require you to lower your standards for your students. Challenge them because our job is to care for our students as difficult as they are, and believe me, you will find out, a lot of them are very very difficult.

—Sandra Feldman, president of the United Federation of Teachers, in an address to new teachers at the Felt Forum, August 25, 1988.

The music director raised his hand, the electric piano sounded, and the several hundred students who had filed into the auditorium minutes before began singing "The Star-Spangled Banner." It was April 13, 1989—the first rehearsal for the 1989 eighth-grade Whitman graduation.

On patrol duty, I walked up and down the center aisle, scanning the rows of students. Scattered about were several dozen who, I knew from my classes, didn't know basic arithmetic, who couldn't write a simple essay, who couldn't understand a short passage from an elementary textbook. Yet, in just over two months, these kids, dressed in caps and gowns, would graduate to high school. I was watching the biggest sham I had ever seen, made even more distressing by the kids' eager anticipation.

Having already decided to pass kids who had not come close to mastering the eighth-grade curriculum, I, too, had a part in perpetuating the lie. I hadn't gotten around to teaching the curriculum to most of my classes, anyway. So many of the kids had tried, and some had improved; others just beat me into submission with their yearning eyes and pleading voices. I felt I couldn't fail them.

Eight long months had passed since I had first walked into Whitman, and, over that time, I had abandoned my hopes, my plans, and my standards for the vast majority of my students. I passed kids to encourage them. I passed them as an enticement to stay in school. I even passed some because I simply saw no point, at this late date, in failing them. Would a student who failed want to continue studying math? Would a student who failed want to come to school? Would a student who failed take it as further evidence that life on the streets offered more rewards than a classroom ever could?

The alternative—failing kids because they did failing work— didn't make much sense to me anymore. I had begun the year convinced that, especially in junior high school, before it was too late, clear standards had to be set and reliably enforced; only then could children get what was necessary from the city's schools. Ignoring failure only cheated the students of an education. After a year in the classroom, though, reality intruded upon such idealism: students and education did not exist in a vacuum. Kids can't learn when their parents don't care; kids can't learn when their teachers aren't given basic materials; kids can't learn when they are uncertain where the next meal will come from or fear the bedsheets will be crawling with roaches. By eighth grade it is too late to begin enforcing standards. What help was a failing grade to a kid too old to sit still for another year in the eighth grade? What use was another year of oversized classes and baffling textbooks with a curriculum that stifled his interests and belittled his fragile skills?

"Before you fail a student," Winfield had said at a late-year faculty conference, "think whether he will be well served by another year here. Are you doing a service to your colleagues who will have to teach that student next year? Are you doing a service to the student who will tell himself he's a failure?"

At our school and most other intermediate schools in the city, students who were fifteen by summer's end automatically moved on to high school, regardless of grades or standardized test scores. Under this policy more than one-third of my students would pass.

Students younger than fifteen when September arrived—fourteen being the typical age for a student completing eighth grade—faced but two criteria for promotion to the ninth grade: passing the citywide reading test in May, and passing three major subjects. On the reading test, a percentile ranking of 21–29 percentage points off the national median was sufficient. Math aptitude test scores were irrelevant in determining promotion from grade to grade within junior high and, apparently, to high school, as well. It seemed inconceivable that anywhere in modern America students would not have to fulfill certain requirements in math as well as language arts. But that's the way it was.

Just as worrisome were the rules about which three majors a student needed to pass. The bottom line: *any* three, even shop or a foreign language. It was possible to fail both math and English and still fulfill the Board of Ed's requirement for promotion. "And if you're overage," one of my colleagues explained, "you pass even if you fail everything."

"Oh, and one more thing," my friend added with a knowing laugh. "That stuff they tell you about the high school applications and how important the eighth-grade marks are? It's all bullshit. A friend of mine who works at the board told me the computer only looks at the seventh-grade marks."

So I had been lying to my kids, and the administration had been lying to me. Two assistant principals had told students, in my presence, that if they didn't pass math, they could plan to repeat the eighth grade. A lie. What we had been telling the kids about how hard they should work the first and second marking periods of the year was equally false. "What a system," I sighed.

"Shows you how much they really care about the kids."

One pragmatic reason militated in favor of promoting students who failed, according to the administration. If students working below eighth-grade level in academic subjects were held back, Whitman would be even more crowded. It was already operating at more than 110 percent of capacity. Nor was there any guarantee, Winfield reminded us, that a student held back would do any better the second time around. Recent research had shown what teachers, myself included, had already seen ample evidence of: holding a kid back did not usually lead to substantial improvement in academic skills. The kids' egos had to be considered, too, according to other administrators.

"People have to understand that when you take a difficult or physically mature kid, sometimes moving him ahead has a far more beneficial effect than holding him back," one assistant principal mentioned. "You say to a teacher subtly: 'If we keep these kids here, we've got another year of the kind of nonsense they pull.' Dealing with difficult kids is one of the reasons people retire in record numbers. They burn out."

Earlier in the year, I had seen ample evidence that rigorous standards, even on citywide standardized tests, were a thing of the past. In January, all eighth-graders in New York took the State Preliminary Competency Test in Writing. Anyone who received a failing mark would be slotted for a remedial-writing class in high school. Since we, the teachers of Whitman, would be grading the papers, we could use this tool to help the most desperate students. Remedial writing courses for many of our students seemed desirable. Yet many of the language arts teachers at Whitman feared that giving failing marks might be interpreted as a damning reflection on the quality of their teaching. And several administrators worried that poor scores on the writing test would also reflect negatively on the school, since these marks, like results of the citywide math and reading tests, were used to judge a school's success.

It was easy enough to pass the students. We—not some objective strangers—would be marking them. We would work in pairs using a grading approach called "the holistic method," passing any student who turned in a "reasonably coherent" paper. We were to disregard structure, and ignore grammar, spelling, and punctuation entirely. "If you can basically get through it, that's good enough," a language arts teacher told us. "Pass the kid."

When the test day arrived, the language arts teachers took one look at the test and panicked. "Have you heard what they did to the PCT [Preliminary Competency Test]? They changed it on us, one frenzied teacher said." The English teacher for my homeroom class entered Room 315 in the middle of the test and read the straightforward directions for Part III, Composition:

Write a composition of about 150 words in which you tell one interesting real-life event from your own life or the life of someone else. In your composition be sure to tell what happened and organize what you write in the order in which it took place.

When he was through, sweat covered his brow, and he looked worried as his eyes panned across the classroom. For as long as he had been teaching, he later told me, teachers had been informed what would be on the test; for years the State Education Department had not deviated from a standard format requiring students to write a persuasive essay, a business letter, and a report. "They changed the test on us," he told my class of 8-5 students. His voice was unsteady. "You were supposed to get the Persuasive Essay, and instead you got the Composition. But don't panic. If you can't think of your own real-life experience, use the story of a friend or a relative. If you can't think of anything, make something up. Just write something."

When he left, a flurry of questions came from the equally distressed students.

"What's a real-life event?"

"Is it something from history?"

"What if you can't think of nothing?"

I reviewed the topic again, explaining that all they really had to do was tell a simple story from their own lives—the first day they went to school in this country; a time when they were frightened or excited; a day when they got to do something special.

After school that day, we marked the tests. In addition to the Composition, each student had been required to write a Report based on facts they were given on bloodhounds, as well as a Business Letter ordering towels from a catalog. Together with an eighth-grade science teacher, I graded the papers of one of the top eighth-grade classes. The school's teacher trainer reminded us what the holistic approach to marking meant. "Spend no more than two minutes reviewing each paper. And those of you on Compositions, be particularly understanding. Remember, they changed the test on us."

There was nothing wrong with the topics the students had selected. Several wrote about parents, siblings, or friends—especially ones caught in drug raids, drug wars, or other drug-related events. Seven students wrote about breaking various limbs. A couple of others related their first experiences swimming or skating, and another told about the many wrongs his grandfather had endured since immigrating to the United States thirty years before. These were vivid and meaningful tales, and the students showed a real effort at communicating them.

What was dismaying was the quality of the writing and our emphatic instruction to overlook its inadequacies. Of twenty-five papers, only two were free of spelling errors. Every paper had mistakes in punctuation and grammar. Most students did not use paragraphs or understand their function. Many of the essays were rambling, some nearly incoherent. One student described a dream about a drug bust in his apartment, but midway through the essay, switched to his mother's journey to the United States from the West Indies. Even his spelling mistakes were inconsistent—his mother arrived on both an "airplane" and an "airplain," once "flighing" another time "fleying."

Even with the holistic guidelines, all but three or four students should probably have failed. But my partner, who had been through this many more times than I, disagreed: "If we're out of line, they'll regrade our papers anyway. Just follow me on the marks we should give." In the end, the two of us failed only two students. The overall results at Whitman later showed 78.2 percent of the eighth-grade students passing the test—nice work, considering that less than half those kids read at grade level.

What the tests mostly demonstrated was how willing educators were to abandon standards they had created. I continued to teach as well as I could and devoutly hoped my students would learn, but I abandoned any effort to correlate my grades with their objective performance. Why should my students suffer because their teacher was not yet cynical enough to play the game? When I turned in my final remarks in May, I realized how far I had come since September. Everyone in 8-1 passed and all but three students in 8-7. Out of 150 students in five classes, I failed only twenty-nine.

Such grades were far out of line with the students' mastery of eighth-grade material, and, indeed, the standardized test results showed just how far behind they were as a group. Even after prepping my students for the test, only 16 percent came up to the national average.

Just before the year ended, I went over the list of students slated to be kept back. There were forty-seven names, about 8 percent of the eighth grade. Of those, the school won exceptions from the Board of Ed for eighteen who had failed the reading test and whose native language was not English. They would be moved on to high school anyway—yet another ironic twist, since reading level was to have been such a critical promotion criterion.

To be on the holdover list in June did not, however, mean that the student would automatically be forced to return to Whitman in the fall. Any deficit—failed reading test or failed majors—could be made up during a six-week summer session. One can only imagine the grading standards there. By the time September 1989 arrived, the list of eighth-grade Whitman holdovers had dwindled down to six.

Several teachers who regularly taught these summer school groups told me that academic standards were even more lax than during the school year. "The summer is magical," one teacher said. "Just another chapter in the watering down of standards."

Shona Sloan, administrator of promotional policy at the Board of Ed, discussed some of these issues of standards and grading with me. "In a district like yours, marks are pretty irrelevant anyway. It's a space issue. If the high school is willing to take them, then the junior highs are always willing to promote them."

"But supposedly there *are* some standards," I objected. "You're admitting that even those standards are not followed."

"Decisions are made that may be in the best interests of the child or, more likely, in the best interests of the school. Not just at Whitman, but all over the city. The age issue is a big part of the problem. It's not appropriate for a teenager to spend his years in a middle school. Eventually, he'll just stop coming." But, she admitted, unprepared students who cannot cope are a major reason for the 40 percent dropout rate in the high schools.

One of Whitman's assistant principals offered another justification. "There are teachers coming into the system who are taking and passing exams and who are close to illiterate, but we are letting them teach. How then can you take exception to moving a child from one grade to another if he hasn't met all the standards?"

The problem with both arguments was that they ignored our purpose and our results: the students' lack of basic knowledge would surely catch up with them later in life. But "later life" would wait until after high school. In New York City, earning a high school diploma was *also* relatively easy.

On paper, the requirements seemed demanding—four years of passing grades in language arts and social studies; two years of math; two years of science; one year of foreign language; seven semesters of gym; one semester each of music, fine arts, and health. To graduate, a student also need pass six so-called Regents Competency

Exams—in global history, American history, reading, writing, math, and science. But, in practice, said Larry Edwards, director of an office called Access and Compliance in the Board of Ed's high school division, "They keep retaking the classes and retaking the tests until they pass." He said, "Believe me, we give them lots of chances."

Students can take the math and science tests seven times; they also have two shots at the American history exam, five at global history and four each at the reading and writing tests.

Painful dilemmas and paperwork filled the final months of the year, but there were also some glorious times with my students. 8-7, which months before had offered only a barrage of plastic dart guns and rattling desks, invited me to a "demonstration" one Thursday afternoon in late April that turned out to be a surprise baby shower. With the help of their language arts teacher, Ellen Yudow, and their social studies teacher, Roman Foster, the class had baked cakes and bought outfits and a blanket for the baby. They acted out a skit about a newspaper reporter-turned-teacher who, against all odds, succeeds in teaching math to her recalcitrant students. "Recognize anyone?" asked the smallest girl in the class who, stuffed with pillows under her shirt, played the role of the very pregnant teacher. The skit, videotaped as a keepsake, was followed by a rendition of "Happy Baby to You," with touching thank-yous from the students. "Sometime we behave like we don't like you, like we think you're bad," one girl said into the camera, "but we love you." "I know I gave you a hard time," said Marlon, "but it's only 'cause I loved you so much." "You're the best math teacher I've ever had," Linda pronounced, "because you showed me I could do something, and you believed in me. No one else ever did." "I know I's been a real pain," said Kevin shyly, "but I did learn how to divide by 10."

Finally, two students handed me a card the class had made. Inside was a poem:

We thank you for the many things you've taught to us this year
We're glad you chose to spend your time by working with us here.
We wish you luck, we wish you health, we wish you hugs and
*   kisses.*
You'll stay with us through our good thoughts and with the best of
*   wishes.*
We hope that you'll return some day, just give us a firm "maybe."
And bring with you for all to see your beautiful new baby!

"Mrs. Sachar," it said at the bottom, "May all good things be yours in the future. Thank you for all the wonderful things you have done for us and just for putting up with us through this year. You will be missed." Every student in the class had signed it. My eyes brimmed with tears.

That last week of April, just before my baby was due, more cards and baby gifts poured in from students. One girl in 8-16 knit booties. Two boys from 8-13 shyly tucked cards into my satchel. There were baby rattles and teething rings and buntings and sweaters, tiny out-fits and another antique porcelain music box from two students in 8-1.

In April, too, came the most recent essays I had assigned. I had asked the students to tell me what they learned in eighth-grade math.

When I read the essays, I regretted not having asked the questions months before. It was obvious, from their heartfelt replies, that the kids desperately wanted to succeed, despite their actions.

I began with the efforts of the students I had come to know best. Reginald, the math whiz of 8-16, told me:

> *So far I'v enjoy is mostly the math, the thing I enjoy least is that I can't learn evything Because I all raedy know the work and the teacher can't teach me anything cause the rest of the class do'nt know the work.*
>
> *I would Be Better of for math I chang my class Becaus I am only doing Baby work, I'm not'n blameing the thecher But I would lik to do more harder work, that way I would learn a lot more than I do know.*

Tiara turned in an essay that I could not have mistaken for any-one else's. After explaining what she liked best and least, she gave me an overall critique:

> *The topic that bored me most is the recent topic probability it makes no sense to me at all, it just seems stupid. Subjects like that make me want to fall asleep in your class. I think if we do harder problems and harder subjects this class maybe can be much more interesting.*
>
> *I want you to know that I got 97 on my citywide math test and that this year I am going to get a perfect score. I also want you to know that even though I started out bad in the beginning*

of the year I plan on doing much better work. I think that you should let me lead the lesson sometime.

Shereeza did not turn in an essay, but wrote a few words, mostly unintelligible, in response to each of the questions on the question sheet. What did she like most? "Ingou deiviso." Least? "I didnt add." What topics would be most important leaving Whitman? "I would leave respect." What topics have bored you? "subtrac because it easy." What would make the math class better? "yes she could learn some fracations." Anything else? "yes"

There was no essay from Pedro, but on the day the students were supposed to turn in their essays we had another conversation.

Approaching my desk empty-handed, he said, "Mrs. Sachar, please, please, please pass Pedro for third marking period."

"But, Pedro, how can I pass you?" I showed him the marks in the book—no score higher than a 50, again. "Are you asking me to ignore your test scores?"

"No, but can't you put in that Pedro try really hard?"

"Well, Pedro, of course I'm taking that into consideration. But you haven't turned in a homework assignment in six weeks."

"But I will next year, Mrs. Sachar. Pedro come back and show you. Next year, I learn it. Trust in Pedro, Mrs. S."

"Oh, Pedro." I put my arm on his shoulder, then sighed and turned away.

Tawana, the umbrella-wielder from 8-12, answered the question sheet as well. "I've enjoyed nothing because you are always picking on me. I've least enjoyed the way your always calling my house."

Anything else I should know?

"Yes, I have a very bad attitude and try to stay away from me or else it's just going to go off."

One of the most astonishing essays—astonishing both for its tragedy and its nonchalance—came from Maria, a bright girl who had been bumped up to 8-7 from the seventh grade in March.

I'm 14 years old I'm going to be 15 in September 30. I have a 21 year old brother and also a 23 year old sister. I would have a little brother who would of been 13 years old but he died on the age of 11 the polar bears ate him. I have a niece and a nephew my niece is 1 years old and my nephew is 2 years old my mother is 47 years old and my septfather is 47 years old too. My real father died by drinking to much achole and I have 5 sept bother and 2 sept sister I have 4 sept niece 4 sept nephew.

Being eaten by polar bears in Brooklyn sounded like an outrageous tall tale. But it was true. Two years earlier, three boys, sneaking into Brooklyn's Prospect Park Zoo after closing, had climbed into the bears' pen. The animals had attacked one of the boys; the other two escaped, but eleven-year-old Juan had been mauled to death. Juan was Maria's brother.

Some of the essays were sprinkled with apologies. "Math class is fun," wrote Marlon. "I learned a lot but I know I have been a real pain. I'm sorry for interuping your class but me and Tasheema don't get along."

Jordene of 8-16 needed special help; I should have referred her for special ed months before. She wrote: "1. So for this year's I enjoyed how to mutep. 2. I have Enjoyed Divien 3. will the topics be about dvien and mulip 4. so for the topics bored me is mulipes." Her answers to the other questions, which she numberd 5, 6, and 7, saddened me the most. "5. is to tlkae to the kids in the class 6. tlake to me 7. yes is speak with the kid." Was she saying that I hadn't talked to *her* enough? Or did she feel that I had ignored the entire class?

"Ignore?" she said when I asked. "What's ignore?"

"Do you feel that I should talk to you more?"

"About what?"

"About math, about you, about anything you want?" I suggested gently.

She looked confused, as if about to cry. I put my arm around her and she smiled awkwardly.

The essays of some kids suggested I was not alone in my frustration. Angelie, one of the most raucous students in 8-16, who was a tough match for any boy, told me, "The kids they make too much nose," and to cope with it, she suggested, "verytime the children make nose you can put them out side."

Kevin's essay was sprinkled with diagrams of angles, arcs, and circles. "I would like my maths teachers should gave us more games like Monopoly and order games, the games are all in the line of maths, the are a topic in maths I like a lot."

And Hartman, a rowdy but very bright kid, wrote pointedly that "We should have more free time to ourselves less notes more quizzes and experiment and more freedom to do what we want and the teacher should help thous students who don't understand."

Saheedra, the top student in the 8–16 class after Reginald, said, "My thoughts is to have two period in math every day so we all could learn more and have experience so we could learn."

Other students revealed illuminating personal details.
Carlia, another 8-7 student, wrote this:

*What I want the teacher to know about me is that I am a very
quiet and sensitive person most of the time. I enjoy math very
much and this is my favorite subject. Usually I like to sit in the
back of the classroom by myself so I could concentrate and get
more work done. As you know, I have an obligation to finish
junior high and go to High School.*

Maxina, whose paper was typed, revealed a personal problem:
"My mother use to talk to my teachers and tell them I have a problem
with raising my hand. Sometimes I get over it and I raise my hand
and I finally got over my problem. Then I get my problem back again
and I can't get rid of it." Karl of 8-7 stated, "I'm a good kid but i get
angry when i don't know how to do math. it makes me mad."

I was disappointed again by my 8-12 students, who hadn't bothered to do the first essay either. This time only six students turned in
papers, the others scribbling a few words the day the assignment
was due.

Most of them showed about as much effort as that of Mark, a boy
who had turned in two homework assignments all year. He wrote:

*So far, what you enjoyed most in this year's math class I en-
joyed the most in this math class in. adding fractions that's the
easiest. so far what have enjoyed them most math? Like I said
it is adding the topics I think are more important is decimail*

In 8-13, only eight of thirty students turned in essays, and the
sentiments mirrored those of 8-12.

In 8-1, many of the students turned in their essays in laminated
folders. Some were typed, and many were personal, with some nice
words for me.

Judith, a well-behaved girl with strong grades, wrote, "I hope
you have a girl because we are the future."

One girl handed me a paper entitled, "Things About Me." She
wrote:

*Let's start off with my behavior. First thing is I like competing
with my test scores from my other classes with the boys. But
there is alway's a catch I'm very fragile and sentimental about
stupid things. I'm very fragile for instance when I fail a test*

(math specifically). The reason I feel hurt is because I try too hard to understand, (and) never succeed. When I succeed I didn't try hard I past my math tests. I try too hard maybe because I want to be an excellent student, and famous, not by my last name but my brillance. I think I'm afraid of math because I put myself down hard when I don't understand something. It seems to me as soon as I hear math my brains just blank out, that's why I'm so difficult to tutor. Thank you for reading my essay (which I did by myself and I hope I deserve the grade I get)

Early in the year, Laurenta sat in the back of the room giving me dirty looks for the benefit of her friends and persisted until they grew bored with her show. Her essay read:

I think the math class would be much better for me if the kids around me show that they are more eager to learn. All the kids in my class are worrying about just passing MATH. I would like to do more than just pass my tests. I would like to score way above passing. I want to make my parents and teachers proud of me.

Unusual for her intensity, Mara socialized with no one and worried constantly about understanding the material, although she regularly scored between 95 and 100 on my tests. She wrote:

Math is one of the most useful and fascinating divisions of human knowledge. It includes many topics of study. For this reason, the term mathematics is difficult to define. It comes from a Greek word meaning "inclined to learn". . . . I believe that I was born to dislike math and nobody can make me or force me to like it 'cause it's a fact of life but I thought after seeing "Stand and Deliver" I would of change but I didn't. Still, I hope to like math and that I'll be able to do it well some day and even to teach it if I have the opportunity.

Shoshona, a distance runner, confided:

Only thing I think you should know, is that at the beginning of the year I didn't like you very much, but as I got too know you better I have grown to like you more than any other subject teacher I have had from this year.

Opening her soul to me in all its adolescent vulnerability, Monica's essay was one of the most powerful I read. After telling me how boring she found math in general, she plunged into self-analysis:

Well I just told you a little about the way I am, but I think I should tell you some more so you could really know me. Well, I can be nice, lovable, and sharing sometimes and next minute around the people I do not like I can be snobby, selfish, crampy, and rude, sometimes even around the people I love. I don't like to bother people who's different from me only the people who bother's me and act stupid at times. Sometimes when I do things I may feel guilty for doing it later on in the day a week or it might just alway's be on my mind. So to forget it, I may do something accomplishable, and nice to know that god is not doing something to punish me for my sins. When I was smaller I was kind of quiet in class, smarter, nicer, giving more help, doing more things but now things have changed I am a different person and not only I know that but my family is beginning to see that. I have changed in ways such as I give less help to others, I am less smarter less nicer, and absolutely less quieter, I curse more often, think about boys more often. To me I have changed in a wrong way my life is a roller coaster to me, things are not going so good. My relationships with my family is different in such ways they say I have got rude and especially my mother alway's tells me "Where is my baby." Mrs. Sachar, I know I have to change, I always say okay I would try because I love my mother and sisters very much and for the day I may be good and everything and the next day I may be back to the same attitude, just like I may study hard one day for math and try very hard to understand the work and the next week or so I am still back to the same old thing goofing off and not trying hard enough to accomplish what I want and what my family would want for me. I hope you understand me Mrs. Sachar that's maybe why I am having trouble understanding some of the math topics that you teach us.

David had been one of the least involved students in the class, often nodding off even when I insisted that he keep his eyes open. His essay explained his behavior. From my earliest teaching days, I did not force the kids to learn or to pay attention; I felt they were old enough to decide for themselves whether my class was worthwhile. Now, that attitude seemed misguided. He wrote:

Math doesn't catch my attention. The topic will have to attract me from the beginning, just like a book. Usually when I fail a test, I fail the next one too. This is because I lose faith and I dont seem to care anymore. But that's not the reason I sleep in your class. I sleep in class because of 1. lazy 2. I am not forced to work. No offense Ms. Sachar. The topic I disliked the most in math class was algebra. I don't like the word and the topic is just to hard. I probably need some counseling. When I'm rejected or left out at home because of my baby brother, I feel the same at school when I'm not helped or never picked to answer a question. Algebra is the topic you didnt make more understandable to me. When I ask questions you seem to don't hear me. . . . The only other thing is that I am not a good multiple choice test taker and that has to do with probability when you don't know the answer. I'll understand you failing me 3rd marking period. I only have passed 2 tests this period and with a 20% on a test nobody deserves to pass with that.

Leroy, I adored. He had arrived in my class shortly after Christmas and struggled the entire time I taught him, but he always smiled at my corny jokes. He said:

Math to me is very heard, but I am still trying my best to pass. I like my math teacher she's very funny but for that, there is nothing else I like about it. I know if I don't do good in math I won't do good in the real world so that is why I am doing my best.

I'm a very nice person, I'm not a mean person. I write poem and write short story. My friends tell me I have to relax and have some fun once in a while. I said to them I do have fun by writing.

Oooh there's one more thing, I also write comic books I have one hundred and ten issue. I think when I'm older I'm going to be a book writer and be good at it. too.

This is the first poem I ever wrote I remember it by hurt:
   Winter winds passing by,
   nothing in sight but the blue winter sky.
   I blow my horn to see the sea
   and all I could see was you & me.

Winston, another charming boy who had tried hard in class to little avail, wrote:

The thing I hate most about the math class is when we are to study for a test. And I really study for that test and it came out into a big disappointment. Then all the other children would get together and compeare their grades and they would laugh at me because I failed the test.

Finally, from Stacey, a heavy-set girl with a baby face and too little confidence:

What I dislike the most in math is that sometimes I don't understand the work and I am afraid to tell you and ask you for help . . . I would like you to go a little slower. I am not dum just slow in math.

   I am not very good in math I am sure you can tell by my tests and my citywide test last year. I hope you know that I am honest. I never cheated on any of my test that you have given to me although I have been tempted if I did cheat that would not be fear to you are my friends are me.

Shortly after noon on May 1, my second daughter, Caroline Gail, was born. Once back in my hospital room, I called Edward Newman, the assistant principal whom I counted among my friends at Whitman. He said he would pass the word on to my students. I had given all of my students my home phone number and told them they could call during the two weeks I planned to be away from school.

When I returned home, I found seventeen messages on my machine from Whitman students. "Have you had the baby yet?" "I hear it's a boy." "I hear it's a girl." "You's naming it after me, aren't you, Mrs. Sachar?" "Congratulations." "Happy Baby to you." "Mrs. Sachar, we don't understand this plotting of algebraic equations on them number lines."

Although the school year did not end until mid-June, the marks for eighth-graders were due by early May. I went back for a half day at school on May 9 to work on records for my homeroom class. There were attendance cards to complete, high school records to file, and grades to enter.

When I came through the front door of the school dozens of kids ran over as word of my arrival spread quickly down the hall. "It's

Mrs. Sachar, she's had the baby." Winfield said nothing as I passed him in the hall. On May 15, I returned to Whitman for good.

Many of the final weeks of school were devoted to graduation rehearsals, singing "The Star-Spangled Banner" and "Lean on Me" and "Lift Every Voice" dozens of times, and, for my kids, playing Budget, bingo, Yahtzee, and Monopoly in class. In 8-1, I had replaced the original textbooks we had been given in October with algebra books. For the last five weeks of the year, at the students' insistence, we plowed through the first third of the book, working at breakneck speed to get to the sections on graphing simple algebraic equations. They couldn't seem to get enough of algebra. Even on blistering hot days, the kids in 8-1 toiled away, hoping to finish the new book before the end of the year.

We spent the last day of the year having an intense heart-to-heart talk. As we sat in a circle, I told each 8-1 student, in front of his classmates, how much he or she had meant to me. "Tiara, how could I ever forget you? You got that near-perfect score on the citywide, just as you promised, and I finally got my lessons timed to within fifteen seconds of the bell, as you'd demanded." She laughed, "Yeah, but you never did let me teach the lesson."

8-7 wrapped up the year with lessons on scale drawing; we noted the dimensions of our classrooms with measuring tapes and plotted the positions of all of the closets, doors, desks, and chalkboards on graph paper. I tried to have an intimate talk with the kids in 8-7, too, but the exercise quickly degenerated into hooting and note-passing.

In 8-12, the year ended much as it had started, with more hairbrushes and umbrellas in evidence than notebooks and pencils. The class had continually disappointed me, and I told them so several times before the year ended. "I hope that those of you who acted up will think long and hard about your behavior this year," I said on the last day of school, "because, in addition to making my life miserable, you cheated yourselves out of a year of math. At some point, you're going to have to take responsibility for your actions." A few kids approached my desk after the final bell rang. "You have to understand, Mrs. Sachar," one girl said. "We hate each other too much to concentrate on your work." Tawana just scowled at me as she left the room. "Bitch," she said, sneering.

As word filtered down to the students that grades had been

turned in and a month's absences would mean nothing on the final report cards, 8-13 dwindled to just a few students—my favorite ones, fortunately. The class had started so well, with eager, attentive students, but the addition of new unruly kids midway through the year had destroyed it, and the kids knew it as well as I.

As they had all year, the students of 8-16 kept me guessing until the final hour of class. They were great one day, awful the next, but when I told them they had come a long way in math and in their growth as human beings, they beamed. Of all of my classes, they had made the most improvement as measured by standardized test scores, gaining five points for a class average at the 20th percentile. A few of the students had made huge strides, from the 7th and 8th percentiles to the 30th and 35th. One boy asked if I thought he was any closer to his dream of becoming a doctor. "You've improved so much, but you still have a long way to go," I told him. "Stick with your classes. Keep your goals right in front of you. You'll get there." One student, fifteen-year-old Sheteequa, stopped coming to class. I heard from her best friend that she was expecting her first baby in three months and no longer saw any point in school.

On June 15, I found a letter in my mailbox. "Dear Ms. Sachar: Please be advised that your services will be terminated as of the close of business on Wednesday, June 28, 1989." It was signed by Winfield. A year as a teacher had taught me the lines of command. I immediately went to see Bob Moore, our union leader.

"Does this mean I'm being fired?" I asked him.

"There was no letter of explanation with this?" Moore said. "I can't believe he did it again."

"No."

"This is just a form letter. They give this to all the TPDs [nontenured teachers]."

Though Moore, always one for action, marched out of his office to look for Winfield, I felt no comfort. Maybe he was wrong. Maybe Winfield thought I had done a lousy job. But no: every untenured teacher received the same letter.

"Why can't the man ever say: 'Thanks for trying,'" I asked Bob. "'Now, here's a letter I'm required to give to you.' I guess that takes consideration and thought."

. . .

The graduation ceremony for Walt Whitman Intermediate School was held at Brooklyn College on June 19, 1989. It was long, with many speeches by people the kids and their parents had never met and too many people on the dais looking as if they might fall asleep under the bright lights. Parents and family members fought off the heat inside the auditorium by fanning themselves with the yellow programs. The best part of the show was the singing—nearly 500 students, many with superb voices, turning "The Star-Spangled Banner" into a magnificent hymn. When the students sang "Lean on Me," they swayed back and forth, arms around each other, heads bobbing in rhythm. If only they would indeed lean on each other in the years to come.

Theoretically the Whitman administration made a distinction between students who were graduating because they had met the standards and those who were being moved on to the ninth grade only because their age demanded it. The latter were not supposed to participate in the graduation ceremonies. Yet there was Shereeza, standing proud, her hair, for the first time all year, silken and unbraided atop her shoulders. I saw several others who did not pass the reading test, and there were many students who had failed the standardized citywide math test as well as their Whitman math courses.

Much as the ceremony bestowed a false sense of accomplishment on some students who shouldn't have been there, I found myself deeply affected. So tall and proud were my kids, especially those who truly deserved to be standing there. Their parents' pride, too, was movingly evident. The students looked regal in their caps and gowns—boys in royal blue, girls in white. If only all of them had done well in school, if only they would make it to the next graduation —the one that really mattered—having mastered basic math and reading skills.

Months before one of my friends at school had explained the reason for the graduation. "For most of them, it's the only graduation they'll ever have. A lot of these kids will never make it out of the tenth grade."

As I left the auditorium that afternoon, my kids crowded around me, grabbing my arm and pleading for one last moment of my time. "Mommy, you've got to meet my math teacher," said one girl, dragging her mother over to see me.

In a courtyard ringed with rose bushes and smelling of fresh-cut grass, I posed for snapshots and signed the kids' yearbooks. I happily accepted kisses from some, hugs from others. Two of my students, boys who had figured out how to convert fractions to percents in the final hours of school, each presented me with a long-stemmed red rose sealed in cellophane.

And then, with the stirring of a sudden summer breeze, the school year ended. I walked to the subway station past festive, chattering family groups, past fast-food restaurants and the lively streets of Flatbush. As I waited on the platform, I knew that, like most teachers, I would probably never see many of my students again.

21

Into the Homes

I want the teacher to beg, to say, "Come on Jimmy, please. Won't you please sit down today? Won't you please take this test? Won't you please give it a try?" Like, without me there, the class is nothing.

—Jimmy, 8-7, Walt Whitman Intermediate School, explaining why he misbehaved in my math class.

A puddle of pink liquid coated the concrete floor, and three bullet holes had webbed the Plexiglas panes of the entry door. As I walked into the Flatbush tenement where my former student, Jordene, lived, two beer bottles crashed to the pavement a few feet behind me.

Two days before I had called Jordene to ask if I could visit. Thursday morning, she had told me, would be a good time.

Often, while I taught at Whitman, I had wanted to visit my students, to create a context in which to place their school behavior and problems, and to meet their families. Home visits might offer me a bit of the education I lacked—into the conditions of poverty some endured, and the special problems newly arrived immigrant families faced. I wanted to visit the top students as well as the ones with behavior problems, primarily to convince myself that the dramatic differences I saw in school were a reflection of striking differences in the kids' home lives.

While I taught, however, inviting myself into the kids' homes seemed a breach of my role as a teacher, an intrusion fraught with potential for embarrassment and one that many kids might feel pressured into accepting. When school was over, however, the students and their parents were free to turn down my requests. I hoped to see a few of those who had given me permission to write about them. Their home lives seemed a critical piece of information for the story I now knew I wanted to tell.

At first, Jordene did not remember me, the math teacher she had last seen two months before, in June. "Remember, Jordene? I taught you math last year?" I had said on the phone.

"Who?" she asked.

"Mrs. Sachar. The one who had the baby, remember?"

"Oh, yeah," she said. "I think so."

Jordene had not graduated from Whitman but had, in Board of Ed parlance, "articulated"—been promoted to high school solely because she was sixteen, too old to spend another year at Whitman. After three years in the seventh grade and one in the eighth, she had failed the reading test for the fourth time, and had also failed several of her academic subjects.

I had just written a letter to Paul Robeson High School, where Jordene was to begin her freshman year in the fall, recommending that as soon as the fall term commenced, she be evaluated for special-education classes. "When I visit you, I want to talk to your mother and father, too," I had said on the phone. I wanted her family to know who I was and to have my home phone number in case they were contacted by the new high school about the special-ed referral.

Jordene was an 8-16 student who was so sweet, quiet, and well-behaved that—given the chaos around her—I all but overlooked her. Once when the class was working on a point-plotting exercise, I was shocked to realize that Jordene did not understand the difference between 2 and 20 or even, it seemed, between 5 and 6: when I asked her to count out 9 red beans from a pile, she put only 7 beans on the desktop. I'd asked her to count again, and she twice counted one bean as if it were two. I had never been sure what her problem was. But there were other signs that she was in need of expert evaluation —perhaps even medical attention—for possible neurological defects. Her speech was slurred; her eyes did not focus. Yet 8-16 had posed so many other challenges—some involving the physical safety of my students—that I had neglected Jordene. I had been overworked and overwhelmed, and it was disturbing now to consider that she was surely not alone in having been overlooked.

When the year ended, I felt especially guilty for having failed to send Jordene for a special-ed workup. She was not the kind of kid to ask for help, nor, I suspected, did her family take a great interest in her schoolwork or understand their rights as parents in the New York City school system. Clearly she had not been helped much by her previous three years at Whitman. Arriving from Jamaica in November 1985, she had been placed in 7-10. Two months later, she was bumped to an English-as-a-Second-Language class for seventh-graders. The following September, she was assigned to a lower seventh-grade section and the next year placed in a class for holdovers. Despite those three years in seventh grade, her standardized test scores had not improved. She scored between the 2nd and 7th percentiles in reading and the 3rd and 5th percentiles in math. For her, the system had not worked at all.

Her academic performance—both in classwork and on standardized tests—reminded me of Shereeza's, but Jordene's was an even sadder case. There was no spark in her eyes, and unlike Shereeza, she made no attempt to do the classwork. Her textbooks kept disappearing, and she could never find a pencil or a notebook. At sixteen, she had almost no skills and no apparent determination to obtain any. Shereeza, at least, was organized and eager. I feared for Jordene's future. She deserved so much more than I or her other teachers had given. A special-ed referral, even at this late date, and a conference with her family might help amend my lapse during the school year.

A wide-eyed boy shyly answered when I rang the bell, but he would not unhook the chain that linked the metal door to the jamb. Jordene had not told me she lived in a building of 700 apartments, and I had not asked for an apartment number. Luckily, someone in the crowded concrete lobby knew where her family lived. Even though it was mid-morning on a weekday, the first floor of the south entrance—one of a dozen entrances to the high-rise—was teeming with children and adults. Three languages filled the hallways—Spanish, Creole, and English.

"I'm Emily Sachar," I finally said, "one of Jordene's teachers at Walt Whitman last year." An older man, presumably Jordene's father, appeared in the doorway behind the boy. He seemed confused to find me on his doorstep. "She in trouble?" he asked.

"No, no, no," I said. "Didn't Jordene tell you I wanted to come visit you?" The man and the boy exchanged a quick glance.

"No," he said. "Jordene not here."

"Oh, well, I can wait for her. Besides, I actually want to see you as much as her."

He said nothing, but released the chain and let me in. The door slammed shut behind us. I walked into a cramped room where a dim-watt lightbulb dangled from an orange cord. There was no other light in the room. Against one wall was a crib; a baby stood inside it in soiled diapers and a soot-gray T-shirt. There were no toys in the crib, just a big box of disposable diapers at one end, leaving little room for the child. The thin piece of orange foam that served as a mattress had no sheet.

Against another wall was a breakfast table covered with a cracking piece of green marbleized plastic. Two bowls with rancid milk sat on it. Flies swarmed around them.

Off to the right was the kitchen, which had a floor of splintered plywood. Insects buzzed near the stove and tiny refrigerator, a small box of an appliance no higher than a grown man's knee. The doors of the kitchen cabinets hung haphazardly; the hinges of two were fastened with paper clips. The kitchen walls were a cheerful yellow, but patches of pink and fluorescent blue were visible where the yellow had cracked and peeled.

I asked if I could sit down and was shown to a couch whose legs had fallen off on the opposite side of the room. A piece of black fabric hung over the one window, shutting out most of the natural light. A television set played loudly in the next room. When I sat down on the couch, it felt moist and sticky and smelled of mildew.

"Well, how is Jordene doing?" I began awkwardly.

"Okay," the man said, not meeting my eyes. He was wearing cut-off shorts, sneakers without laces, and an unbuttoned plaid shirt. Sitting on the concrete floor, he shrugged.

"I actually came here to talk to you about her. I think she may need some special help in school."

"Yes, mmmm," he answered, staring off into the middle distance.

"I don't know exactly what the problem is, but I think that when she gets to Robeson, they should test her to see if she might qualify for special help." I paused. "She is going to Robeson, isn't she?" He said nothing.

I had intended to show him or his wife the letter I had written to the high school guidance staff, but now I suspected that I might be handing him a document he couldn't read. To avoid embarrassment, I decided to put the letter on the kitchen table when I left.

"Jordene's at the high school," her father said. Two scars cut across his left cheek. Although his skin otherwise was smooth and his body slim, his graying hair made him look like a man in his sixties, considerably older than the other Whitman parents I had met.

"Oh, it's orientation time, isn't it?" If Jordene was at school, that was a good sign—she was interested enough to make an effort to get to know her new high school. Of course, that also meant that she would probably not return for several hours.

"Who else lives here?" I asked. "Is Jordene's mother home?"

"She's not well," he said abruptly, staring at the window ledge.

He rose from the floor and shouted, "Yvonne." A black-haired woman with deeply wrinkled skin shuffled from behind a curtain into the living room. Her back was hunched and her hands trembled; she might have been sixty years old. I offered her my arm and suggested she sit down. Clutching it, she sank into the couch. "I'm Yvonne, Jordene's mother."

She picked up a can of insecticide and sprayed aimlessly into the air. She had spent the morning in the bathroom, she said; she had not been well for months. Every few seconds, a toothless smile directed at no one in particular flitted across her face, like a nervous tic.

"I was Jordene's math teacher last year. I'd like to talk to you for a minute." She wasn't looking at me, either, but I kept talking, explaining about the letter, Jordene's problems, and how I hoped that something could be done to help her to do better in school or learn a trade.

Jordene's mother nodded, but said nothing.

"Have you or your husband ever been down to Whitman?"

She shook her head. "I was sick. I couldn't go."

Just then, the curtain rustled again and an older girl, who looked remarkably like Jordene but with gleaming, focused eyes and a spunky step, joined us. She extended her hand.

"Hi, I'm Claudette," she said. "Can I help? I heard what you were saying about Jordene, and you're right. She really does need help, but Mama and Daddy can't go up to the school. Mama's too sick and Daddy's usually sleeping or working."

Claudette and I spoke for nearly an hour. Her parents never budged from their positions. She told me that she was two years older than Jordene, had just graduated from Flushing High School in Queens, and was planning to begin studies in the fall at Kingsborough Community College in Brooklyn. She described the rest of the family. There was Clyde, seventeen, who was in his junior year at

Jefferson High School in Brooklyn; Sophia, fourteen, a sophomore at Robeson; Selma, thirteen, a student at Cunningham Junior High School; Daisie, eleven, also at Cunningham; and two-year-old Christian. Sophia would be at the same school as Jordene in the fall, and she liked to keep an eye on all her brothers and sisters. That, at least, was one piece of good news.

Her mother, Claudette told me, was forty-two years old. She did not know how old her father was, and he didn't offer to answer. Nine people—seven children and the two parents—lived in the small apartment. "We have no choice," Claudette told me. "It's hard in this country."

She explained the sleeping arrangements. The six older children slept in the twin beds and one double bed crammed into the next room. The baby slept in the crib, while the mother and father slept at opposite ends of the couch.

"It's a little close," she said, "but we all get along." She rolled her eyes.

Claudette told me that Dudley, her father, had arrived in New York in October 1985 after losing his job as a worker in an aluminum-siding plant in Jamaica. Yvonne had been a home attendant for elderly women until she grew ill four or five years ago. She had never seen a doctor here. The last baby had been born at home and had not been immunized. "We don't have the money for it," said Claudette. Everyone in the family had Green Cards, but when I asked whether her parents had applied for public assistance, Claudette just shook her head. "They don't know this city," she said. "They're afraid of trouble."

Since the family's arrival here four years earlier, some good things had happened. Her father had found a job as a security guard at Hunter College, working the graveyard shift and earning twenty-five cents over minimum wage per hour. She, Jordene, and Sophia had all found steady employment during the summers through the city's youth employment program. Their salaries were just a few pennies over the minimum wage, but they earned enough to buy groceries for the family and winter coats for themselves every other year. The family also had found a church, a storefront Seventh Day Adventist congregation, within walking distance of the apartment.

Jordene's academic problems, Claudette admitted, had stumped the family. "I try to help her, and sometimes she gets it, but not usually. She wants to learn, though, if someone will take the time to teach her."

Yvonne, who had her eyes closed as she slouched on the couch, suddenly sat up. "She likes to read and she do have friends," the mother said, then closed her eyes again.

What did they think of Whitman?

"Seems like a good school," Yvonne answered.

"Seems good enough," her husband added. Had he or his wife ever gone to an Open School night?

"What?" he asked. I explained that the two Open School nights each year were for parents to meet teachers, retrieve report cards, and meet other parents. Dudley had never been inside the school.

"Do you have any plans for your children?"

"I believe they will pick it on their own," he said. "They must pick something for themselves."

Was life here better than in Jamaica? Everyone in the room chuckled, even the baby boy, offering a welcome change from the bleak conversation in a dilapidated room. "It's much better over here," Claudette said. "Over there, you just have a trade."

"People don't learn to be nurses and doctors there," the father added.

"But we don't know what to do about Jordene," the mother said. "She's the only one who has problems, but at least she behaves herself."

"I have no good idea of the things in this city," Dudley added. "We don't know the ways here." There was no animosity in the room, just confusion and incomprehension.

When I asked to meet the other children, Claudette escorted me into the back bedroom. There, one older brother and three younger sisters, naked but for their underwear, lay across the beds watching a game show on a black-and-white television set. Draped across their windows were sheets of black fabric: might these be makeshift efforts to hide from the housing authorities? They had listed only four occupants on the lease of the apartment, Claudette confided, for which they were paying $500 a month. "It's impossible here," she sighed. "We have to move."

I said my farewells and asked Claudette and her parents to call me if I could help with anything. I left a copy of my letter referring Jordene for special testing, and I wrote a note to her, which I asked Claudette to deliver, along with a hug from me.

Dudley, Yvonne, the baby boy, the older brother, and Claudette all followed me to the door, a yearning sadness in their eyes. They said good-bye and watched as I walked down the hallway and around the corner to the bullet-worn Plexiglas front entrance.

. . .

In the ten months I worked at Whitman, the consistent impression given by my bottom classes was that most parents had no interest in the academic part of their children's lives. But the visit to Jordene's home suggested that for many the problem might not be lack of interest, but rather an overwhelming fatigue, and even more pressing problems. Before the end of the first marking period, I'd sent letters to nineteen parents whose children I intended to fail. There were personalized descriptions of the academic and behavioral problems each child was having in my class. The parents were invited to visit me at school to see how we could work together to solve them.

I heard back from only one parent. It was the extent of our contact all year.

> *Dear Emily Sachar:*
> *I would like to thank you for the interest that you have shown in my son. I have spoken to Albert already and he said that he will try to study harder. I also ask that you help him in any areas that he needs extra help.*
> *Once again, I thank you for your show of interest. Let's keep in touch.*
> *Very truly yours,*

The parents of those children in the worst shape never replied, even to follow-up postcards sent after the first-quarter grades and encouraging them again to arrange private conferences with me. When various other parents scheduled appointments, most simply did not show up.

I made frequent calls to some parents, especially in the early months of school. After three weeks of classes, I phoned more than thirty parents whose children did not know the times tables, to explain that almost everything we would study that year required the ability to multiply and divide; with flash cards I had purchased they could help their children learn the tables at home. Every one promised to send $3 for half the cost of the flash cards, and to work with their children after school. Two weeks later, only three students had brought money. I distributed the flash cards anyway. Still, not one of those students mastered the multiplication tables. Most explained that their parents did not have time to work with them.

Parents were also encouraged, through frequent school notes, to attend PTA meetings. But in a school of more than 1,700 kids, the Whitman PTA had nineteen members, with no more than thirty people showing up for the regular meetings.

At the Open School nights, only a third of my students' parents showed up; those who did generally were from my 8-1 and 8-7 classes, parents of kids who posed the fewest problems and did the best work.

Now that the school year was over, however, I phoned several of the students who had most intrigued me during the year or to whom I felt particularly close, explaining that I wanted to write about their time in my classroom and their lives at home. All, with their parents' permission, agreed to see me. Several invited me to their homes for dinner. In addition, there were students like Jordene with whom I had unfinished business. I planned to use the summer vacation to attend to it.

Two students, I was especially eager to visit—Crystal of 8-12 and Kevin of 8-7. But they had moved during the summer and their phones had been disconnected. No forwarding number was available. In fact, when I attempted to get in touch with all my students to tell them about the impending publication of a series of newspaper articles on our year together, I discovered that fully a third of them had moved.

By the end of September 1989, I had visited the homes of twelve of my students. Six of those—Jordene, Reginald, and Shereeza of 8-16; Tiara of 8-1; Pedro of 8-13; and Jimmy of 8-7—told me that I could write in detail about their academic and home lives. "I has nothing to hide," said Reginald. "Tell it all. Maybe you help someone else."

"Mrs. Sachar, how you getting on?" Jimmy asked, hugging me tightly. "I been missing you, Mrs. Sachar."

I had expected to find many brothers and sisters, but when I arrived inside Jimmy's well-kept sixth-floor apartment one sunny afternoon in July, only Jimmy and his mother were in the living room. Though small, it was immaculate, with a clean white shag rug on the floor and a series of prints of winter scenes in black frames lining the walls. Opposite the tan couch, a stereo sat on a shelf against one wall. Several chairs—one of red velour, another green leather—were positioned across from the couch. A coffee table held little trinkets. The room was cozy, neat, and welcoming.

Jimmy's mother invited me to sit down and offered me a glass of water before she took a seat in a straight-backed chair. Jimmy sat next to me on the sofa. "So, Jimmy, what's new?" I asked, patting his leg. I wanted to talk to him about his disruptive behavior in my class, but not right away. Four times that year, his mother and I had discussed his "I have to pee" antics, but his behavior never improved. Finally, in March, he was transferred out of 8-7 and into 8-5, with no explanation. As 8-5's homeroom teacher, I still had to deal with him daily, though at least it wasn't forty-three minutes at a time. Being at a distance from Jimmy's academic problems had improved my relationship with him in other ways. I was curious to hear how he now justified his behavior.

"I'm doing great, Mrs. Sachar. Just great. School's great. Friends are great. Everything's just great."

"Oh, Jimmy," his mother said, a disgusted edge to her voice. She turned her head away.

When I had spoken with her on the phone, Jimmy's mother had always been cooperative and concerned. Unlike some parents who defend their children vehemently, she always accepted my reports. But often there had been no answer when I called, and I asked her why.

"It's my job," she explained. She worked as a service attendant on Amtrak trains, serving drinks in the club car. Although she was off three days a week, she worked seventeen and eighteen hours at a stretch the rest of the time, most often on the New Orleans train that left New York City early in the evening and returned to the city the following afternoon.

"That must be hard on both of you," I said, "being away from each other so much."

"It's not hard on me," volunteered Jimmy. "If you just come home and do around the house what you're supposed to be doing. A kid like me just calls a friend and hangs around. I don't think about what's happening with her."

"It's not a great job for a woman," his mother said, "coming home in the dark and all, but the pay is good." She brought home $395 a week, she said, and also had rental income from a home she owned in Florida.

"Money's not the problem in this household," she said. "Jimmy is."

"Oh, Ma, what you ragging on me for now?"

She had lived in England, where her ex-husband, Jimmy's father, remained. They had separated before Jimmy was born, and she had come to the United States eight years later. Jimmy was an only child with a life considerably more stable than that of many of his classmates. Except for one year at a school in the Bronx, Jimmy had attended the same elementary school in Brooklyn for three years and gone on to Whitman for sixth, seventh, and eighth grades.

Except—Jimmy also had sickle cell anemia. "It so happens that my mom has it, too," he confided. "But it's no big deal. If there are a hundred cells, the white ones eat the red ones. Sometimes you just don't want to get up. You put your head down for a rest, and you don't wake up for eleven hours. Not always, though."

Sometimes, his mother reminded him, the complications were severe. He had had a case of frostbite in 1986, she said, that was so exacerbated by the disease that he had had to spend a week in the hospital. Lately, she added, he had developed "other problems."

"It can get kind of bad, Mrs. Sachar," Jimmy said. "Do you know what an erection is?

"When I was six or seven, I got these erections for, like, a half hour, and they were kind of bad, but not that bad. Then, they started lasting for, like, fifteen or twenty minutes. But now, I can get one at, like, four in the morning and it might last until nine the next day."

"That sounds awful."

"Sometimes, I just need my momma to hold me, the pain is so bad. And when I have to pee and it can't come out, that's really something." His face twisted suddenly, as if he were in pain, and he put his hands over his groin. Jimmy's frequent pleas to go to the bathroom obviously had a lot to do with this bizarre side effect of his disease. His comic act in class was simply a way to cope with this physical agony.

"Can't they do anything for it?" I asked.

"He has transfusions twice a week," his mother said. Jimmy would go to the hospital for four or five hours, she told me, and have dialysis to thin his blood and diffuse the blood clot that doctors suspected was causing the condition.

Jimmy's description of his ailment suggested that he had been told only as much as he could handle: "It's no big deal." But with each additional incident detailed by his mother, the picture emerged of his progressively painful disorder. His constant routine of "I have to bathroom," was not a disciplinary problem, but a medical one. He received regular dialysis treatments, with fluid infusions to prevent clotting and crippling cramps. His pain was real and dreadful—and no one had told me a word about it. He might have had a crisis in my class, and I would not have had a clue to its nature. He probably had a life expectancy half that of any normal child, and no one in the entire school, Board of Education, guidance staff or social services had thought to mention this to his teacher. Or perhaps even they had never been informed.

I no longer saw a problem child before me, but a child who could stand for all of them: helpless, trying against all odds, and losing more ground each day.

"I try to help the boy," his mother said, "I really do. But sometimes I just can't help. He need so much from me."

"So, do you miss school, Jimmy?" I asked awkwardly after a long silence.

"Yeah, like a lot, you know?"

"What did you think of Whitman? Was it a good place for you?"

"I always say Whitman is a good school. Everyone has a good purpose there. I have many experiences there—sad days, bad days, good days." His voice trailed off.

"It can be a rough place sometimes. I know. It was for me, too."

"Yeah, I think the teachers has a hard time with the kids," Jimmy agreed, looking at the floor. "Some kids curse at the teachers, throw things at them, right. It's pretty bad, I guess." He stopped for a moment. "Some teachers are not too strict. When they's strict, the kids find out the teacher won't take no garbage. Teachers who is lame is the ones who get the kids' love."

"Like me?" I asked. "I guess I was pretty lame."

"It's like, some kids is easily led not to pay attention. In your class, we never know who would mess up next. The fun part was we all knows you was a rookie. You use to tell us some wacky things. We was like, all right, we could bug out—we could teach her about the do's and the don'ts. We had a chance to teach you something. You know, Mrs. Sachar, everybody cuts class, but nobody cuts your class. It was fun in your room."

I laughed. "But fun for the wrong reasons, it sounds like. Jimmy, do you remember acting up in my room last year?"

"Oh, no. Not this again," his mother said. "He did it to you, too? That's just what I'm talking about, boy. You're always cutting up and giving trouble for the teachers. You probably led the gang around that school." To my surprise, her eyes filled with tears. "You know, he does it to all the teachers. He has no respect for education, does he?"

She stood up and asked Jimmy to bring me his progress report book from his new high school. "Take a look at this." She handed me the blue booklet with the words "Behavior Report" in black ink on the cover. "The worst ever," one teacher had written after a recent math class. "Late again and loud!" another teacher stated. "Rude, insolent behavior," was a third appraisal. "He belongs in a special class."

"No respect for the teacher and no respect for me," Jimmy's mother said. Now she was weeping.

"Oh, Momma, why you always sitting down to cry? It's stupid to cry. It don't help no one."

"It helps me," she said, choking on her tears. The room was quiet for a long time. "I just don't know what you want from me, child."

"I don't want nothing from you, Momma. Just a brother or a sister, and some respect."

"Oh, child, don't start talking like that. He's always asking for a brother, like he's lonely or something." Her eyes rolled upward. "Honey, I'm not going to have another baby just 'cause you're lonely."

She turned to me. "The boy is a chronic liar. I can't tell you how many times I get home, it's the middle of the night, and he's not here. He's out on the street with some gang of kids. When I'm away, they come in and blast the music. All these things behind my back. He always tells me he has no homework. The boy just lies and lies and lies."

"Oh, Momma, it's not as bad as that."

"Don't talk back to me, boy." Jimmy hung his head and clicked his tongue in disgust.

"I don't know," she went on. "I worry so, he's not doing anything with his life. Two calls every week, I get from the school. I think maybe he's the worst kid in the whole school. I want to put him in a home for discipline."

"Then do it, do it. Stop talking about it and just do it," Jimmy snapped.

"I'm not talking to you, boy. You're just a lying little kid." She was a beautiful woman with a svelte figure. She wore tight jeans, and a cowl-neck sweater, and her hair was tied up with a graceful bow. But her face contorted with anger, and suddenly it was not pretty at all.

"She has some nerve," Jimmy said to me. "She waited one year to buy me a pair of tennis shoes. And she lets her boyfriend come here and beat the shit out of me. I told her, don't do that again or I'll put the social worker on you. There was this night when she hit me with her jeans jacket and the zipper cuts me straight, like this, across my face." Jimmy's hands made the sign of a knife slashing his cheek.

"Okay, you want to hear the real story?" his mother replied. Her lips were tight and she spoke so forcefully that spittle formed at the corners of her mouth. "I get home one night, right, after two nights of no sleep on the train, and I'm ready to fall over. It's nine or ten o'clock at night. I get home, and no Jimmy. So I go outside in the front of the building. Again, no Jimmy. I give up and go to sleep, and then I wake up the next morning, around three or so, and who's there but Jimmy, sleeping on the couch in his clothes." She looked at him hard. "So, you're right, lying boy, I took my jacket and hit you in the face with it and told you to go to bed decent, not lying all over the couch in your soiled clothes. So then, you know what he says to me? He says, 'I'm going to your job and I'm going to tell them you hit me in the face with a bottle.' He's carrying on and carrying on. He's going to tell my supervisor I'm child-abusing."

Jimmy objected. "But, Momma—"

"Don't argue with me, child. I was late for work that day and you know it."

For nearly five minutes no one said a word. Then Jimmy broke the stalemate. "Oh, Momma, it's not so bad. We love each other, right? Things is okay most of the time."

Jimmy's mother gazed fixedly at her small, sickly son, then, her voice breaking, she addressed me passionately.

"I'm angry for what he's doing to me. It hurts me. I don't want to spend my days off sitting in the school hearing about what a lousy kid I've got. That's what I had to do today. I was supposed to go to this seminar to train for a new promotion, but instead, I get called down to the school for a suspension or something. I lose the day's pay.

"He's the only child I've got, and I don't want him to be out on the street as a tramp. But if someone says, 'Let's jump in the river,' Jimmy says, 'Fine, let's go.' He don't think for himself. And then, at the school they say he's got no respect for anyone. When I sat there today and the teacher stopped talking, I just wanted the earth to open and the chair to disappear with me in it. All I hear is how nasty he can be. My friends, they say they don't know what's wrong with him."

"Nothing's wrong with me, Ma. Really. I'm just plain old Jimmy, the boy you always knew." Jimmy started laughing maniacally, as if he were performing again for the kids in 8-7, playing for a reaction. I was quiet.

"I never say, 'You must look at a book.' I always say he can go with his friends. He never has a dirty pair of clothes. He wants everything name-brand. If it's not $50, $85 for a pair of pants, he's not going to wear it. So, okay, I get it for him. I say the day he doesn't get what he wants is the day he's going to kill me. I don't go to parties. I've got no time for friends and company. I'm always dealing with him."

"All she does is rub it in. Why don't you stop nagging, Ma? If I'm getting on your nerves so much, just get rid of me. It can't be much worse than this."

Tears rolled down her face and onto her jeans, making dark splotches on the blue denim. Jimmy, too, seemed so vulnerable, his real emotions much closer to the surface than I had realized when I taught him in 8-7. "He always says he'll do better, but he doesn't. I feel like I've failed."

"Come on, Ma. You didn't fail. You don't see me selling drugs on Tilden Corner, do you? I'm nice enough in other people's eyes."

"But you're not nice enough in the eyes of me." He watched as she reached for a fresh tissue. "Oh, Ma, cut the crying. You're always crying."

The tears kept flowing. "You're supposed to love him and cuddle him and hold him and say, 'Hi, Baby.' And then, as soon as you turn your back, he lies and cheats and talks back to the teacher."

"Oh, Ma, you want me to be a saint."

"I tell you, sometimes I just don't feel like coming home from work. Sometimes I just want to end it all right there on the platform. I just feel so depressed. What bad news am I going to get today?"

Abruptly, she sprang from her chair and walked into the kitchen. A few minutes later, I heard the sizzle of grease in a frying pan. "You want corn or beans?" she yelled to Jimmy.

"Corn, Momma."

"You know, Jimmy," I said, alone with him, "there's nothing wrong with admitting you need help once in a while, from a teacher or from your mother. You don't have to act up every day to get attention. Your mom really loves you, but she needs some respect, too. Think of how she feels when it's a school night and she comes home and you're out with your friends and you haven't even tried to sit down to do your work. Don't you think that worries her sick?"

Jimmy just shrugged. But I could finally see why. It wasn't all his fault. He felt his mother didn't understand how much he needed her, and why. He wanted a momma to send him off to school in the morning and to welcome him home in the evening. He wanted someone to share the lonely and volatile moments of adolescence. He needed someone more than most. Nor did he understand the pain his mother lived with—all alone but for him.

"Jimmy," I asked, "what did you really want from me last year? If you had to go to the bathroom, why not politely raise your hand instead of running around crazy?"

He looked thoughtful, then began pacing the room. "I guess I just wanted you to plead with me, like when I stand up and yell that I have to pee, I want you to say, 'Please, Jimmy, sit down. Please let me teach.' I want to feel like the biggest shot in the room, like I'm fresh, like you and everyone else in the room wants me to be there.

"I know I hurt the teachers' feelings," Jimmy continued, shrugging his shoulders. "But I don't mean it bad. I just do it the wrong way." He touched me lightly on the leg. "Right, Mrs. Sachar? You don't think I'm a bad kid, do you?"

"No, Jimmy, I don't. But I think if you could discipline yourself, you would be much happier. I'm sure it's hard with your mom gone so much of the time. But you're old enough to know the right way to behave in a class. You know that running around screaming that you have to urinate is a childish way to behave, don't you? Especially since if you really had to go that often—if your mom or doctor had told me there was a reason—I would always have let you. But you were usually only fooling. The kids may laugh, but it's not really a laugh of friendship."

"Yeah, I know," Jimmy said quietly.

"So why do it?"

"I just want the kids to say 'He's fresh, he's cool, I'm not going to mess with him because he's fierce.' I want to be like Bill Cosby. But, you know, Mrs. Sachar, I'm just an all-round good guy with a nice future in front of me."

"I hope so, Jimmy, because you're sure a smart kid. You could do something great with your life if you start to buckle down. And I bet you find the kids will like you better just the way you are."

Even as I spoke the words they sounded like platitudes, well-intended but irrelevant. Jimmy needed a mother who wasn't away half his life. He needed real friends, not these classmates he was forever trying to impress with his cavortings. And it didn't help that he was so much smaller than the other boys in his class.

Jimmy wanted to show me the rest of the apartment, and together we saw his mother's large bedroom behind the living room, and his room: a converted walk-in closet behind the kitchen. He invited me to stay for dinner, but I wanted to get home before dark. The area had a reputation for dangerous drug-dealing, particularly at night.

At the door, Jimmy gave me another tight embrace, saying, "You'll see, Mrs. Sachar. I'll make it to the Court of Supreme. And you can tell all your friends you had that judge, Jimmy Jones, in your math class."

22

Dr. Pedro

Every day, when he leaves here, I go down on my knees and pray to God for Pedro's mind opening up. He have so many problems. But God promise to help. God tells me he opens up Pedro's head and lets the learning go in.

—Maria, mother of 8-13 student Pedro.

Just five blocks from Walt Whitman Intermediate School, in a once beautiful pre-World War II building that had deteriorated into cracked plaster walls and splintered marble floor tiles was Pedro's apartment. The hallways were dark, and the walls gray, but the building was nicely located, across the street from an attractive city park with new softball fields and a well-maintained playground. Flatbush Avenue, a busy commercial strip with a bustling Macy's and the only Sears store in Brooklyn, was two blocks to the east. Elementary, intermediate, and high schools were all within a six-block walk.

Pedro's apartment was abuzz with friends and relatives when I arrived late one September afternoon. A little girl about ten years old sat at a kitchen table, studying. Two boys stood in the doorway of the kitchen, eating snacks their mother handed out. Pedro, with his usual uneven gait, came to greet me from a room somewhere inside the apartment. "Mrs. S.," he said, putting his lanky arms around my neck. "Pedro so happy you here."

I entered a linoleum-floored room just beyond the breakfast area.

It was filled with furniture—two plastic-covered couches sitting back-to-back and too many chairs to count piled atop a well-worn plywood dining table. Velvet paintings in ornate gilded plastic frames hung crookedly on the walls; blaring from a corner was a television set mounted on a high shelf just below the ceiling. Pedro's mother, Maria, joined us, yelling at the younger boys to turn off the TV.

She was short and heavy-set, with a pink paisley apron tied tightly around her waist. Her hair was knotted in a bun, and she was sweating from her work in the kitchen. Friends and relatives, she told me in hurried Spanish, were always stopping by for dinner, and some were expected soon. I introduced myself; I never met either of Pedro's parents at Whitman.

"So, Pedro, how's everything going this year?" I asked as his mother first pressed her hands together, as if in prayer, then patted her son on the knee.

"Fine, Mrs. S. You know Pedro. Pedro always fine."

Five people suddenly appeared at the door and walked into the living room, speaking loudly in Spanish. Pedro's mother stood up and gestured at them to be quiet.

"*Una periodista,*" she said. "*La maestra de matemáticas de Pedro.*"

The people in the doorway stood still, almost transfixed, and I realized that Pedro's mother had yet to speak to me in English. I hoped we wouldn't need a translator. "*¿Habla ingles, Señora?*" I asked, desperate to remember what few words of Spanish I knew.

"A little," she said. "*Un poquito.*"

I hadn't wanted to rush right in with my questions, but Pedro's mother seemed too busy for small talk. Food was sizzling in the kitchen, and now her company had arrived. "Well, I just wanted to know what you thought of Walt Whitman."

"Some of her friends told her I would get killed in that school," Pedro offered, "because I'm a defensive and there are a lot of kids looking for trouble. She always go down on her knees and start praying. But she never thought bad of it."

"Pedro responsible," his mother added. "He never say, 'I don't want to go to school.' He's sick? He still wants to go. And I always tell him, 'Don't use the drugs.'"

I was eager to talk about Pedro's problems in school. He had spent his entire young life in the New York public school system, but his eighth-grade year was his first in a regular English-speaking class. Until then, he had always been in bilingual and English-as-a-Second-Language classes. Only in seventh grade did he pass—just barely—the test for admission to the English-only program. He scored at the 21st percentile, just one point above the cutoff. Not only was his grasp of the English language poor; on the standardized math test, he had scored at the 5th percentile.

"When Pedro starts at school, Pedro never learning," Maria said. "He no get the work. His teachers say he needs help, but I not know what to do with Pedro mind. He such a good boy, but he just no get the work."

"Oh, Mrs. S.," Pedro said, laughing. "Pedro do some silly things. Mom send me to the store to get corn flakes, and I forget and buy bread. And she tell me to get shampoo and I get ketchup. Pedro have a silly head."

Pedro's cumulative record included one page from his elementary school labeled "Guidance Data," with his personal and social behavior rated in several categories. He had received mostly satisfactory ratings, but the accompanying comments were discouraging— in kindergarten, "He has a language handicap"; in first grade, "Pedro is trying hard to improve. He is easily distracted and is a slow learner." He repeated first grade; a similar comment followed. "Pedro tries to please. Great help around classroom. But has great trouble with schoolwork." In fourth grade, however, a teacher wrote, "Pedro has greatly improved in reading and math. He needs to control aggression." On another page, the same teacher noted that Pedro "reverses letters." The only reference to testing of any kind was "Guidance referral, 1985," but there was no indication whether Pedro's case had ever been reviewed by the school's guidance department.

In elementary school, on a scale of E for excellent to U for unsatisfactory, his marks were all Fs and Gs—fairs and goods, at least passing. At fourteen years old, he was two years older than the norm when he started seventh grade; he consistently earned passing marks, including 65s in math and 80s in language arts. Such marks, I knew by now, were often meaningless; many bore little relation to a student's actual academic progress.

"Pedro sometimes come to me and he say, 'Mommy, I have nothing in my mind.' It sad. Pedro problem is my problem."

"She's a mother," Pedro said. "She feel it bad when I mess up."

A few years ago, Maria brought her son to a psychologist at a public health clinic. "This medico ask Pedro many questions and Pedro answer many things. The medico say, 'I don't have any problem with Pedro. He a good boy.' We never go back."

"But he said I don't have nothing in my head," Pedro added. He frowned and shrugged his shoulders. "You know about Pedro, Mrs. S. If the teachers say something, sometimes I no get anything they say. I try, but I no get it."

"Tell me what you've been doing all summer, Pedro." He had spent the summer, he said, doing the same things he did the rest of the year—especially helping an elderly woman who lived on the first floor of the apartment building. "She just lonely old lady, and she love Pedro." The woman had just turned eighty-five, and he ran errands for her and helped straighten up her apartment. "Most days, we just sit together," Pedro said. "We keep each other company. Saturdays, I take her to have her hair done."

"Does she pay you for all that help?"

"Sometimes she gives me a dollar, sometimes a quarter, sometimes five dollars. Pedro bored in the house. I don't care if I get the money."

"That's Pedro," his mother said, her hands again in a gesture of prayer. "I have to pray for him." She knelt on the floor for a moment, her hands pressed together and her eyes closed so tightly the lids quivered. After a moment, she pulled herself up to the chair. "In every school, he help the teacher so much and then he don't do his work."

This neat, orderly home bubbled over with warmth, and it was hard to understand why it was always so difficult for Pedro to be on time for school. He shared a room with his two younger brothers, eleven and thirteen, both of whom did well in school and were always there on time. The parents' bedroom was next door to the boys' room, and Maria said that Pedro's father always awakened him before leaving the house.

"I shake him and shake him, but he no get up," his mother sighed. "Pedro a tired boy. What to do?"

"Daddy would set his alarm for seven o'clock and put the volume up real loud on the radio, but I no hear it." That sly smile I had seen so often at Whitman was back on Pedro's face.

With that, he announced that he was hungry. We followed his mother into the kitchen, where every counter gleamed with cakes, cookies, and frothy delights. Perhaps a dozen people were crowded in, eating and talking, while a radio blared Latin music over their conversation. In the midst of all the chatter and noise, the little girl still sat at the kitchen table, meticulously copying a paragraph into her notebook. She was Pedro's cousin and often stopped by, he said, to do her homework. "She always saying it quieter here than in her place."

We went back out to the couch, and Pedro munched a pastry as we talked.

"So, Pedro, have you given any more thought to what you want to do when you're finished with school?"

"I still want to be a doctor, Mrs. S. I gonna study real hard and do all my works and homeworks. I graduate from high school and then to college. I leave it in God's hands. It's up to Him."

"I didn't know you wanted to be a doctor. Do you know that, after college, you'll have to go to medical school for four more years?" I said.

"No, Mrs. S., just college for Pedro. Then I be doctor."

"No, Pedro, really. After college, you have to go to medical school. It's a long haul. It's great to try, Pedro, but you're going to have to start working harder than you did last year."

"I let the people decide. I never say I think I'm smart because then people say Pedro think he so great. But just between Pedro and Mrs. S., yeah, Pedro pretty smart. Pedro going to make it to *médico*. I'm very friendful."

"Why do you want to be a doctor, Pedro?" I asked.

"I want to take babies out. I want to save lives. There's a lot of bad abortions in this country. That's my dream, to stop the killing. My mother prays for me to be *médico*."

Pedro turned to the television set, where a distracting detective story was unfolding. I asked him who else lived in the apartment. His brothers had left the room but we could hear them jumping on the beds in the room next door. His mother was chattering loudly with friends and relatives in the kitchen. His father still had not come home; Pedro said he was trying to find work driving for a taxi service.

Along with his immediate family of five, a grandmother and grandfather, an aunt and a cousin also lived in the apartment. The grandparents slept on the couches in the living room, while the aunt and cousin shared a room with the boys, "two in each bed," Pedro explained. There was a twin bed and a bunk bed in his room, which was strewn with clothes and old copies of *El Diario*, the Spanish-language newspaper. No schoolbooks were in sight.

Considering how poorly Pedro performed in math, it was surprising how precise he was on the details of his family's finances. They paid $372 a month for their two-bedroom apartment (a rent that seemed particularly reasonable given Jordene's situation; her one-bedroom apartment in a rundown filthy building was badly located compared to Pedro's, yet cost $130 more a month). Pedro's father collected $431 unemployment insurance every two weeks; the family income was less than $900 a month. Both parents—his father, thirty-nine, his mother, forty—were from the Dominican Republic. They had met in New Jersey after immigrating to the states in the late 1960s.

Pedro, like Jimmy, asked me to stay for dinner, but once again I had to get home to my own family. I gave him a big thank-you hug and thanked Maria, who sent me off with a pile of pastries and a six-pack of soda for my family. "Instead of dinner," she smiled.

Pedro followed me to the stone spiral staircase at the end of the hall. "You think Pedro can be a *médico*, Mrs. S.?" he asked, with that same desperate tone I had heard when he asked me not to fail him. "You dig in and learn those times tables and start plugging away in your math and science classes," I replied. "Then maybe you can make that dream come true."

"You'll see, Mrs. S., Dr. Pedro could give you your next baby. Dr. Pedro. Dr. Pedro." As he walked back to his apartment, I could hear him muttering the words over to himself.

When I got outside, I looked up to the second story, searching for Pedro's apartment. There, in the window, he was. Leaning out, he shouted to me, "Dr. Pedro, you see, Mrs. S., Dr. Pedro."

"Now, Teeta, she's a mouth almighty, I always says. You got to keep her mind going," Tiara's mother was telling me. "One day, I woke up and Teeta there was reading a book, you know, maybe four years old or something. Once she starts running her mouth, you just got to give her more and more work. That's Teeta, she's a mouth almighty."

We sat in the gracious living room of a classic Victorian home in the wealthiest section of Flatbush, not far from Brooklyn College. The parquet floors were ringed with a delicate braided pattern of several types of wood and had been recently varnished. A bookshelf in the room was filled with classics. Freshly cut firewood sat at the base of the fireplace. White curtains, starched and uncreased, hung in the two bay windows at the front of the house; the wallpaper was bright and pretty with big prints of violets. The dining room was being used as a study hall for three of the nine children who lived in the house. The kitchen was austere and clean, only a few patches of plywood showing where the linoleum was worn away. An old gas stove stood out several feet from the wall. Like every room in the house, the kitchen was alive with laughter and children.

"I always say, it doesn't matter what money you've got. It matters what you do with what you have," declared Norita, Tiara's mother. As if to demonstrate, she ordered three of her children to line up and present their completed homework. "Too sloppy," she told one of the girls. "Go do it again. You know better." The child dutifully went back upstairs.

Norita turned to me. "You don't keep a hand on the child, the child will keep a hand in your pocketbook. If you teach the child to love the books, he won't need the money."

Her daughter Tiara was neither the best behaved nor the most attentive of the students I had taught. She could be a tiresome show-off, and had a playful wit that often turned cruel. Too many times to count, other girls in 8-1 were reduced to tears after a confrontation with her. Yet she was surely one of the brightest students I taught at Whitman and often one of the best-performing, though her grades turned mediocre whenever she neglected her homework and study assignments. Her mind was alive with curiosity. I couldn't help liking her, even when she embarrassed me by yelling out that my lesson was too easy, too short, or too dull.

All year, I had hoped to meet her parents, but they never came to our open houses. That, in itself, was curious. There was a dependable correlation between a student's success in school and the interest shown by parents. Nor had setting up this visit been simple. Tiara had said I could come only if I first cleared the request with her aunt, in whose home she and her eight brothers and sisters had been living for nearly a year.

Although Tiara's aunt consented, she would, in turn, have to clear the scheduling with Tiara's mother, who proved nearly impossible to reach. On the day of the visit, I had still not spoken with Norita, and half-expected to be turned away at the doorstep.

Instead, she gave me a hug, apologized for not phoning back, and warmly invited me in. Norita Barnes was a large forty-year-old woman impeccably dressed in an A-lined floral dress, with perfectly coiffed hair and a light touch of makeup. Before the conversation turned to her daughter, she told me about herself but would say nothing about her husband, Tiara's father. She had grown up not far from the house in which we sat and had had her first baby at twenty. Her children ranged in age from five to nineteen, and not all of them had had an easy time of it in school. Her eldest daughter lived at home, and had just returned to high school after dropping out several years before. "She realized there's nothing out there for someone without an education," Norita said. "So she's back. And I always tell them, 'You got to stay in school to make something of yourself.'"

Another daughter was away in Pennsylvania in the Job Corps. The others attended various schools throughout the city.

Tiara's aunt, Norita's sister, also had two children. Her husband was very strict, and helped her keep all the kids in line. "They need it," Norita said. "Look at me. I immediately started making babies. I had no young life, no fun. I don't want my kids doing that. There's not a lot of time in life, if you mess it up young. You got to be involved with your children, with their schoolwork. Now they know more than I do. Once I decided to go back for my GED [General Equivalency Diploma], and Teeta here had to help me. I had cobwebs in my head. I'm not embarrassed to tell you, I needed my daughter to help me." Tiara smiled broadly at the compliment.

"Does Tiara get more attention than the others?"

"I don't show her any more favor than I show the rest. When they do good, I reward them as best I can. Teeta's got the sharpest mind, but the others have sharp minds, too. You have to find it in each of them."

The two youngest daughters lined up for their mother's signature on homework. "You'll have to excuse me," she said, turning to review the children's workbooks, before signing the bottom of each page.

"I don't make much money working as a home health aide, but that's okay because I'm home every afternoon, three o'clock sharp. A mother's got to be home for her kids, even if it means they don't get as many clothes. I always says a momma's got to show her kids a lot of care."

Tiara stood up and began doing pirouettes and arabesques around the room. She had written in an essay, I recalled, that she wanted to be a dancer. "How's the dance going, Tiara?"

"Great. Ballet, tap, jazz, modern—I'm doing it all at King." She was now a freshman at Martin Luther King, Jr., High School, just across the street from the LaGuardia High School of the Arts and Juilliard and Lincoln Center. It was still a big street to cross.

Norita Barnes resumed her story: her own father had died when she was a year old. Her mother remarried, but her stepfather was usually out of work, so her mother worked as a housekeeper. "I think she also worked in a brush factory. She was always tired, that's for sure." Norita dropped out of high school when she was seventeen. "I just quit."

"It must be really hard with nine kids," I said.

"No harder than when you have one or two. There's just more to spread the money on. But it hasn't been easy, either. We lost our apartment, that's why we're here with my sister, and I haven't been lucky finding anything else. But my kids won't suffer—they might not get winter coats every year, but they trade around. It will work out."

I wanted to talk with Tiara, as I had to Jimmy, about her behavior at school, but first, I asked her about her life at home.

"It's okay. I have to do my work, but I have lots and lots of friends." She rattled off a list of names.

"You know, Tiara, I've always wondered why you picked those kids and not the ones like you at the top of the class."

She shrugged. "They ain't stupid, Mrs. Sachar. Just because they don't get good grades don't mean nothing." I changed the subject.

"You know, Tiara, you really made me laugh sometimes last year, when you kept pointing out my mistakes in class. But what were you really up to?"

Fixed in a ballerina pose, she answered, "I'm not used to doing the class without the Aim, and sometimes you forgot to put it on the board. If I didn't tell you, no one else was going to say nothing. And that scientific stuff. I don't know when we're ever going to make big numbers into small numbers and move the decimal over and put it in a power of 10. So I had to tell you it was stupid so you wouldn't spend that much time on it. You needed me, didn't you?"

"Do you always think you know best?"

"Yes," she retorted. " 'Cause I do."

And how did it feel to be voted Class Clown of the eighth grade? "I know I was real funny and all, but if I had my choice, I'd rather be voted most talented." She did a few more pirouettes.

"Are you really as cheery as you seem all the time? I don't think I've ever seen you depressed."

"Nothing ever really gets me down. I have many, many, many, many, many, many friends. If anything, I have too many. I don't have any big problems, just little problems."

"Like what?"

"Like what to wear to school the next day. The only day I felt lost was the first day of high school at King. But I found someone to help me, and it was great after that."

Tiara was one of the few intelligent kids I had met who did not seem consumed by self-doubt and uncertainty. Others at Whitman were more mature than she; none seemed so carefree. I wondered how she would cope as life became more complicated. Inevitably, she would face adjustments more daunting than a simple switch in schools; the mean streak she occasionally revealed likely came from insecurity she wanted to hide. As I watched her twirl around the room, I realized she would never allow me close enough to know.

"You must be proud of Tiara, Mrs. Barnes," I said.

"I am, I am. She's friendly, and she's not a troublemaker. It's true, sometimes her mouth gets the better of her. But she's a good-hearted person. I tell you—though, when that mouth of hers turns, she can get into trouble." Norita Barnes recalled that day I remembered so well when she had been called to school because Tiara had been tormenting one of her classmates. Tiara had thought the whole episode quite amusing. "We had to go up to school because Teeta let her mouth get beyond her. She had the girls all riled up. The assistant principal told me Tiara was such a smart girl, but this was her way of making sure her friends didn't know how smart she is."

"It's not true, Mrs. Sachar. I don't care if people knows I'm smart."

"I told her that way of acting wasn't right," Norita Barnes continued. "I know what it's like to be picked on. I have no patience for that sort of nonsense. If she didn't know it before, Teeta sure knows it now. She's lucky I didn't punch her in the teeth. When it happens to someone else, you don't know how bad it feels to get picked on."

Tiara interrupted her mother. "She had an attitude, that girl. She never wanted to be with anybody. She never wanted to answer you when you talked to her. No smiles from that girl or nothing."

"So, what difference does that make?" her mother said. "You start talking that way, I'm going to choke you something bad." She reminded Tiara, despite her bravado now, how contrite she had been that day. "She didn't want her uncle to know about it. He does the discipline around here. He's a real no-nonsense person. He'd put her on punishment—no phones, no movies, no friends, no company."

Tiara rolled her eyes. "You ain't kidding."

Mrs. Barnes had ambivalent feelings about Whitman. "They can use some help with that school," she ventured. "The teachers are overworked. They pay you a lot of attention, but they's still overworked. The school is cleaner than it was, but it's still pretty bad."

"You ain't kidding. That school is a mess," Tiara concurred emphatically.

"And it was bad that the kids didn't have a lunch period. But I think their new principal is really going to turn things around. That man Winfield, right? And Green, the new chancellor, he's going to fix things up real nice." She was the first parent I had met who knew the names of the principal and the late chancellor, Richard Green, who had died of a heart attack in May 1989.

"But I always say, even if he doesn't, if you try, you can learn. There's good teachers everywhere. I tell my kids: if you want to clown around, join the circus. Don't waste the teachers' time. When you go to school, you got to get something out of it."

Tiara invited me upstairs to see her room. Large and airy, it had a bunk bed and a red shag rug. "I dance around in here," she declared. The house had three stories, the top two filled with bedrooms, with ample space for everyone to move around in and for the children to study.

We finished the tour on the top floor, at Norita's bedroom, and I thanked her for permitting my visit. "No problem. I always say, we got nothing to hide. Just say nice stuff about Teeta here." She gave her daughter a bear hug, and the two started dancing the fox-trot.

Tiara had never demonstrated any affection toward me, and today was no different merely because I had come to visit. "Bye," she said matter-of-factly after walking me downstairs. "Find me in ten years. I'll be famous."

"I hope you are, Tiara. Just don't give up on that math you're so good at." She smiled and went inside, never looking back.

Reginald was waiting for me when I pulled up in front of his apartment building. He was fooling around with three boys I recognized from 8-12. I couldn't imagine why they would be happy to see me since I had failed them all in the final marking period of the year. "It's Mrs. Sachar," one of the boys yelled. "How's the baby?"

"Hey, how are you guys doing?" I replied.

"Look, Mrs. Sachar, new gold," one boy said, flashing a necklace with 'Ahmed' carved across a thick plate of gold.

"Tell her great stuff about us," Hudson urged.

Reginald smiled.

"It's great to see you, Reginald."

He led me into his building, the ornate lobby of which still displayed the remnants of Art Deco grace. But the elevator reeked of urine. Reginald's apartment was right next to the elevator bank. Holding the heavy black door open for me, he introduced me to his mother, Veronica.

She was a beautiful woman, tall and svelte, who looked much younger than her fifty-one years. She wore a red crêpe de chine dress, and shiny black patent-leather high-heeled shoes. Her hair was pulled back tight with a barrette and around her neck on a thin chain she wore a gold crucifix.

She led me down a short hallway to a doorless area that served both as their living room and the boys' bedroom. The couch and chairs, all covered in white imitation fur, were encased in transparent plastic slipcovers that she insisted on removing before we sat down. The room was immaculate. It was divided by a tinkling curtain of large red metallic beads. Behind the curtain was a makeshift bedroom with two large cots, one for Reginald, the other for his older brother, Larry. Pictures of naked women adorned the walls. "Don't look at that, Mrs. Sachar," Reginald blurted, embarrassed.

Veronica brought out cake and coffee, and I asked how she and her sons had come to the United States.

"It's a long story," she began. "First we came up when Reginald was a very small baby, then we went back to the Bahamas and didn't come back for good until 1985." Larry and Reginald were her only children. Looking a bit sheepish, she explained that they had different fathers. In 1972, Larry's father died. Reginald was born two years later. She had never seen or heard from the father in years, and Reginald had never met him.

"It hasn't always been good for us here. At first, they starts telling me Reginald is handicapped. In my country, a person that's handicapped is a person in a wheelchair. I said he don't do anything stupid at home, how can he be handicapped? They said his reading was bad. I said they must know best, so do what they think. 'Just don't jeopardize my boy,' I tell them."

Reginald picked up the story. He started school at a nearby elementary school in a fifth-grade special-education class. He had been well-behaved in my class and seemed intellectually keen. Why had they put him in special-ed? I asked.

"I had problems then. I had a bad attitude and I like to fight. I wasn't like I am now."

His mother interrupted. "I couldn't take that teacher he had. It's not my nature to complain, I don't like to embarrass people. But she gave him that handicap. She made him bad. He had never been bad before."

Had she complained to school authorities? "That's not me. I have to trust the school. But I decided to get him out of there and try somewhere else, so I put him in another school."

"Is that when the reading problems started?"

"Kind of, but I always has had problems reading. Not math, but reading."

"What did they do for you at the new school?"

"Nothing really. Reading's been real bad for me. I just sat there, kind of bored, not really learning much." At the new school, too, he was placed in a special-ed class, a designation that followed him to Whitman as a sixth-grader the next year. "The reading stayed bad, but the math was okay. Math was always easy to me, easy to learn."

"What is the problem when you read?"

"I don't know. I just don't get it. I read the words, I can make out what they say, but then I don't know what they mean."

Reginald's reading difficulties always seemed perplexing to me because what I saw of his writing was not so bad: he could organize his thoughts and communicate them, even though his spelling and grammar were weak. When he had to recite what he had written, however, he struggled like a very young child just learning to sound out words. His 17th percentile showing on reading aptitude tests suggested that he had little comprehension, as well. And his scores on standardized math tests indicated that the difficulties he had in math were not in computation or concepts but in dealing with word problems.

"I guess being in 8-16 was pretty frustrating for you," I said. "We had to go pretty slow there with the math."

"When you had them puzzles, it was okay," Reginald replied. "But I never moved ahead, I just stayed where I was. It wasn't the right class for me for math, that's for sure. I guess it was the right class for reading."

Reginald spoke of his other math teachers at Whitman, particularly one who had taught him most of the math he had learned so far. "Mr. Katz taught stuff for eighth and ninth in sixth grade. I wish I could have been in his seventh-grade class. But I'm too quiet. I don't like to argue, so they just didn't put me there."

I asked Veronica what she thought of her son's reading problem. "I don't know much about it, just what Reginald tells me. There was one year in Jamaica when he didn't go to school at all because we kept moving around. Maybe that hurt him."

How were things going at his new school, Roosevelt High? "There's lots of reading. They're trying to help me again, but they don't get my problem." In math, he was getting good test marks— an 80 and 85 so far—but "what use is it going to give me to study integers and the commutative property and order of operations? I learned this stuff in sixth grade." Science, he said, was a joke unless the kids were doing an experiment. "The kids mess around a lot, but the topics is good." They had been studying balance, force, distance, and speed, he said. "And the experiments—I wish we be doing experiments every day."

How was the social life at Roosevelt? "The reason I like this school is because I don't know anybody. That's good for me. Sometimes people want to make friends with me. I just don't pay any attention. If you don't have any friends, they won't lead you the wrong way."

At Whitman, Reginald had hung out with the tough kids in 8-16. "Those kids, they went the wrong way. I don't hang with them anymore." Two of his friends from Whitman were "dealing drugs now. There's drugs in my new school, too." His mother interrupted. "A couple of weeks ago, there was a shootout on this block and someone was killed. A drug fight or something. When it's dark, Reginald has to be in the house."

"If they don't get mixed up now, they won't get mixed up later," she continued. "I brought them up in a religious home. My boys know not to lie to me. I don't complain, and I don't borrow. I like to see my kids clean. I am involved in their education, I want them to have one thing to be a master in. I use the big one to pull it out of Reginald. I need him to be the father figure. The big one checks on the homework, he does the discipline."

"My brother had almost the same problem as me in his reading," Reginald recalled. "What my cousin did for my brother, my brother is doing for me. My brother says he wants me to be more and better than he."

"It sounds like you guys get along really well."

"We have a lot of arguments, but we never have a fight. I love him. I respect him. I'm more scared of him than my mother."

Veronica began to talk about her own school days. She had dropped out of school in Jamaica when she was sixteen. "I always say I want to go back and get my equivalency. But work and school at the same time? That's hard. The boys need me here." She worked days, she said, as a home attendant.

I asked her how she had created such an attractive apartment. "I can take a cave and make it a beautiful place. Nothing you see before you is new, not a thing. I bring home $250 a week and if I want something, I put away a little every day. I go with my $10 to put it on layaway and I pay it off, a little at a time. I never live over my means. I deny myself of a lot of things just for my boys. I hardly save anything, but the boys have what they need. "I cannot choose for them. What they choose for theirselves, as long as it edifies them and it's the right channel, I am with them."

Reginald said that his twenty-year-old brother hoped to be a lawyer, but had decided to get a master's degree in criminology first. "I am affected by him," Reginald admitted. "I see how safe he plays it, and I see that is a good thing."

"What do you want to do with your life?"

"I'm trying to cut a record. I want to get it copyrighted. A friend of mine works on it with me. I wish the schools gave more music. I didn't get music in the seventh or the eighth grades, and not this year either. I'd like to play the piano. I've always wanted to learn. I'd like to learn to read music, too. When I sit down at the piano, I can play it, like the tunes come to my ear and I feel it at the keys, but some people tells me that doesn't really count for much, that's not the right way."

"That counts for a lot," I said. "Lots of people would love to be able to play music by ear." Reginald shrugged.

As I rose to leave, Veronica Pinkert asked if I wanted to see the rest of her apartment. She showed me a spacious bedroom, another impeccable combination of crisp curtains, a neatly made bed, and religious artifacts on the wall. She opened the bathroom door. "If there's anything that gets me down, it's a dirty bathroom," she said, picking up a sponge to give the hot pink sink a quick onceover.

Reginald insisted on riding the elevator down with me and walking me to my car. As I shut the car door, he went back to talk to the boys from 8-12 who had greeted me when I drove up. For all that Reginald said, he was obviously still drawn to tough kids. Nevertheless, he struck me as a kid who could avoid the fate awaiting so many on those streets. He was aware of his reading problem and wanted to work on it. And he had a mother who clearly paid close attention to the details of her sons' lives. A little luck was all he really needed.

Two weeks into the 1989–90 school year, I phoned Shereeza Moodan's home. It was late on a Monday afternoon, and I expected an adult to answer the phone, since the kids should be in school.

"Yes?" I instantly recognized the voice at the other end.

"Shereeza, this is Mrs. Sachar, your math teacher." Silence. "Honey, why aren't you in school?" I was suddenly worried that the special-ed placement we had worked out had fallen apart.

"Can't go," she said in that strange voice that was always so hard to understand. Whether it was her accent or her rough English, I could barely make out her words.

"What do you mean, you can't go?" I heard her breathing on the other end of the phone, but again she said nothing.

"Shereeza, I called because I want to come visit you, but we've got to figure out a way to get you back to school. You're supposed to be going to a good new place this year, aren't you?"

Was her mother home? I asked. No, she was alone. "They home later," she said.

I told her I'd call back. There was a pause, then I said, "Are you okay, sweetheart?" She didn't reply, and hung up.

Three days later, I went to visit Shereeza. Like several of the students I had visited, she lived in a handsome building that still bore witness to an elegant past—pink marble columns lined the hallways, though they were now covered with graffiti; the tiled floors, a handsome checkerboard pattern on black-and-white, were thick with dirt. One of the original chandeliers still hung in the lobby, its crystal facets pock-marked and laced with spider webs.

I climbed three flights of stairs to Shereeza's apartment and was greeted at the door by her mother, Ransawtie, a small-boned, plump woman in a short-sleeved print dress. She quickly looped her long black hair into a bun and clipped it at the top of her head. I followed her slowly down a hallway to a spacious living room with a couch, two chairs, and, at the rear, a mahogany dining table. A console television set was tuned to *Wheel of Fortune*. A man who appeared to be in his twenties, still wearing his nightclothes, was sprawled over one of the chairs, his eyes on the screen. As soon as we sat down, a young child of about two, with huge brown eyes, ran over and clung to Ransawtie's skirt. Shereeza's mother called for her eighteen-year-old daughter, Ransoutie, to join us.

The language barrier, I saw, was going to be a problem. Ransawtie seemed to be speaking English, but her accent was impenetrable. She also spoke a Guyanese dialect, according to her daughter, and she switched back and forth between the two.

Shereeza wasn't there. It was a Thursday morning, and her mother said she had left her for her first day of school.

"Why hasn't she been in school until now?" I asked. The fall term had begun nearly a month before.

"She's afraid of fall," her mother said, presumably referring to Shereeza's limp. I began to explain who I was and why I had come to visit. "Ask us anything," the daughter said.

So I did. I asked about the man in the chair. His name, Ransoutie said, was Surendre. He was sixteen and one of Shereeza's brothers.

"He dropped out because the teacher refused him in school. He can't write his name." He had stopped attending school at thirteen, while the family still lived in Guyana. What did he do all day? "Watch TV." Ransoutie shrugged.

After each question, Shereeza's mother would answer in her thickly accented English, then her daughter would translate. All eleven of Ransawtie's children came with her to New York in 1986, several years after her husband died at forty-two of "a liver problem." Between 1961 and 1978, she said, she had had a baby at least once every two years. Six of her children still lived with her in this two-bedroom apartment. As she talked, two mice scampered across the floor and disappeared into a space between two floorboards under the television set. I flinched, and the little girl's eyes followed the mice; Ransawtie and her daughter gave them a fleeting glance, then looked back at me. The room in which we sat was not dirty, but it had the sour odor of soiled diapers.

One of Ransawtie's older daughters had marital problems—"her husband beats her," Ransoutie said—and two others were married, with children. Her nineteen-year-old unmarried daughter had a baby and both lived here with the family. That was the little girl, dressed only in a diaper, who clung to her grandmother's skirt, occasionally glancing at the television set.

Why had the family come to the United States? "Make a better life," the daughter said. "Things very expensive in Guyana and you can't get many things." Her mother interrupted, and Ransoutie interpreted. "She says, how can I maintain all these kids there?"

I asked about Shereeza's eye. "Do you know what is wrong with your daughter? Does she have a medical problem of some sort?" Her medical records at school had said nothing about the limp or the lazy eye; "Dental caries" had been the only mention of a physical ailment. Ransawtie shrugged. "When she was three years old, the eye dropped down." She said nothing more about it.

Shereeza's cumulative record file indicated a fairly stable school life in Guyana; she had attended the same school for six years. On her last report card, her attendance had been "good"; her appearance "neat and tidy"; her relations with staff and students "good"; her conduct "very good"; and the quality of her work "average." However, under "Examinations passed," the record said "Nil." At the Kildonan Primary School, Shereeza had taken English language, mathematics, social studies, general science, agricultural science, home economics, woodwork, and motor mechanics. No grades were reported for these subjects. Under the heading General Remarks were the words, "a very quiet and co-operative student."

Ransawtie's analysis, spoken through her daughter, was more down-to-earth. "Shereeza can tell you the TV story, but she never pick up a book. She's always saying, 'Momma, I'm a trying, but I don't know why, I can't catch it.' We don't want her to miss her education. But a few days back, when school's a starting, she say she couldn't find the school. And there is a problem—she just don't like to study."

What did her mother think of her daughter's grades? "They seem good," she replied. For years Shereeza had been given passing marks in most of her subjects at Whitman. "She think she good," her sister said. "I tell her she's not. The teacher just say that to make her feel better. She say I'm wrong."

I asked the daughter why, at eighteen, she was not in school either. "I had to drop to help my mother pay the rent," she said. After quitting Erasmus Hall High School at age sixteen, she said, she had attended a six-month course at a private business school. She was now paying back a $6,000 loan at the rate of $50 a month. "I want to go to college, but I don't know now. I have to help too much with my mother. I don't want to work at a store forever. I have other dreams." She was working as a cashier at a children's clothing store on Flatbush Avenue, taking home $27.50 a day for a ten-hour day. She was often paid in cash, she said, and did not know whether she was earning less than the minimum wage. "What's that?" she asked.

Just then, another woman entered the living room, walking with the same slow gait as Shereeza's mother. She wore a low-cut pink nylon robe, and as she walked over to the little girl, her robe fell open, exposing her breasts. She grabbed the child's arm, picked up a hairbrush from the wooden coffee table, and began vigorously brushing the little girl's hair. The child whimpered in pain. "Shut up," the woman said.

"Maybe you explain this," asked Shereeza's mother suddenly. She lifted the sheet that hung as a curtain behind the television set. Behind it was her bedroom. "What is this?" It was the letter from the Board of Education, informing them that Shereeza was to attend a special school for learning-disabled kids in Brighton Beach. I was a bit stunned by the school's location; it was at least forty-five minutes away by public transportation—a long ride for any student, but especially trying for one as weak and vulnerable as Shereeza.

"Where did you go this morning when you took her to school?"

Obviously, Shereeza's mother did not understand the special-ed referral or that her daughter was to attend a new school.

"To Erasmus," her sister answered.

"She's not supposed to be going to Erasmus. They found a place for her in a special school where she'll be able to learn more. Look, I'll show you on the form."

Everyone in the room was staring at me. No child in this family, I learned, had gone to high school anywhere except Erasmus.

"Where is this school?" Shereeza's mother asked.

I explained, but was not sure she understood. I promised to find her a bus map and mail it, with directions.

"So, tomorrow she not go to Erasmus?" Shereeza's mother asked me. I didn't know what to say. Certainly Erasmus was better than nothing. Shereeza's mother obviously did not know the city or the school system well enough to understand how to get her daughter to the new school. And, from what she had said about her children's education so far, she did not seem troubled when they were absent from school for long periods of time.

"I can't afford taxi for Shereeza," she finally said. "How much this bus cost?" I told her it would cost one dollar, but that Shereeza would probably get a free pass eventually and until then might be able to show her schoolbooks and ride without one.

"Here, take my phone number and call me if you need help." Ransawtie and Ransoutie smiled in thanks.

A few days later I phoned to ask if Shereeza had received the map and bus information I had sent. The brother who answered the phone refused to let her speak to me. "I'm taking care of it," he said. "Shereeza will be fine. Don't bother us anymore."

23
Epilogue

Just think of teaching three classes in a row and you won't miss it so much.

—A Walt Whitman teacher, speaking to me in October 1989.

The television reports and newspaper headlines screamed out the city's latest appalling crime. On March 7, 1990, eleven-year-old David Opont had been dragged off his path, beaten, and critically burned. After failing to accept drugs from a thirteen-year-old neighborhood bully, the slight, hard-working Brooklyn boy, a recent arrival from Haiti, had been forced into an abandoned building, tied to a radiator, beaten, and doused with a flammable liquid. Then he was set on fire and left to die. With his clothes aflame, David broke free, ran out of the basement, and stumbled into a nearby auto body shop, where mechanics snuffed out the flames. It was nearly too late. Third-degree burns covered more than half of his body, and in the weeks to come he would need multiple skin-graft operations.

At the end of the first day's newspaper report was a familiar name. When the incident occurred, just two hours after sunrise that Wednesday, David had been on his way to Walt Whitman Intermediate School.

Several of my former Whitman students phoned me in the following days to see if I had heard about the incident. "Mrs. Sachar, you hear about the burning boy?" one girl asked. "I tell you, Mrs.

Sachar, it's not safe around that school. You know, one day last year, a boy with a gun followed me to school. I knows he had a gun and I just kept on walking. Maybe it was the same boy that did this."

"Whoever it is, I hope they catch him soon," I said.

"Lots of kids around that school be bad, Mrs. Sachar," she hurried on. "They like to pick on the little kids from Whitman. It's a game to them."

In the days immediately following the incident, public officials reacted with horror. Then-federal drug czar William Bennett called the attack on David "about the worst thing" he had encountered since his appointment. Former first lady Nancy Reagan, who had spearheaded the "Just Say No" antidrug campaign during her husband's presidency, was "deeply saddened by this tragic story."

More details of the attack on David Opont came out in the following days. Accused of the crime was another boy, living in a foster home, who, for months, had not been seen at his school, Jackie Robinson Intermediate School, also in Flatbush. At thirteen, he was assumed to be a dropout. He was described as a surly, thuggish boy who, attempting to win the respect of older kids, intimidated, beat up, and extorted money from younger children. Several reports said that he spent his days playing video games in arcades on Flatbush Avenue. Not long before, in an effort to ingratiate himself with older toughs in the neighborhood, David's assailant had stripped naked and run across the rooftops of Brooklyn tenements. He liked to collect stray dogs and, after beating them into a snarling fury, set them on one another. A neighborhood youth told reporters that the thirteen-year-old boy once picked up a dead cat and chased a group of small children down a street with it. On another occasion, he had emptied salt and garlic shakers on restaurant chairs, then mixed the contents with ketchup before pushing the chairs in to the table. Unsuspecting patrons then sat on the mess.

The school this boy was supposed to be attending, and its principal, quickly became the subject of investigations by both press and school officials. What had happened to the dropout prevention program that was to have kept the offender in school? Why was it that funds earmarked for programs to help children like him somehow got spent on things not directly tied to improving their education? Just what was the agenda of the principal, Vergie Muhammad, a Columbia University-educated Muslim who patrolled her school in headwrap and camouflage jacket? In the weeks to come, the Board of Ed reported that in the spring of 1990 Muhammad refused to accept $342,000 in federal funds for remedial programs for students because doing so, she said, would create "negative peer pressure" for students. Board of Ed officials, meanwhile, alleged that Muhammad simply didn't want to fill out the stack of necessary forms and had deliberately failed to submit them in time to qualify for the programs —charges that left many parents reeling. In September, Muhammad volunteered with one other principal out of the 998 citywide to participate in a four-to-six-month retraining program initiated by the city's new schools chancellor, Joseph A. Fernandez.

It was more than a year since I had left Whitman, and during that time I had heard often from teachers and administrators that life at the school was improving, the kids working harder and behaving better, and that the neighborhood, too, was on the upswing. After the Opont incident and after further discussion with teachers and former students, I could only conclude that such reports were the wishful thinking of adults as terrified as the kids by deteriorating conditions. The realities were grim as ever. Teachers' cars were being vandalized and burglarized at record rates. Brawny teens from Erasmus Hall High School, some of them Whitman alumnae, were still coming by to taunt the "babies" at Whitman, while Whitman kids, in turn, were beating up on even smaller kids from PS 399, the nearby elementary school. And then had come this final outrage—an eleven-year-old child nearly burned to death by a thirteen-year-old bully. What would happen next?

When I spoke with some former colleagues in May, I heard that the 1989–90 school year had been one of Whitman's most difficult in a long time. One winter afternoon, gunfire from the street pierced the basement cafeteria windows. A teacher told me about a fight with razors between two girls that spring; another told of a boy stabbed with a compass on the way to class.

In certain ways, it had been easy to extricate myself from Whitman. I deposited my last Board of Ed paycheck in the bank one day at the end of August 1989, and then returned to newspapering. Some of my fellow teachers were right in saying that only when you *can't* leave teaching, when it is your life's work, can you begin to appreciate the enormity and difficulty of the teacher's task.

Most of my former students lead lives far more difficult than my own, often leaving cramped apartments and parents and relatives as needy for help and direction as they are. Many walk to school in constant fear that a crack addict may be looming around the next corner, ready to pounce, like the young hoodlum who jumped on

David Opont. They are often mindful of their own academic shortcomings. They wonder if the school system serves them well, and
puzzle over what they can do about it when it serves them badly.
They want to know who can help them. They are dreamers, and
sometimes their dreams seem reasonable, even if for many, they are
still beyond reach. Dr. Pedro and Jimmy in the Court of Supreme—
what will happen to the kids who fail to achieve these goals? What,
as their teacher, did I do to help or hinder?

On Sunday nights, the phone occasionally rings with one of my
students at the other end of the line. Kevin, the boy who threatened
me with the letter opener, called just after New Year's Day, 1990, to
"say hi," as if our months apart had erased the angry confrontations
we had, as if he had forgotten how shaken I was by his conduct. I
still find it hard to talk to some of the kids who threatened violence,
and I found it hard that Sunday night to talk to him. How personal
should I get? Do the kids still see me as a math teacher, or now that
I am no longer marking their homework, am I a confidante and a
friend?

I asked Kevin how his artwork was going, for I had discovered,
in the last months of school, that he was talented and particularly
adept at drawing comic book heroes. "Okay," he replied but made
no effort to carry the conversation further. He just stayed on the line,
his breathing audible. Was he hoping that I would give him permission, with a personal question, to tell me that, no, things were not as
good as he had always said? Perhaps he merely wished for some
nonthreatening small talk, a little comfort in a lonely moment.

"Are you still living near Whitman?" I asked. "I tried to call you
a few months back. I'd love to see you." I had never visited Kevin,
but I knew from other students that he lived in a squalid tenement
near the school. His father supposedly was a longtime drug addict.
"No," Kevin said. "I'm living with my aunt now." Where, I asked?
Maybe I could visit, bring some drawing materials. Perhaps he would
explain what had been behind the knife incident that had so alarmed
me. "I'm living in East New York now," he told me. It was a neighborhood several miles from Whitman. "I'd love to see you," I said
again. "No, Mrs. Sachar, it's real bad over here. I can't let you be
coming here."

"Well, tell me about school," I said after a long silence. "It's
okay." "Math going all right?" "No." As our desultory conversation
drew on, I heard pots clanging in the background and a woman's
voice shouting for Kevin. "Well," he said softly, "it's been good talking. Bye." And that was that.

I felt at loose ends after Kevin hung up, as I so often do when other students say good-bye after odd phone calls at odd hours. I feel between us that same impenetrable distance I felt so often at Whitman, undiminished by my desperate wish to be close to the kids. They either weren't interested in an emotional relationship with their teacher, I concluded sadly, or weren't sure what to make of my awkward overtures.

I tried to call Kevin several times after his January call to me. His phone number had been disconnected. None of the other students in 8-7 knew where he was or how to reach him. I have not heard from him since that wintry Sunday night.

In the spring of 1990, another of my 8-7 students called. Could I, she said, sing "Happy Birthday" to her? It was late in the evening, and her mother had not remembered all day that it was her sixteenth birthday; she had just gone to bed. "I guess my sweet sixteen wasn't so sweet," the girl said. "Could you just sing it so I know somebody's thinking about me?" I could hear her crying as I sang.

I miss her, and Kevin, and so many of my other kids. I long to run into them, and I find myself examining nearly every black teenager's face on the subway or the street. I am delighted when I think I have spotted a former student and frustrated when I discover that I am mistaken.

One day in December 1990, I did spot one of my students, Tameeka—the girl who had shouted, "Shut the fuck up and let the lady teach" during one of my early days with 8-16. There she was with her mother, in front of State Supreme Court in Manhattan, her head dropped in apparent shame.

"Why're you here, Tameeka? You testifying in a case?"

"No, it's my case, Mrs. Sachar."

"*Your* case? What do you mean? What did you do?"

"Nothing."

"Tell her," her mother demanded. "Tell her now."

"Robbery," Tameeka said, stammering. She looked away.

"Robbery? What kind of robbery?"

"With a knife."

"Why?"

"I don't know. No reason."

"Who did you rob?"

"Just a girl. She didn't get hurt or nothing."

"What did you take?"

"We didn't get nothing. They got us."

Tameeka told me her lawyer had worked out a good deal for her

—a five-year probationary sentence in exchange for a plea to a misdemeanor. What could I say?

"Well take care of yourself, Tameeka."

She nodded, and she and her mother walked away.

Other students call from time to time, to brag about how well they're doing or to ask for help with their math work. There are other mementos of the good days, too, and they grow more important with time. In my jewelry box are some of the gifts the kids gave me, the "I ♥ Math" button from Pedro, the "No. 1 Teacher" pin made for me by two girls in 8-1. I hold dear the "Kids Are Leaders, Too," button that I wore almost every day the last few weeks of the year, when I finally felt that the kids were not the enemy. I have all the cards they sent for my daughter's birth and the Christmas cards and the thank-you notes for showing *Stand and Deliver*, and other small treasures.

The unhappy memories remain, too—the words of some of the black teachers who disliked me then and, I have heard, still detest me; the feelings of incompetence and helplessness that gripped me the first half of the year; the sad stares of Shereeza or Jordene as they struggled to write a sentence or figure out whether 30 or 300 is the larger number.

My eighth-graders, most of whom I last saw on graduation day, are attending high schools all over New York. Some have kept touch with each other; all but a few have lost touch with me. The 8-16 student who had a baby just before the new school year opened phoned to tell me of the birth. Her daughter was named for Tameeka. The new mother told me that she had dropped out of school and was living on welfare, like her own mother. Two of my other students have also dropped out of school; but they told me when they phoned that they had found jobs.

Five of the six students whose lives and academic trails I continued to track are enrolled in various school programs. But Jordene remains a mystery. I phoned Paul Robeson High School, where she was to spend her ninth-grade year, and asked if they had received the special-education referral I had sent. They hadn't—the registered letter must have been misplaced, I was told. Jordene had been enrolled in regular-education classes. When I tried to phone Jordene's home, her phone had been disconnected. I dropped by her apartment hoping to find her in, but the only ones at home were the baby and one of the older boys. Visiting again several months later, I found the family gone.

I have heard from other students as well; their letters responded to a newspaper series I wrote about my year at Whitman. They were required to read it as a class assignment. Some agreed with what I had written. Some didn't.

I didn't like what you said about some people in your articular. You were talking about things that shouldn't be talk about. So I resent the things you said and the only thing you should have talked about were the good things instead you talked about how much trouble the school put you though.

There are a lot of studence are against what you wrote but I feel you should have the right to speak out. Maybe then they will try to fix the schools.

My cousin told me about your teaching. She said that you teach lowsse, and she said that your article was not so interesting all those silly games you use to make up my cousin say's that you could of done better than that.

I have been reading your articles and I find them very interesting the things you write in your articles are the truth about Walt Whitman. But it is not the school that makes it bad, it is the students that make it look bad.

Hi, Ms. Sachar. You were my eight grade teacher. I was in class 8-16, your wounderful class. I read all of your articles in the newpaper I think that all of it is not true! Ms. Sachar, my Jonior high school was not bad. You were a woandeful teacher. I alway respected you, and you gave me a good grade on my report card. You were always on my back to do my work. in your newspaper. you said that kids were always picking on you. Maybe you were trying to boss people but that was not you job. your job was to teach them. If I were in your shoes I would have suspended a lot of stundents. However to me you were a very good math teacher and a good friend.

I'm glad somebody wrote about one of the dirty schools in brooklyn. I went to Whitman for 2 years and the desks and chairs were all broken up, the classroom had paper all over the floor and some window was broken in the winter time. It's about time somebody told the truth.

In October 1989, I returned to Whitman to talk to principal Claude Winfield about teaching, his school, and his job. Although I had scheduled a two-hour block of time with him, our interview started nearly an hour late and ended abruptly after forty minutes, when Winfield said he had to leave for a meeting. When I asked for a return visit, he politely said there was nothing more to discuss.

Our discussion was deeply disappointing. Winfield quickly discounted the problems I had experienced teaching in his school, saying all I had needed was a better understanding of math. A trained mathematician himself, he launched into a ten-minute discourse on the complex theories behind division of fractions, suggesting that had I offered such theories to my students, they would have learned more. I had hoped for candor, including an honest appraisal of his school and its many problems. Instead, Winfield pushed piles of papers at me listing the myriad accomplishments of the school and its students: Industrial Arts Teacher of the Year—New York City Technical Education Association 1986; District-wide Storytelling Contest, 1st Place, 1989; Women's History Month Poetry Contest, 1st Place, 1987, and so on. Impressive though they were, I knew that these accolades resulted from the efforts of but a small handful of teachers and students. What, I asked Winfield, of the vast majority who were not achieving?

Winfield's rejoinder was that I couldn't possibly know much about the school or about teaching after only one year at Whitman. "There was a lot I didn't let the other teachers tell you," he said. "I felt you should come back as a journalist and ask."

"Like what?" I asked, annoyed. Surely I had at least seen the reality of classroom life at Whitman. "Yes, that's true," he conceded. "In that sense, you saw a true reality. You can't change what goes on when the door closes." I sensed he felt that classroom experience offered a very inadequate means by which to evaluate his school; this struck me as bizarre. Where else did one learn about a school and its students?

He talked about numerous special projects during the 1988–89 school year and some new ones that had just started. One of these— a joint program with Brooklyn College to train math teachers to work with inner-city kids—would have been especially useful to me when I was teaching at Whitman. The school's principal since 1984, Winfield kept returning to the school's successes, even citing the accomplishments of students five or six years after they left—alumni who had made it into good colleges or prep schools; three former Whitman graduates who were semifinalists in the prestigious Westinghouse Talent Search science competition; a student accepted at Hunter Campus High School.

Without question, I had seen some superior, even brilliant work by highly motivated students during my year at Whitman—one student placed second in a citywide storytelling competition; the student poet who was selected to read her work at the memorial service for Chancellor Richard Green. But these students were the exception. To focus on them while ignoring the vast majority who were struggling to read and write or do basic math computations seemed to ignore the essential problem.

While working at Whitman, I had always felt that the programs of which Winfield seemed so proud were little more than window dressing masking the real agonies that were the everyday working reality of the school. I could understand why the administration wanted such projects—they gave opportunities to "exceptional" kids at both ends of the curve and provided bright spots of hope for the rest of us to contemplate. Unfortunately, most of the students I taught had not been touched by these programs, and neither had I. One teacher told me of Winfield's reaction to a program the school had hosted at which Whitman students traded ideas about student life with children from a predominantly white school in Canarsie, a section of Brooklyn. Winfield did not introduce himself to the visitors when they arrived at his school nor, my friend said, did he seem interested in what the kids thought of the program. Staff from the Brooklyn borough president's office had been invited, too, and Winfield reportedly asked only about their reaction. "What did the Brooklyn borough president think?" he wanted to know. My friend was dismayed: "Doesn't he ever ask: 'What did the kids think?' "

Yet there was no denying that Winfield, like so many principals around the city, faced daunting tasks year after year. During the 1986–87 school year, for instance, he had been forced to accept hundreds of sixth-graders from a neighboring district, bringing Whitman's register to well over 2,300 students. On many of the days I taught, he could understandably do little more than respond to a continuing flood of discipline problems—many so severe they threatened the safety of students and staff.

Yet, as I sat in his office that October day, Winfield appeared colder and more opaque than ever, sitting across from me at an uncomfortable distance, never removing his dark glasses. Was he afraid that honest answers to my questions might get him and his school in trouble? Or were his eternally optimistic answers the only truth he knew?

Whitman's enrollment the year after I left was down 200 students, to about 1,500. That was still 150 students over capacity, but represented a big victory for Winfield, who had made a reduction in the student population one of his most important goals. There were, as ever, many teachers new to the school—almost one in six, four in the math department alone.

More upsetting news from the school came several weeks after my October discussion with Winfield. Financial irregularities discovered in the District 17 office resulted in the laying off of eight Whitman teachers in the middle of the 1989–90 school year. There was no money, the district claimed, to pay their salaries. To the teachers, this was devastating; finding jobs midway through the school year is virtually impossible, especially for those with little experience. The layoffs occurred in three rounds, each of which forced a reorganization of the entire school. So the students, too, were tormented; amost every one got at least one new teacher, while some students saw their entire programs rewritten. "It's been a tense year," Vikki Kowalski told me. "When you reprogram a school three times, you're going to fray some nerves."

Despite picket lines set up before school hours to protest the continual layoffs, the cuts continued. Finally, citing complete financial disarray throughout the entire district (the city's fourth largest), the city's new schools chancellor, Joseph Fernandez, overruled the school board in late March 1990 and appointed three trustees to make all personnel and financial decisions. The district, he charged, had run up a $1.3-million deficit in its $70 million budget. It had also failed to spend nearly $2 million in special state and federal money designated for after-school and remedial programs. Other details surfaced. One of the reasons Whitman had such antiquated textbooks was that money to purchase new books was allocated to schools only four months before the end of each school year, insufficient time to place book orders for the next year. So the money was spent on other items.

District 17 was not the only one with personnel and financial woes. Other districts around the city were just as poorly managed. The Board of Education, since August 1989, had assigned replacement teams to run District 4 in East Harlem, District 16 in Brooklyn, and Districts 9 and 12 in the Bronx. In every case, the move was the result of large budget deficits or gross underspending of funds designated for students.

Yet, Whitman looked neater and cleaner during my October visit than I remembered it. The walls in the hallways and in many classrooms had been freshly painted; the rooms in which I had taught were no longer awash with graffiti. And the corridors seemed less crowded. The mentor program for new teachers, which had started more than three months late during my year, started only two months late in the 1989–90 school year because funding for it came through earlier.

But the layer of crayon that had covered some of my chalkboards still remained. Kids were still fighting and running recklessly through the halls, and a few classes looked completely out of control. The day after my visit, in fact, a teacher who was attacked by intruders while I was at Whitman was assaulted again and soon decided to give up teaching altogether.

To contend with the overcrowding, the kids were still being assigned to the auditorium once a week, where they watched the same videos as the year before. Lacking a locker room, students still took gym classes in their street clothes, and eighth-graders still had to endure a 5½-hour school day before lunch.

I miss teaching. Because I hope some day to return to the classroom, I have been reluctant to let go of the tools of the trade. One shelf in my den holds workbooks; another has bags of smiley-face stickers; a third, dice and protractors. Next to my computer is a filing cabinet filled with the photocopied puzzles I used at Whitman. "Get rid of the stuff," a friend advised. "The year is over. Get on with your life." But I can't bring myself to throw them out, nor do I want them moldering away in my basement.

"You got bit by the bug, didn't you?" Bob Moore, the school's UFT rep, said to me one afternoon over lunch. "You saw the agony. But you saw the glory, too."

"I guess that's right," I told him. "I've never been so close to real people." By which I meant: It's hard to fake it in teaching. Kids make you own up to what you are and what you're trying to do.

Nowadays, the closest I get to a school is watching the comings and goings of its students from the outside. Still, I can't help hunting for my kids. Teachers tell me it will happen somewhere, some day, when I least expect it—"Mrs. Sachar," the father of two will yell out, "you were my math teacher at Whitman, weren't you?"

Then we'll rehash the old times—the stink bombs and the panicked hallways and the magic moment when Budget produced both a new $95,000 winner and a little comprehension.

Until then, I take comfort in the victories of my year at Whitman, however sporadic and few in number. For at least a handful of students, I want to believe that I did make a difference. And for all of them, I tried.

Acknowledgments

During my stint in teaching and in the writing of this book, I have been blessed with help from many friends and professionals. This book would never have been completed without the careful and sensitive hand of my editor, Elaine Pfefferblit, and her aide, Michael Sanders. My most literate friend, Peter Tauber, also substantially improved the manuscript. And Herbert Kohl, author of *36 Children* and many other books, offered invaluable suggestions.

A number of people at the Board of Education made it possible for me to undertake this project, and I owe each of them a debt of thanks. Robert Wagner, Jr., former president of the board, blessed the project at the onset, encouraging me long before I had a job to write about everything I saw in the classroom. The late Chancellor Richard Green also could have nixed the project, but encouraged me to teach instead. Over my years covering the board as a reporter for *New York Newsday*, James Stein, director of the board's Office of Appeals and Reviews, provided an ongoing flow of story ideas, including this one. So did Richard Guttenberg, now president of Outward Bound in Masssachusetts.

At the board, a number of administrators explained various aspects of teaching and school management when my year as a teacher was complete. Among the most helpful were Shona Sloan, former administrator of promotional policy; Robert Tobias, director of the Office of Research, Education and Assessment; Susan Zakaluk, director of mathematics; Thomas Ryan, executive director of the Division of Human Resources; Mary Schearer, testing administrator; and Lawrence Edwards, director of the Office of Access and Compliance.

Thanks also to Claude Winfield, principal of Walt Whitman Intermediate School, for allowing me to teach in his school even after he knew of my plans to write about what I had seen. And thanks to several of his assistant principals—Edward Newman, Vikki Kowalski, Ronald Novins, and William Berkowitz, the latter now retired— each of whom was helpful to me during my time at Whitman.

Several teachers and professionals at Whitman whom I hold in particularly high regard also helped me survive my first year of teaching as well as the writing of this manuscript. They include Barry Kantrowitz, Sylvia Culler, Roman Foster, Gloria Holloway, Ellen Yudow, Vivien Nobile, Sharon Cohen, Bruce Hanson, Barry Friedman, Joel Fried, Joann Thompson, and Bob Rich.

Thanks also to Paul Heller, a high school social studies teacher, for his continuing support and myriad explanations about the operating details of New York City schools.

Also supportive of this project, and infinitely sensible, was Sandra Feldman, president of the United Federation of Teachers. Also at the union, I want to thank Neill Rosenfeld, Susan Amlung, Bert Shanas, and staff attorney Randy Weingarten for their thorough answers to questions during the year and afterwards.

Three editors at *Newsday* and *New York Newsday*—Donald Forst, James Toedtman, and Anthony Marro—agreed to grant me a leave of absence of sufficient length to allow me to complete this project without forfeiting my job. And I thank them also for issuing no requirement that I write about my teaching experience. At *New York Newsday*, I also owe thanks to Deidre Murphy, assistant metropolitan editor, and to Richard Galant, deputy metropolitan editor and assistant managing editor, for providing invaluable help in outlining and editing the newspaper series that served as the dress rehearsal for this book. Several of my colleagues also provided a constant stream of encouragement and editing suggestions, most notably columnist Paul Vitello, director of special projects Robert Friedman, and reporter Nina Bernstein.

At Columbia University, noted math textbook author and professor Bruce Vogeli, and his colleague Frances Bolin, spent hours explaining their view of math instruction in troubled city schools, for which I thank them. Dorothy Geddes, a professor of education at Brooklyn College, was also very helpful.

For keeping my computer up and running, especially at one point when I nearly lost all my diary notes from the first semester of school, I am thankful to my dear friend and technological wizard John Varkony.

Many others paid painstaking attention to the manuscript and to the project, including my husband, Mitch, my brother-in-law Robert Muller, my sisters Ann and Sally, my mother, Nancy Sachar, my father, Byron Sachar, and my literary agent, Jane Dystel. Special thanks as well to Patricia Eilenberg for dozens of Sunday morning pep talks; to Sara Lessley for dozens of Sunday afternoon pep talks; and to Amy Coopersmith, Deborah Marchini, Randall Forsyth, Mark Wenneker, Susie Luten, Jane Stein Kerr, Wendy Eisenberg, and Suzanh Hannon, just for being dear friends.

And for giving me so many warm smiles at the end of guilt-ridden, weary days, thanks to my darling daughters, Amy and Caroline.

Finally, to the students and parents profiled in this book, I am deeply indebted. They shared their thoughts, writings, homes, and histories, and I will remember them always.

About the Author

Emily Sachar was born and raised in St. Louis, Missouri. She earned a bachelor's degree in economics from Stanford University in 1980. She has been a reporter for *Newsday* and *New York Newsday* since 1982, and has received numerous awards for reporting and writing. She is a two-time winner of the nation's most prestigious education-writing award, the Grand Prize for Distinguished Education Reporting, for her coverage of the New York City public school system. She also has won a New York Press Club award, the coveted Peter Khiss Award for Outstanding Reporting on New York City Government, and a Newswomen's Club of New York Front Page award, all for her coverage of public education in New York. She lives in New York City with her husband and two young daughters. This is her first book.